Speaking about Godard

Speaking about Godard

Kaja Silverman and Harun Farocki

with a Foreword by Constance Penley

NEW YORK UNIVERSITY PRESS

New York and London

NEW YORK UNIVERSITY PRESS
New York and London

Library of Congress Cataloging-in-Publication Data
Silverman, Kaja.
Speaking about Godard / Kaja Silverman and Harun Farocki : with a
foreword by Constance Penley.
p.   cm.
Includes bibliographical references.
ISBN 0-8147-8065-2 (hardcover : alk. paper). —
ISBN 0-8147-8066-0 (pbk. : alk. paper)
1. Godard, Jean Luc, 1930–   —Criticism and interpretation.
I. Farocki, Harun.   II. Title.
PN1998.3.G63S56   1998
791.43'0233'092—dc21   98-12701
                                 CIP

New York University Press books are printed on acid-free paper,
and their binding materials are chosen for strength and durability.

Manufactured in the United States of America

10 9 8 7 6 5 4 3 2

Contents

Foreword

If you are going to speak about Godard, or at least try to speak about Godard—it's not easy—you would do well to begin by seeing the beauty of Harun Farocki and Kaja Silverman's conversational gambit. The filmmaker and the film theorist decided to construct a dialogue around a close reading of eight Godard films, in chronological order, beginning with *My Life to Live* (1962) and ending with *New Wave* (1990). Like *Gay Knowledge*'s Emile Rousseau and Patricia Lumumba, played by Jean-Pierre Léaud and Juliet Berto, they set themselves a program of analyzing sounds and images, of collecting and critiquing. But Farocki's and Silverman's project is far more inductive than that carried out by the characters of Godard's 1968 film, the discussion of which forms the hinge chapter of this book. Their close reading follows the unfolding of the films as if the two were sitting at a flatbed, with the benefit of a filmmaker's eye for the formal issues of shooting and editing and a theorist's attention to the relation of text and interpretation.

By adopting this viewing strategy Farocki and Silverman found that films contain many scenes that do not fit smoothly into the kinds of arguments one normally makes about them. To speak about a whole film, and not merely the elements that help ground an interpretation, allows for a productive contradiction between text and interpretation. The dialogue form richly dramatizes that contradiction, showing interpretation to be not so much a matter of empirical correctness, but rhetoric, philosophy, and politics as well. And it is a form that is especially appropriate for speaking about films made by Godard because he is a director who always tries to find the "argument" for a film by approaching it from several directions, without a pregiven intention. He discovers the argument in the recorded sounds and images instead of producing it through them. The dialogue form also offers a way to approach the film from several directions, and allows for the failed attempts as well as the successful ones to be kept.

As early as the mid-seventies, film analyst Raymond Bellour declared that the close analysis of film had become an art without a future. "Analysis in Flames" states bluntly yet elegiacally: "In truth there are no longer, or should no longer be, any analyses of film." What's behind this wish in the guise of a prediction? First, there's the paradox of having to stop the moving image to study it and of only being able to document the stylistic and narrative complexity of the film through selected "stills." And then there's the problem of how to write in such a way as to freeze the image in the reader's mind and then make it move again. Finally, there's the difficulty of deciding whether one's close analysis is too close. Film analyses are not often good reads, weighed down as they are by all the lists, charts, and diagrams necessary to give a complete inventory of the film's elements and their interactions. How do you determine, in each particular instance, "how to make the strategy of analysis comply with its stakes"? After a certain point, it becomes a mere academic exercise (although still fascinating and fun to do in a film classroom) to demonstrate that one can and has constructed a full and accurate catalog of a film's elements. But Bellour is a dreamer, so he lets himself dream of a future form of close analysis, perhaps not on paper but on video or film, in which strategy and stakes are matched, and that would contribute to advancing film theory as well as cinema itself.

Speaking about Godard comes as close to that dream of film analysis as anything we can imagine on the contemporary critical scene. Yes, the movement of Godard's films does get reduced to "stills" in this book, but the lovingly detailed descriptions—with one voice building on the other, agreeing, demurring, qualifying—make them move again. And the strategy of analysis complies beautifully with the stakes: we come away from the reading of any one chapter with a three-dimensional mental map in our head, a virtual geography of all the film's images, sounds, and dizzyingly complex motifs, rhymes, counterpoints, and patterns. We also understand the artistic, philosophical, and political questions and answers that are being posed and resolved through that figurative and narrative patterning. Farocki and Silverman's close analyses are exhaustive without being exhausting, and just close enough not to become didactic formalism on the one hand or speculative interpretation on the other.

As one reads through *Speaking about Godard*, it becomes clear that the dialogue strategy emerged from the nature of the object itself, again inductively. It takes two to analyze a filmmaker who always proceeds by twos. Here are just a few of the pairs that organize Godard's films: sound and image, light and dark, stillness and movement, structure and chance, male and female, fiction and documentary, classicism and modernism, actor and character, rich and poor, heterosexual and homosexual, victim and agent, secularity and spirituality. As philosopher and film analyst Gilles Deleuze points out, Godard is not a dialectician. His preferred conjunction is not "or," but rather "and": "What counts with him is not two or three, or however many you like, it's AND, the conjunction AND. . . . The AND is neither the one or the other, it is always between the two, it is the boundary. . . . Godard's aim is to 'see the boundaries' . . . to make the imperceptible visible." Godard's politics, Deleuze says, is no longer a macropolitics of large groupings but a whole micropolitics of boundaries. Farocki and Silverman map many of the boundaries and much of the territory between boundaries in Godard's cinema. But their discourse itself also dramatizes the infinity of ways in which "and" can signify. Together—yet apart by sex, language, nationality, and training—the two authors of this book disprove the most fundamental law of mathematics: they show that one and one can sometimes add up to much more than two.

Why choose to speak about Godard? For Farocki, whose filmmaking has been said to combine the poetry and visual imagination of Chris Marker with the rigor of Alexander Kluge, Godard has always been a guide. It is crucial, for him, that Godard doesn't define himself against commercial cinema; rather, he has torn down the walls separating art and business. At the same time, Godard is also the only French filmmaker who was permanently affected by May '68, never returning to making the kinds of films he was making before '68. Farocki also finds Godard's particular kind of auteurism exemplary: whereas other directors require an elaborate technology to make a city, a landscape or an apartment their own, Godard needs only his imagination; we must only look through his eyes to find a city of the future in Paris of the past, or a murder in a pair of oversized scissors. Farocki also feels that he learned most of what he knows about quotation from Godard. Generally films either colonize the texts they cite, or fail to integrate them. Godard, however, always permits the books and paintings from which he quotes to maintain their autonomy, while at the same time making it possible for them to reverberate in new ways. Finally, Farocki is moved by Godard's fidelity—by his return in film after film to the same concerns, whether that is shooting with natural light, the enigma of human movement, or the use of repetition. And, as in every good relationship, each return is both a renewal and a transformation.

For Silverman, a semiotic and psychoanalytic film theorist whose passionate scholarship has discovered some of the most original and compelling relations between visuality and sexuality, the choice of Godard is a natural. No other contemporary filmmaker has carried on such a sustained or aesthetically rich exploration of the psychic and social implications of sexual difference. But Silverman also values Godard because of his remarkable capacity to surprise us out of our usual ways of thinking. No other contemporary filmmaker has so challenged the interpretive strategies of film scholars who want to understand the relation of the shapes and flickerings on the screen to the subjectivity of the spectator, to the institutions of cinema, and to the social context in which films are produced and consumed. Silverman wanted this challenge. She wanted to work with a body of films capable of cutting the theoretical ground out from under her own feet, over and over again. To maximize the destabilizing potential of Godard's films, she began reading them in exactly the way he makes them. She gave up trying to know in advance where she was going, and opened her eyes and ears. And before long she found herself in a strange and wondrous land, where the quotidian leads to the sublime, where the fall never happens once and for all, and where it is by displaying a woman's naked buttocks rather than covering them that one best protects her against the advances of strangers.

It should not go without mention that this book is by, for, and about unabashed cinéphiles. The love of film suffuses Godard's work from the beginning, first American cinema, then the films of revolutionary comrades around the world, and more recently the films of his immediate predecessors in French art cinema such as Tati and Duras. But we've always known about Godard's love of film. Farocki and Silverman have their own fair share of cinéphilia and they put it to work in analyzing these eight films. When they speak about Godard, they are concerned above all else with the *performance* of the text, with the unfolding, over time, of that complex and never-to-be-repeated structure of inimitable sounds and images that comprises each of his films. Farocki and Silverman attempt to do something that has seemed nearly impossible: to theorize through description. They ask us to think, with them, *through* color, light, music, movement, face.

This book not only shows us anew what it means to love cinema, it also reveals the startling degree to which Godard's films are about love itself, especially when they are most insistently political. And by the end of Farocki and Silverman's conversation about Godard, by the time you have realized that these dialogues are love letters, you can't help but be persuaded by their implicit argument that Godard-the-modernist's turn to classicism and ethics has only deepened the political dimension of his filmmaking practice. This may seem a surprising claim. But those who read this book to the end are likely to find that their notion of the "political" will never again be the same.

CONSTANCE PENLEY
University of California
Santa Barbara

Acknowledgments

We would like to thank Eric Zinner for his unwavering support for this book, which began even before either of us had a clear conception of what it might be. We would also like to thank our exceptionally overqualified research assistants, Amy Zilliax and Greg Forter, for their resourcefulness, assiduity, editorial acuity, and passionate intelligence. They have earned the right to have research assistants of their own. Finally, we are indebted to Marian Stefanowski, who produced the film stills included in this book.

A shorter version of chapter 3 appeared in *Text zur Kunst* no. 27 (1997): 21–40, as "Worte wie Liebe." A slightly different version of chapter 6 was published in *Camera Obscura* no. 37 (1996): 93–122 under the title "In Her Place." A few paragraphs of chapter 7 come from a piece entitled "To Love and to Work to Love: A Conversation about *Passion*," published in *Discourse* vol. 15. no. 3 (1993): 57–75.

one

Nana Is an Animal

My Life to Live/Vivre sa vie (1962)

HF: *My Life to Live* (1962) consists of twelve episodes telling the story of Nana (Anna Karina), a young woman whose beauty—as Patricia Highsmith would say—is dangerous, but only to herself. Pimps, johns, and artists find in her face and body the incarnation of their dreams. As a consequence, Nana's life is not hers to live.

KS: At the beginning of the film, Nana works as a shopgirl in a record store, but earns so little that she can't pay her rent. She dreams vaguely of becoming a success in the movies or theater, but before long slides into prostitution. As is customary in the movies, Raoul, her pimp (Sadt Rebbot), does not treat her well. Not surprisingly, then, Nana falls in love with someone else, and decides to break off her relationship with Raoul. But before she can do so, Raoul sells her to some other pimps. A quarrel ensues, and Raoul and one of the other pimps casually eliminate Nana. The film ends with a two-minute-long close-up of her corpse, which has been brutally reduced to a few seconds in the American version.

HF: Unexplained omissions occur between and within the twelve episodes. These are not omissions of the usual sort, which delete unimportant moments, or create significant gaps, but more the kind one encounters in a documentary film. With them, the film says something like: "We did not see our heroine during the next two weeks. When we met her again, she was . . . " They confer upon what we are shown the status of found fragments, rather than produced elements. As a result, no scene is subordinated to any other. Instead, every sound and image is equal. Our analysis should respect this democracy of being.

Credit Sequence

KS: The three shots over which the credits are displayed show us Nana's head first in left profile, then from the front, and finally in right profile. In each of these shots, Nana's neck and the edges of her profile are illuminated, but her face is heavily shadowed. By shooting from three different sides, the camera attempts to penetrate the mystery suggested by this darkness.

HF: The lighting is studied in this sequence, as in art photography. It makes an image out of Nana's face. However, the sequence has one strikingly documentary feature, which is the unprofessional flare of light with which it ends. Such a flare would normally be edited out of a fiction film, but is often included in a documentary film as a way of establishing the verisimilitude of its images. By virtue of this feature, as well as of the camera's attempt to be exhaustive in the views it provides of Nana's face, these shots represent something like police photographs, or a physiognomic study. They offer a documentary of a face.

KS: Insofar as the three credit shots represent a documentary of a face, they tilt the film in the direction of Karina rather than of Nana. It is the mystery of the actress rather than the mystery of the character which is being plumbed. But these images are not purely documentary; they are also elements within a fiction film. Consequently, it would be more appropriate to say that it is the mystery of Nana *as the mystery of Anna Karina* which is at issue here. In this respect, these three shots are emblematic of the film as a whole. More than any other work, *My Life to Live* proves the truth of Godard's claim that, since "an actor exists independently of me . . . I try to make use of that existence and to shape things around it so that he can continue to exist" within the character he plays.[1] But Godard does not base the "truth" of Nana on the "truth" of Anna Karina because, like

Brecht, he abhors method acting. Rather, he typically asks of his actors that they let their "reality support his [fiction]."[2] Godard construes the category "reality" differently from film to film, but here it would seem to designate something like "soul."

HF: As in the passport photo, the "truth" of Karina is assumed to reside in her face—or, more precisely, her eyes. Godard seems to believe the old adage that the eyes are the window to the soul. On several occasions in the film, the camera studies Karina's face in this way, and sometimes she looks back. In so doing, she defends herself, but she is simultaneously exposed.

KS: Over the last of the three credit images, Godard writes Montaigne's maxim: "*Il faut se prêter aux autres et se donner à soi-même.*"

HF: To me, this means: "You'd better take care of yourself on earth, for there is no higher force who will do it for you, and no heaven in which your tragedies will be redeemed."

KS: The translation in the English subtitled version of *My Life to Live* renders the maxim: "Lend yourself to others and give yourself to yourself," which privileges the self over others. Literally translated, Montaigne's words would be better rendered: "One must lend oneself to others and give oneself to oneself," which weakens somewhat the hierarchy of self over others implicit in the English translation. However, in an interview about the film, Godard offered a gloss on Montaigne's aphorism which completely transforms its meaning. He said, "*My Life to Live* will prove Montaigne's saying that you have to give yourself to others and not only to yourself." This gloss not only eliminates the distinction between "lend" and "give," but—if anything—privileges the other over the self. This productive misreading of Montaigne will be crucial to our understanding of the film.

1
A cafe. Nana wants to leave Paul. The pinball table

KS: In the first shot of the film proper, Nana/Karina sits with her back to us at a restaurant counter. We thus now see her head from the only side not depicted in the credit sequence, and so complete our tour of that part of her body. We also pass almost imperceptibly from actress to character, from documentary to fiction.

HF: Most of the rest of this tableau consists of alternating shots of Nana and her estranged husband, Paul (Andre S. Labarthe). Both are sitting at the restaurant counter, and both have their backs to the camera. Sometimes we can see Nana's reflection in the mirror in front of her, and once Paul's as well, but in neither case distinctly. Because their faces are withheld, there is also an interesting divorce of sound and image in this scene. The dialogue doesn't seem to come from the characters; Paul's and Nana's words hover over them, without a bodily grounding. The exchange at the counter represents a conversation of perhaps twenty minutes, but it summarizes the events of three or four years. We learn that they have a child, who has remained with Paul; that Paul is chronically poor; that Nana has begun working in a record shop, but has show-business ambitions; and that Nana started learning English, but gave up after a time—unlike Paul, who has continued with his music. Years of quarrels are also reprised in the acrimonious words they exchange, particularly in Nana's "It's always the same thing," and "I'd just betray you again."

KS: We also discover something very crucial about Nana: we learn that she wants to be regarded as special. Paul is disappointing in this respect; he thinks that "everyone is the same."

HF: Twice this scene makes a creative use of the "pickup." A pickup is when the same line is spoken at the end of one shot and the beginning of the next, and it is used by filmmakers when shooting to give themselves more flexibility during the editing process. Just before complaining that Paul doesn't regard her as special, Nana twice says: "You're mean, Paul"—once as we look at his back, and once as we look at hers. Shortly afterward, when Paul remarks that his parents like her, Nana responds: "I bet." We see her looking out of frame in his direction, as she asks: "What's that look for?" A moment later, she repeats the same question, as Paul looks out of frame in her direction. These repetitions are a bit like reverse jump-cuts, underscoring the fictiveness of the narration. Also, by uttering the same words twice, Paul and Nana emphasize them; it is as if they are so important that they warrant a violation of the rules of filmmaking. A device which is usually purely technical becomes semantic.

KS: These repetitions indicate a desire to communicate which is generally missing from this exchange. Although the conversation provides a crucial exposition, it is for the most part a striking example of what might be called "empty" or "narcissistic" speech.[3] Except for these two pickups, the characters do not really address each other. On both sides, the conversation is characterized by a bitter egoism, each character insisting on his or her rights and grievances, and scoring points at the other's expense. This is formally signaled in several ways. First, although in other conversational situations in *My Life to Live* the camera insistently pans and dollies from one participant to another, here it shows Nana and Paul in separate shots, as if to stress their isolation from one another. Also, one character's body fills up the frame in each shot, as if to suggest that there is no room for the other. In each one, then, Paul or Nana says "me, not you" to the other. Finally, the insistence with which the camera shoots them from the back encourages us to see that Paul and Nana have also turned their metaphoric backs to each other. Nana at one point says: "The more we speak, the less the words mean." Significantly, in light of the Montaigne epigraph, Nana does not offer anything to Paul in this scene, but rather requests a loan of two thousand francs from him. He, of course, refuses.

HF: Godard's decision to leave these characters' faces out of most of this scene also represents a striking example of that art of omission to which *My Life to Live* is dedicated. The film is like a drawing which consists only of a few lines, yet in those lines we can see an entire body, or a complete landscape. This is a kind of *via negativa*—a portraiture through negation, through what isn't there, rather than through what is.

KS: At the end of Episode 1, their quarrel ended, Nana and Paul move to the front of the restaurant, where they play a game of pinball. This event is shown with a single shot, which—in keeping with their temporary reconciliation—includes both of them.

HF: Nowadays, our ears have grown accustomed to hearing a dense sound background when we go to the movies, but—apart from the voices of Paul and Nana—in this shot we hear only the pinball machine, or perhaps the steps of a waiter in the background. The silence is astonishing—it's as if Paul and Nana are under water, or in another world from our own.

KS: As Nana takes her turn at the pinball machine, Paul recounts perhaps the most crucial of all the film's stories, although we won't understand that until later. The story was written by one of his father's pupils, and consists of the words: "A chicken is an animal with an inside and an outside. Remove the outside, there's the inside. Remove the inside, and you see the soul."[4]

HF: Paul introduces his anecdote with the words: "I don't know why, but suddenly I remember a story father told." Godard also does not know why, and does not want to know why, this story finds its way into *My Life to Live*. Inspiration, not premeditation, is his artistic credo. And "inspiration" means allowing things to come together from the most surprising sources.

KS: Before Paul recounts this story, the camera pans to the left until Nana is in center frame, and Paul excluded from the image. And after Paul finishes speaking, it holds on Nana for approximately ten seconds, before fading to black. During these ten seconds, the silence deepens. In both of these ways, the film insists upon the relevance of this story to the figure of Nana.

HF: I agree, but the special way in which the face of Nana and the story about the chicken are put together should not be forgotten. *My Life to Live* gathers together different elements—a clip from a film, lines from a Poe story or a pulp novel—and quotes from them in a way which maintains their difference. One could compare the film in this respect to a Picasso image, in which a feather representing a bird lies side by side with a piece of wallpaper designating hair. Such *objets trouvés* can be put to analogical purposes, but—because they still insist upon their specificity—the result is always a bit startling or "weird." Although undeniably connecting Nana with the chicken, *My Life to Live* shows us how miraculous it is that one thing in the world should be able to explain another.

KS: We will see later that the film accommodates relationships between the most divergent of terms, since it does not predicate those relationships on the basis of identity.

2

The record shop. Two thousand francs. Nana lives her life

KS: Episode 2 consists entirely of one extended sequence shot. Some days have perhaps elapsed since the previous episode, but we are not told anything about them. We are shown only a few consecutive minutes in one of Nana's working days at the record shop, during which nothing of particular importance happens. Yet from this single shot we learn that Nana is broke, that she takes no interest in her work, and that she yearns for a different life.

HF: At the same time, the camera does not really "characterize" Nana; it is more interested in how she moves. It says: "If we can find out how she moves, that will be enough." And it does something like an experimental dance with her.

KS: The camera seems more narratively motivated than that to me. In an early interview, Godard maintained that the camera in *My Life to Live* does not spy, trap, or surprise Nana, but "simply [follows] her."[5] However, it often does much more than that. It pans to the left in Episode 1 in order to be in place before Paul tells his story. It is as if the camera knows even before he begins that the story will be significant for Nana. And in Episode 2, the camera starts tracking to the right even before Nana has taken a step in that direction, in confident anticipation of her doing so a moment later. At another point in this episode, it pans to the right by the record stacks, more quickly than Nana can go there, again certain that she will follow. Even in life, predictions can quickly turn into determinations. Within cinema, there can of course be no question of "free will" on the part of a character; the enunciation always dictates every step a character takes, and every word she utters. But the enunciation can be "for" or "against" the narrative which it induces, and, in the case of *My Life to Live*, we would have to say that something lies ahead for which it can't wait, literally, and perhaps metaphorically.

HF: Bazin privileged the long take because he believed it to involve less discursive intervention than montage—to be less freighted with signification, and therefore more "real."[6] The sequence shot in Episode 2 is the very opposite of this; it not only anticipates Nana's movements rather than simply following them, but it also generates a surplus of meaning. Nana has only to walk back and forth a few times behind the record counter to indicate everything that her job entails, and how little interest she takes in music and her customers. But at the end of Episode 2, as the other shopgirl reads aloud from the pulp novel, the camera pans rapidly first to one window, where it remains for about ten seconds, and then to another, where it stays even longer. Now it exercises no control over what comes within its field of vision. Most of *My Life to Live* seems almost timeless, but the two window pans offer the unstaged reality of a particular day in 1962.

KS: Earlier in the film, the documentary—Karina's face—led to the fiction—Nana's soul. Here the formula is reversed: the fiction leads back to the documentary.

HF: In these two pans, the camera has a skillful neoprimitivism akin to the earliest days of cinematography. It stares wide-eyed through the window, like a prehistoric animal. Now it really does hope to capture things in their "virginal purity."[7] And that is something which can only be seen with eyes from which the scales of culture and experience have fallen—eyes which have been, as it were, washed clean.

KS: Just before the camera effects its journey to the window, Nana says of the book her colleague is reading: "That looks fabulous!" Her colleague responds: "The story is silly, but it's awfully well written." The words she reads suggest that this is a world of purple prose, a world in which the characters achieve that quality of "specialness" or heightened reality Nana craves.

HF: Here we have another dramatization of the *objet trouvé* principle. One just has to open a book—even an unknown one—and the words will speak to you, like the faces of strangers, or the details of a street. *My Life to Live* is full of such wonderful and terrible moments, in which uncanny connections occur.

KS: The novel from which Nana's colleague reads is also about speech. The presumably female first-person narrator triumphs over her masculine interlocutor with a well-conceived verbal formula. The text reads: "He gazed at the turquoise, star-laden sky, then turned to me. 'As one who lives intensely, logically you . . .' I interrupted him: 'You attach too much importance and power to logic.'"

For a few seconds, I was filled with a bitter sense of triumph. Forgotten, my broken heart. Forgotten, too, the need to put on a brave face. Yes, a distinctly elegant way of escaping this dilemma." This represents another striking example of empty speech, analogous in its one-upmanship to the conversation in Episode 1.

3
The concierge. Paul. The Passion of Jeanne d'Arc. A journalist

HF: This episode begins with Nana trying to sneak into her concierge's booth to grab the key to her own apartment. It becomes immediately evident that she has been locked out due to unpaid rent. (Again, Nana neither gives nor lends. Instead, she owes.) A struggle ensues, first with the concierge, and then with her male assistant. Meanwhile, two children dance the twist. Their continuous movements provide something like a time measurement, comparable to the pendulum of a clock.

KS: Most of this scene is filmed with an overhead camera, which pans first to the left, and then to the right, as Nana runs with her key toward her apartment, and is then dragged back to the street by the landlady's assistant. Again, the camera moves more quickly than Nana does, its anticipation of her action suggesting both foreknowledge and narrative impatience. The camera could even be said to spy upon and to trap Nana, since its vantage point and its high-angle pans associate it with a surveillance apparatus.

HF: At the same time, the camera's overhead position is indicative of a certain emotional distance from the feelings experienced by Nana herself. It is laconic about the concierge drama, and does not share Nana's hope or disappointment.

KS: Nana has nowhere to spend the night, and decides to go to the movies. But first she sees Paul, and he gives her some photographs of her son. Nana is eager to see the photographs, but loses interest in them as soon as she determines that the child resembles Paul more than herself.

HF: *My Life to Live* cuts to a shot of a movie marquee with the words *Jeanne d'Arc*. A few seconds later, we see an arm placed around Nana's

Fig. 1

shoulders in a darkened movie theater, but are offered no clear image
of its owner, and no narrative explanation as to who he might be.
Later, after looking at images from the scene in which Jeanne d'Arc
prepares for death in Dreyer's version of her story, we see Nana walking with a man toward an illuminated restaurant in a high-angle long
shot. Again we are offered no clarifying close-up of the man. Nana
says: "I've said good-bye." The man responds: "I bought your cinema
ticket." Nana answers, definitively: "Too bad." Astonishingly, with
these few details Godard tells us everything we need to know. Nana
has allowed a stranger to put his arm around her in a movie theater in
exchange for her admission, and now wants to shake him off. The man
is not individuated because he stands for many men—because Nana
routinely solves her monetary crises with arrangements of this sort.

KS: The scene inside the movie theater is one of the most important
in *My Life to Live*. First, *Jeanne d'Arc* is a silent film. *My Life to Live* also
aspires to become a silent film. Second, like *My Life to Live*, *Jeanne*

d'Arc is simultaneously a documentary of its actress's face, and a fiction film about its eponymous heroine. More precisely, it uses the reality of Maria Falconetti's face to support the fiction of Jeanne's story. Finally, the scene Nana watches from *Jeanne d'Arc* enacts the same paradigm suggested by the story about the chicken in Episode 1: spiritual realization through death. There can now be no further doubt that this is the fate awaiting Nana. *My Life to Live* twice cross-cuts between a close-up of Jeanne's face and a close-up of Nana's, much as the camera focuses on Nana's face during the narration of the bird story. With the second of these close-ups, the relation between the two women becomes mimetic: the tears in Nana's eyes mirror the tears in Jeanne's (figure 1). The point at which this mirroring relationship is established comes immediately after the priest asks Jeanne what her deliverance will be, and she answers: "Death."

HF: The parallels between Nana and Jeanne seem more diegetic to me.[8] Nana knows that she is in a crisis, but she doesn't entirely understand why. She goes to the movies in the hope of finding out; after all, Jeanne d'Arc is also a woman in trouble. But in fact this is not a situation in which art comments upon life, but only one in which life imitates art.

KS: *My Life to Live* shows the word "death" twice during the projection of *Jeanne d'Arc*—once before we see Nana's tear-filled eyes, and once after. The second time, that word is available only to us; it is thus Godard, not Nana, who insists upon the relation between her and Jeanne. This repetition also represents an unequivocal enunciatory intrusion in a second way. The word "death" appears only once in Dreyer's film, and when it does so, it is printed in black against a white background. The second citation is added by Godard to the bottom of the image of Jeanne, as her lips form the word "death," and it assumes a different form. On a second viewing of *My Life to Live*, this repetition represents the most emphatic enunciatory anticipation of what will later happen to Nana. If the film has until now given us nothing to justify the metaphoric alignment of Nana with Jeanne, that is because it is what Nana will become, not what she is, which links her to Jeanne. It is also because Nana's soul or spiritual meaning will—even subsequently—be shown to exceed her. *My Life to Live* ultimately gives us access to something that is "of" her, but not "in" her.

HF: The comparison, then, doesn't imply an essential similarity.

KS: Exactly. The equation which the film sets up between the two women bypasses what is most specific to each as a person.

HF: Perhaps one might say that the relationship between Jeanne and Nana is at this point primarily "morphological." Both have "talented faces." With the cinema machine which scrutinizes faces in such an unprecedented way, something new has come into the world: the facial talent. Once God was believed to select a few people for great and meaningful things—people like the illiterate Jeanne d'Arc. Nowadays one's appearance can be a vocation: a vocation which the bearer of the face cannot understand, but has to follow.

4

The police. Nana is questioned

KS: Episode 4 consists of three frontal shots of Nana's head against a brightly lit window in a police station, intercut with two reverse shots of a policeman typing up a report detailing her theft of some money dropped by a stranger at a newsstand.

HF: In the first shot, we see Nana in medium close-up, with a great deal more "air" above her face than is customary in filmmaking today. She is as a result strangely decentered. With each of these shots, the camera moves closer to Nana, until her face completely fills the frame. The policeman is concerned with Nana's identity—with her age, her occupation, her address—but the camera with something very different: her soul or "essence."

KS: This scene ends when the policeman asks: "What will you do now?" Nana does not provide a direct answer to this question. That answer comes instead in the form of the next episode, in which she for the first time turns explicitly to prostitution as a way of solving her monetary crisis. Instead, Nana says: "I don't know . . . I . . . I is an other." With this quotation of Rimbaud's famous line,[9] Nana might be said at least for the moment to surrender precisely that category upon which she has until now so strongly insisted: the "me." She at least dimly apprehends that what most profoundly defines her is a constellation of relations which, although internal to *My Life to Live*, is external to her. It is for this reason that the camera is able to approach something else, what we have agreed to call Nana's strangely impersonal "soul."

HF: Like the credit sequence, this scene ends with a white flare. The arrest scene refers back to the credit sequence in two other ways as well: Nana is again filmed against light, and at one point turns her head so that she is shown in profile.

KS: Through these parallels, Godard once again reminds us of one of the ways in which Nana is an "other": we are obliged to look for her "essence" in the face of Anna Karina.

HF: This scene also plays with the similarity between filmmaking and police work. The noise of the mechanical typewriter suggests that it is a difficult and never entirely appropriate job to document life, whether in a police station or on a film set. And in both settings, one never knows when the meaningful will surface within the murmur of everyday life. Will it be when Nana trades sexual favors for a bed, when she cannot pay the rent, or when she picks up a bill which someone has dropped on the street?

5
The boulevards. The first man. The room

KS: Episode 5 for the first time gives us a number of point-of-view shots. Previously, the camera has always remained exterior to Nana—sometimes markedly so, as in her apartment courtyard. This episode begins with a traveling shot of a street lined on both sides with prostitutes. It is as if Nana is riding down the street in a bus or a taxi, and considering what it would mean to be a prostitute. The camera makes a swish pan from the left to the right of the street, as if Nana has turned her head. In the next shot, the camera dollies backward, facing Nana as she walks. She looks to the right, and, as the sound of her footsteps continues to be heard, we see what she sees: first a white wall with graffiti, and then (as the camera tracks further in the direction Nana is walking) a prostitute standing against the wall. We are given another shot of Nana walking and looking, this time to the left, and again we then see what she sees: a prostitute standing against a wall. There is a fade, and then we see Nana walking once again down the street. Now she is more the object than the subject of the look. She is shown in profile, against the wall, like the prostitutes she earlier observed. A moment later, a customer asks: "How about it?", and Nana agrees.

HF: What impresses me about this sequence is that Nana slips so imperceptibly from conventional life into prostitution. We never know at which point in this sequence she makes the decision to begin selling her body. It is as though Godard means to blur the dividing line—to suggest that it is not so easy to determine where conventional human interaction ends, and prostitution begins.

KS: A number of earlier events in the film could even be construed as prostitution, such as Nana's exchange of sexual favors for a roof over her head, or the transaction with the movie spectator. But the film itself insists in the intertitles that this man is officially her first customer, obliging us to mark the moment that she acquiesces to this solicitation as the beginning of her career as a prostitute. Given that, what is most striking about this sequence is that it contains another dramatic example of enunciatory anticipation. In shooting Nana against the wall, even before the man enters the frame, it might even be said thereby to "make" her a prostitute. This would of course be true in any case, but few films would acknowledge their complicity so directly.

HF: Part of this shot cannot be immediately incorporated into the narrative, again encouraging us to look with freshly-washed eyes. Before we see the first prostitute at whom Nana looks as she walks down the street, our look travels with hers slowly across the white expanse of the wall, with its mysterious graffiti. Like the unstaged shot of people walking on the street outside the record shop in Episode 2, this is an image which somehow doesn't signify, an image which says only "wall," or "graffiti."

KS: Inside the hotel room, there are three more shots from Nana's point of view: the shots of the turned down bed, the bar of soap resting on a folded towel, and the customer's hand inside his trouser pocket (figure 2). These three shots unequivocally signify "bought sex."

HF: At the same time, they pull away from the narrative in the way the wall and the graffiti do. They are somehow autonomous from the scene in which they occur.

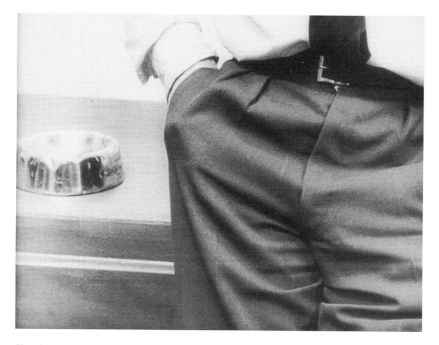

Fig. 2

KS: It is almost an obligatory feature of the legend of the prostitute that she will give her body to anyone who can pay, but will kiss only those she loves. Nana also attempts to withhold something symbolic from the sexual exchange—to keep part of herself for herself. What prostitution signifies in the film is brilliantly rendered by the ensuing struggle between Nana and the man. It means total egoic surrender. Prostitution signifies the negation of that psychic entity which is so conspicuously on display in the first few episodes: the self or "me."

HF: The struggle between Nana and her customer is shown in a very stylized way. Nana flutters her eyelashes, and opens her eyes unnaturally wide. She is Madame Butterfly in Puccini's opera, or—better yet—Louise Brooks in Pabst's *Pandora's Box*. But this stylization precipitates in the spectator a very visceral apprehension of Nana's panic.

KS: Godard says something in an interview about *My Life to Live* which would seem very germane to this moment: "How can one render the inside? Precisely by staying prudently outside."[10]

6

Meeting Yvette. A cafe in the suburbs, Raoul. Gunshots in the street

HF: Most of this episode takes place in a cafe, where Nana talks with Yvette (Guylaine Schlumberger), a professional prostitute, and meets her pimp, Raoul. Yvette offers the standard liberal alibi of the prostitute in the form of a narrative of her life: she was forced to sell her body by economic circumstances beyond her control (the disappearance of her husband, the hunger of her children). But Nana refuses to defend herself through such an alibi.

KS: Instead, she uses the occasion to make a radical declaration of responsibility. She tells Yvette: "I think we're always responsible for our actions. We're free. I raise my hand—I'm responsible. I turn my head—I'm responsible. I am unhappy—I'm responsible. I smoke—I'm responsible. I shut my eyes—I'm responsible. I forget I'm responsible, but I am." This is a surprising speech in a film in which the predetermination of the subject is so fully foregrounded. But through it, Nana effects a certain transcendence: a transcendence of the liberal alibi, and—beyond that—of the role of victim. She assumes full responsibility for her life in the face of her extremely limited agency, which is perhaps the very definition of ethical being. Jeanne d'Arc does the same in the clip we see from Dreyer's film. Submitting herself to the death which in her mind is decreed not only by her captors but by divine will, as if it were a fate of her own choosing, she makes her martyrdom a victory, and her death a liberation.

HF: Nana goes on to insist upon what might be called the "thingness" of things. She tells Yvette: "Everything is good. You only have to take an interest in things. After all, things are what they are. A message is a message. Plates are plates. Men are men. And life is life."

KS: The subtext is: "And a prostitute is a prostitute—regardless of how she came to be one."

HF: Nana is also saying: "Don't let yourself be seduced. There is no resurrection. Things are themselves, not metaphors for some higher meaning. And there is freedom in this knowledge. We can liberate ourselves in understanding that our world is not a trope for a world to come."

KS: This is because, although *My Life to Live* is a very spiritual film, its spirituality is strangely secular. It is of course only under such a condition that a Christian martyr and a prostitute could be made mimetic of each other.

HF: Nana's little speech also represents an implicit commentary on all those images in the film which we are encouraged to look at with newly-cleansed eyes—upon all those images which resist narrative or symbolic incorporation into the film, such as the shot of the white wall with the graffiti, or the unstaged street scene. Of course, as *My Life to Live* shows, such moments never last very long. After Nana finishes speaking, Yvette goes to get Raoul, and the interpretive machine begins again. Significantly, what starts the wheels rolling once more is a song. At moments of difficulty, songs always seem very existentially meaningful.

KS: The theme of the song is something like "poor but in love." It is the story of an ordinary couple who work in a factory and live in a shack by the railroad tracks, but whose personal happiness irradiates even the lowliest detail of their lives. As the song begins, Nana looks first at a man and woman sitting at a table across from her who seem the very embodiment of this couple. She then glances to her right, and sees a young man standing at the jukebox, who seems to have chosen the song. He, too, seeks such happiness, and Nana could help him find it. Finally, her look falls on two figures representing a very different set of heterosexual options: Raoul and Yvette. The choice is clear: money or love. And once again Nana chooses money.

HF: There is a very skillful choreography in this scene. As Yvette and Nana enter the restaurant, and sit down at a table, the camera holds on Raoul, playing pinball by the door. Consequently, we don't know anything about the room. It is crucial that its spatial dimensions be mapped out for us, since near the end of the episode, the camera will do something which would otherwise be illegible: it will simulate a shooting gun through a series of rapid-fire jump-cuts which move us from the table where Nana is sitting to the door. So, after giving us time to register Raoul as a new but significant presence in the film, the camera first pans quickly to the left, over the restaurant counter to Yvette and Nana, and then—as Yvette walks over to kiss Raoul—from Nana back over the restaurant counter to Raoul. It thereby clearly delineates the space between Nana's table and the door.

KS: The moment when the camera becomes a firing gun represents a startling slipping of the enunciation into the diegesis. For a few seconds, it is practically an agent in the narrative. This slippage is emblematic of the film as a whole, in which there is an extraordinary blurring of the distinction between fictional and enunciatory determination.

HF: For a moment, after the firing-gun sequence, we become involved in a parallel narrative, much as we do during the playing of the "poor but in love" song—a narrative about politics or gangsters. Then we exit this narrative, and are back in the main story. In later Godard films, this digressive predilection will be given much freer reign, and will sometimes almost engulf the main narrative.

KS: Near the end of this scene, Raoul insults Nana in order to find out if she is a "lady" or a "tramp." More specifically, he assails her image of self, her "me." "You parrot anything," he says, "You're ridiculous. . . . You look stupid, and your hair looks awful." Nana, who has journeyed considerable distance from the egoism of Episode 1, laughs unoffendedly, thereby proving that she is a "lady," or—as the film will later put it—"good."

7
The letter. Raoul again. The Champs Elysées

HF: Episode 7 takes place entirely at a table in a unidentified restaurant. At the beginning, Nana sits alone at this table, facing the camera. She is writing a letter to the Madame of a brothel, asking for a job. Behind her is what appears at first to be a window opening onto the Champs Elysées, but later can be seen to be photographic wallpaper replicating such a view. At the moment that we understand this *trompe l'œil*, the photograph ceases to function as a representation of the Champs Elysées, and becomes a signifier for Paris in its entirety. The shot of Nana writing then says something like: "Paris. A woman. A letter."

KS: In classic cinema, the letter is often a privileged vehicle for conveying the interiority of a character. If it serves that function in *My Life to Live*, we would have to conclude that Nana's interiority is astonishingly banal, hinging upon such concerns as how tall she is, and how quickly her hair grows. The contents of the letter are completely incommensurate with the tragedy of Karina's face. This scene helps us to understand better why, as we are told in the bird story in Episode 1, the soul can be found only when the inside as well as the outside has been taken away.

HF: Again, Nana confides her desire to be special. But Raoul responds that there are only three kinds of women: those with one expression, those with two expressions, and those with three expressions. This is his way of telling Nana that only superficial distinctions separate one woman who sells her body from another—in other words, that the category of specialness does not obtain within the class of prostitutes.

KS: Significantly, however, when Nana asks Raoul what he thinks of her, he answers: "I think you are very good. You have great goodness in your eyes." *My Life to Live* thus places the categories of "goodness" and "specialness" in diametric opposition to each other. It also makes "prostitution" a synonym for "goodness," thereby clarifying how that activity can be posited by the film as the agency of Nana's spiritual realization. But what the categories of "goodness" and "specialness" signify is not yet entirely clear.

HF: After Raoul sits down across from Nana, the camera pans from left to right, and right to left, sometimes lining up Nana's face with the back of Raoul's head, sometimes separating them. The camera is a chance generator here. It explores some of the possible constellations available in the given "two people sit across from each other and talk together." Later, it takes up a position to the right of Nana and Raoul, and pans back and forth between them, exploring other visual possibilities implicit in this given. After Raoul asks Nana to give him a smile, and she manifests resistance to doing so, those two characters engage in a "look fight," to see who will win. Now the camera occupies a position midway between them, as if to avoid taking sides until the fight has been decided. But when Nana smiles, it pans so that she alone is in center frame.

KS: Nana has lost at the level of the diegesis, but won at that of the enunciation.

HF: At the end of Episode 7, Nana asks Raoul: "When do I start?" Over a nocturnal image of traffic on the Champs Elysées, Raoul answers, melodramatically: "When the city lights go up, the streetwalker's end-less beat begins."

8
Afternoons. Money. Washbasins. Pleasure. Hotels

KS: This episode begins as an apparent extension of the conversation at the end of the previous one, in that Nana continues to ask questions about prostitution, and Raoul continues to answer these questions. However, certain differences immediately make themselves felt. At the beginning of Episode 8, it is daytime, not evening, and Raoul and Nana are driving through the streets of Paris, not leaving the restaurant. More importantly, Raoul's voice-over here has none of the melodramatic inflection of the preceding episode.

HF: This accelerated montage offers something like a cinematic user's manual—a "How to Be a Prostitute in Paris in 1962" film. But we learn less about prostitution itself than the rituals and activities surrounding it: medical inspections, taxes, varying rates, time restrictions, sanitary precautions, birth control and pregnancy, etc. Once again, reduction is an important organizing principle. Although there are more shots in this episode than in any other, the camera is throughout very discreet: it is always stationary, and the entering and exiting of characters from the frame emphasizes that there are restrictions on what it can see. The world of prostitution is only available between the shots.

KS: Prostitution is also a socioeconomic institution, and that—for the most part—is the view which is offered here. Still, it's clear that this aspect of prostitution is not primarily what interests Godard, any more than the corporeal transaction. *My Life to Live* is concerned with prostitution as a mechanism for enforcing a particular psychic condition. "Must I accept anyone?" asks Nana, over an image of an older man kissing her neck. "The prostitute must always be at the client's disposal," responds Raoul over the same shot. As the film cuts to an image of a younger man undressing, Raoul continues: "She must accept anyone who pays." As *My Life to Live* helps us to understand, accepting anyone who pays does not merely imply assuming as one's own the desires of the culture or Other, something which every subject necessarily does. Rather, it means having no

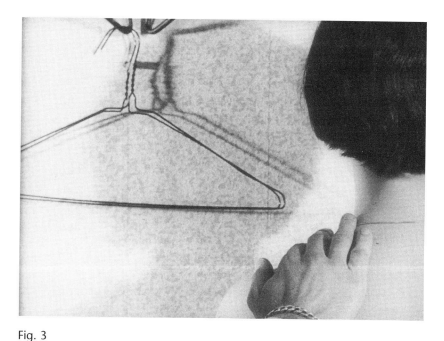

Fig. 3

desire but to satisfy the desire of *any other*.[11] It signifies the end of all personal desire, and so the demise of subjectivity as such.[12]

HF: But her customers don't seem to gain much in the process. They are scarcely even individuated. After Raoul says: "[The prostitute] must accept anyone who pays," he adds "this one . . . [or] this one" over the image of the undressing man, as Nana goes in and out of frame. The implication is that the men with whom Nana sleeps are so indistinguishable from one another that an image of the same man can be used to signify several men. In this respect, they are like the stranger in the movie theater.

KS: Godard deindividualizes Nana's clients in another way as well. A moment after the undressing shot, Raoul repeats the words "this one . . . [or] this one," over a shot of Nana standing in extreme right frame before a wall, on which a hanger is suspended. We see only part of her head and shoulder. At first there is no signifier of masculinity with which to associate the words "this one." Only with the final repetition of those words does a male hand reach into frame and place itself on Nana's shoulder (figure 3). Again, the category "customer" undergoes a radical devaluation. It is as if a symbolic male hand rests at all times upon Nana's neck, which can be indiscriminately actualized by any male hand.

HF: Whereas events in *My Life to Live* generally unfold in real time, in Episode 8 there is an incredible speeding up of the narrative. Weeks or possibly even months are covered. Also, although Raoul's voice tells Nana what she can expect from a life of prostitution, the images show her already living that life. The soundtrack describes the future, and the imagetrack depicts that future as if it were already happening.

KS: The camera can't wait for Nana to live through the remaining hours or days before she fully accedes to a life of prostitution. It demands that she begin immediately.

9
A young man. Luigi. Nana wonders whether she's happy

HF: At the beginning of Episode 9, Raoul describes in voice-over what happens during a typical day off in the life of a prostitute. The rest of the episode shows us the very different kind of day off to which Nana has become accustomed: her pimp doesn't take her to the country to visit a child, nor does he later take her out to dinner or to the movies. Instead, she is obliged to accompany him to a bar where he has a business meeting, and wait for him till he has finished his conversation. This scene makes very clear that Raoul does not regard Nana as in any way special.

KS: However, it introduces a new character, the young man (Peter Kassowitz), for whom Nana *is* special. When he finds out that she would like a cigarette, he provides her with a box of Gitanes. And Nana responds with a dance which represents the only diegetic realization of her show-business dreams, as well—significantly—as her moment of greatest self-affirmation.

HF: Nana is not the only performer in this scene. Luigi (Eric Schlumberger), a character who has no other narrative function than to cheer Nana up when her pimp ignores her on her day-off, offers his virtuoso rendition of a boy blowing up a balloon. It is typical of the *nouvelle vague* to give an actor free space in this way to show what he can do, and to revel in the resulting overflow of exuberance. Raoul Coutard's camera even moves backwards as Luigi blows up the imaginary balloon, so that it has room to expand. These two performances operate at the expense of the narrative. In fact, we almost forget in this scene that we are watching the story of a woman's slide into prostitution. And during the performance, there is a moment which escapes not only narrative, but semantic determination, a moment which is completely surreal. The camera cuts from a shot of Nana dancing to a dolly shot of a wall, a window, and a radiator. It moves vertiginously around the room, as if intoxicated, coming to another wall, another window, and—finally—Raoul and Luigi conversing at their table. Retroactively, we understand that the shot records Nana's point of view as she dances around the room, but for some seconds we gawk again in that wide-eyed way at the sheer "thingness" of the walls, the windows, and the radiator.

10
The Streets. A bloke. Happiness is no fun

KS: As in Episode 5, Nana is once more shown waiting for a customer on the street, and then—having secured him—discussing the price of her services with him in a hotel room. And just as the customer earlier complained "There's never an ashtray," here he objects: "They could have supplied chairs." However, whereas in Episode 5 Nana was like a traveler in a strange country, whose language she could hardly speak, now she is a long-time resident of that land, with a professional command of the idiom; she keeps up a steady patter of conversation with the man as she attempts to determine what he would like her to do, and manifests no surprise when he asks for a second woman.

HF: Nana goes down the corridor of the hotel in search of one, opening one door after another. No erotic secrets are revealed in the process. The female inhabitants are for the most part naked, but pose more like artists' models than prostitutes.

KS: A few moments later, Nana returns with another woman, who discusses money discreetly off frame with the man, while we look at

Nana beginning to undress in front of an illuminated window. Nana asks: "Shall I strip too?" The man responds, off-frame: "No, it's not worth it." "So I'm to do nothing?" Nana protests. "I don't know," answers the man ambiguously. Nana's wish to be special here finds a powerful reverse expression. Not only does she belong to the category of prostitutes, which is earlier established as a profound leveler of differences, but she is even passed over in that capacity for someone else. When this scene is put side by side with the shots over which Raoul's voice utters "this one . . . (or) that one," prostitution again emerges as the most extreme form of subjective negation: as the eradication both of desire and the self.

HF: Nana sits down in profile before the window, her head a small shape in the bottom of the frame, and lights a cigarette. Her insignificant position in the image seems an index of her general unimportance in the eyes of her client. Then the camera reorders the priorities of the scene: it dollies toward Nana, and tilts down, until she fills the center of the frame.

KS: Once again, Nana loses at the level of the diegesis, but wins at the level of the enunciation.

HF: After a long hiatus, we once again hear the suggestive notes of Legrand's music, which saturate Nana's image with pathos. Not many details are disclosed about Nana's life in this episode, but we have the feeling that we are learning something profound.

KS: Now, at last, we understand why prostitution represents the very quintessence of "goodness." The meaning of the story about the chicken which Paul recounts in Episode 1 is also retroactively available: the "soul" can emerge only after the "outside," or demands of the body, and the "inside," or "me," have been removed. This double eradication implies death as inexorably as being burned at the stake.

11
Place du Châtelet. A stranger. Nana the unwitting philosopher

HF: This episode takes place almost entirely in a Paris restaurant, and consists of a conversation between Nana and a philosopher (Brice

Parain). The camera cuts back and forth between the two conversationalists over an extended period of time, with only one variation: at a certain point Nana looks at the camera. At the beginning of the conversation, she is wearing the *fin-de-siècle* black velvet and white fur coat she earlier wears on her day off. However, she is not accompanied by Raoul, and at a certain point she introduces the topic of love, with great emphasis, suggesting that something has changed in her life since she sat dejectedly on the bed in the hotel room.

KS: This scene already points ahead to the next one, in which the young man reads aloud to Nana from Poe's *The Oval Portrait*. Nana seems to be happily in love, which is the condition, par excellence, of "specialness." This reversion to her earlier obsession is Godard's way of suggesting that one does not accede without protest or resistance to the egoic surrender suggested by the previous episode. We begin to understand why a certain amount of textual violence is necessary to bring about the enactment of that paradigm.

HF: The conversation begins when Nana, having joined the philosopher at his table, finds herself immobilized in her attempt to speak by a certain self-consciousness about what she wants to say. In response, the philosopher recounts a story from Dumas's *Twenty Years Later* about Portos, a character who thinks for the first time in his life after setting a bomb in a cellar, and is as a result killed by the falling debris. In so doing, he adds another *objet trouvé* to the large collection of found objects in *My Life to Live*.

KS: I like to think that this story is somehow reflexive. Portos is like the Hollywood action film, which would be destroyed if it stopped for a moment to register the processes of thought. *My Life to Live*, on the other hand, is a film which can accommodate a philosophical conversation without being incapacitated.

HF: It also helps us to believe that a prostitute can think about how to put one foot in front of the other without losing the power to walk. Indeed, this scene has so many realistic details—both characters, for instance, sometimes speak at the same time, or one interrupts the other by speaking more loudly—that it makes one imagine that a prostitute and a philosopher actually *are* speaking together about what words mean. But when Nana looks at the camera, we remember that we are seeing Anna Karina at work.

KS: Nana's anxiety that her words will not communicate her intent reintroduces a topic which was first introduced in Episode 1: the topic of empty speech. Nana tells the philosopher that it would be better to live without speech, since the more we talk, the less the words mean. This is almost an exact repetition of what she says to Paul. But the philosopher objects that we can't live without speaking, not only because without speech we couldn't communicate, but because without words we couldn't think. He then advances an existential model for approaching "true" speech.[13] "True" speech is what the philosopher describes as speaking "in a way that is right, doesn't hurt, says what has to be said, does what has to be done without hurting or bruising," or what Nana calls "[speaking] in good faith." Significantly, the philosopher's verbal ethics once again entails spiritual realization through the death of the everyday. This death means "detachment," a signifier which implies the withdrawal of cathexis from the things that normally engross us most fully: the world and the self. In other words, it signifies something like the abandonment of desire and the abdication of the "me."

HF: Here, however, the agency of death or detachment is not prostitution, but silence. The philosopher tells Nana: "I believe one learns to speak well only when one has renounced life for a time. That's the price . . . one must pass through the death of life without speech . . . there is a kind of ascetic rule that stops one from talking well until one sees life with detachment." Silence does not involve the kind of subordination to the will of another implied either by prostitution or death at the stake.

KS: And the extinction about which the philosopher speaks is not final, like that which awaits Nana, but leads to "resurrection"; it is the condition for living again, more profoundly. From "everyday life" one rises, through the death of silence, to a life which the philosopher calls "superior." It is somehow surprising that this conversation occurs here, since the possibility which it holds out is seemingly negated in the next episode. At the end of the film, we find not "true" speech, but unbroken silence; and not the death of the everyday, but Nana's literal demise.

12

The young man again. The oval portrait. Raoul trades Nana

HF: In Episode 12, *My Life to Live*'s aspiration to become a silent film is finally realized. The first scene in this episode consists of three parts, separated by fades, in which Nana and the young man converse with each other in a hotel room. In the first and the last, what they say is communicated through intertitles, referring us back to Dreyer's *Jeanne d'Arc*.

KS: But the silence of this episode is not the silence about which the philosopher speaks in the previous one, or even the silence of literal death. Here there is linguistic communication, but it is represented via the *graphic* rather than the *phonetic* signifier.

HF: Significantly, this is also the only scene in *My Life to Live* to dramatize an amorous relationship. It seems that Godard means us to understand the silence through which Nana and the young men converse as the language of love. The middle part of the hotel scene, in which silence gives way to speech, would thus seem to be definitionally "unloving."

KS: In that section of Episode 12, a male voice reads aloud from Poe's *The Oval Portrait*. Since the young man is shown reading from a Poe volume, we at first assume that we are hearing his voice. However, the speaker suddenly identifies himself as Godard by addressing Karina directly, as her husband and director. *The Oval Portrait* "is our story," he says, "a painter portraying his love."[14] As you have just suggested, the crucial concept here is not "love," but something which is at least in this context implicitly opposed to it: "portraying." *The Oval Portrait* tells the story of an artist who paints his wife's portrait, and thereby robs her of life. Godard seems to be telling us that he, too, seeks to subsume his wife to a mortifying representation.

HF: There is another reason why Godard compares the Poe story to his and Karina's story: in both cases, there is a rigid role division. In *The Oval Portrait*, the man paints, and the woman is painted. Similarly, Godard films, and Karina is filmed. And, during the brief interlude during which Godard and Karina are present in person in *My Life to Live*, the man talks, and the woman listens. There is a Svengali, or rather a

Sternberg idea at work here: the woman has "talent," but she herself does not understand it. Only the male artist can conjure the timeless masterpiece out of the woman's quotidian flesh.

KS: We have of course heard the *Oval Portrait* story many times before in *My Life to Live*. The narratives about the chicken, Jeanne d'Arc, the artist's wife, and Nana herself are all about the same thing, what might be called the "unmaking" of a subject. The philosopher could also be said to offer a version of this tale, but his version differs significantly from the others. Not only is the death he celebrates voluntary and temporary, and not only is it the vehicle for arriving at "true" speech and a superior kind of subjectivity, but it is also not gendered. In the story which is usually related in *My Life to Live*, on the contrary, death is involuntary and permanent; it provides access neither to "true" speech nor a higher form of subjectivity; and it is inflicted by a man or a group of men upon a woman. A woman's subjectivity is eradicated by and for a masculine other.

HF: When Godard says "this is our story," then, he would seem to mean not only *The Oval Portrait*, but *My Life to Live* in its entirety. He would seem to be comparing himself not just to Poe's artist, but also to Raoul, and Nana's nameless clients.

KS: Godard also likens himself to these male figures every time he shows his camera running ahead of Nana. He says: "I cannot wait for the moment at which Karina has been subsumed to my image of her—the moment at which the last brush-stroke has been painted, and the portrait is complete. I long for the moment in which specialness will yield to goodness, in which Karina will be completely Nana."

HF: But in this episode, there is often a poor match of text and image. Karina is not always filmed in a way which permits us to align her with the words Godard reads aloud (figure 4). This frustrates our attempts to create an analogy between Nana, the artist's wife, and Karina, on the one hand; and Raoul, the artist, and Godard, on the other.

KS: In Episode 12 of *My Life to Live*, Godard dramatizes his attempt to "speak" or "paint" Karina—to subordinate her subjectivity to his meaning. He even literalizes the first of these metaphors by reading aloud in an otherwise silent scene. But unlike the painter/husband

Fig. 4

in Poe's story, the filmmaker/husband cannot completely assimilate his model to his art. Cinema's abstractions are never as absolute as those of painting; a film can give us the "portrait" of a woman only in the guise of the "model." And because Karina's body and voice provide the necessary and ineradicable supports for Nana's fiction, she, too, becomes one of the enunciators of *My Life to Live*. Godard himself suggests as much in Episode 12. Through the nonmatch of Karina's body with the Poe text, he allegorizes all of the ways in which she might be said to "talk back" from the site of Nana, transforming the authorial monologue into an intersubjective dialogue. Godard also reverses the Poe story at the end of *My Life to Live*. Whereas in *The Oval Portrait* it is the wife who dies, and her artistic equivalent who survives, here the formula is reversed: Nana is murdered, but Karina lives on.

HF: In the last sequence of *My Life to Live*, Raoul is shown driving Nana and the other pimps toward the location where Nana will be exchanged for an agreed-upon price. Along the way, we are shown more documentary details: the Arc de Triomphe, shoppers on a Paris street, a

Fig. 5

crowd lined up outside the screening of Truffaut's *Jules and Jim*. These images say: "This is a true story. These events really happened."

KS: And then documentary once again emphatically gives way to fiction. Long before Nana and the others arrive at the location for the rendezvous, the camera has taken up residence there. It rushes to the scene of Nana's death, as if toward a long-awaited fulfillment, and waits for the narrative to catch up with it.

HF: Within minutes of Nana's arrival, she has been first exchanged, and then indifferently murdered, in the most radical denial imaginable of her "specialness" (figure 5). Raoul drives away, leaving her lifeless body behind. The other pimps do the same. Only the camera remains with Nana, and for two long minutes it pays homage to her "goodness."

KS: Nana is an animal with an outside and an inside. Remove the outside, there's the inside. Remove the inside, and you see her soul.

two

In Search of Homer

Contempt/Le Mépris (1963)

KS: *Contempt* (1963), a film shot in cinemascope, tells the story of a group of people who are involved in the making of a movie based on *The Odyssey*: a producer, Jerry (Jack Palance); a scriptwriter, Paul (Michel Piccoli); the scriptwriter's wife, Camille (Brigitte Bardot); a translator, Francesca (Georgia Moll); and a director, played by, and named after, Fritz Lang. It derives its basic story line from a novel by Moravia, *A Ghost at Noon*.

HF: The producer in Moravia's novel believes that the Anglo-Saxons have the Bible, but the Mediterranean countries have *The Odyssey*.[1] This is a strange idea; it allows Frenchmen and Italians to claim Odysseus as their prototype, but tells Americans that they must be content with Adam.

KS: It is in keeping with this subdivision of the cultural heritage that Moravia's producer decides to shoot the film in Italy rather than in Greece. But early in the novel, we learn that he has commissioned a German filmmaker to make the film (p. 76). It seems that texts do not respect geographical boundaries.

HF: Godard appropriates this detail from Moravia, and gives it a narrative rationale: He has Jerry explain to Paul early in *Contempt* that a film about *The Odyssey* must have a German director because Schliemann discovered Troy. Classical Greece can apparently only be reached via contemporary Germany. And he makes the scriptwriter French, and the producer American. In *Contempt, The Odyssey* thus travels even further than its protagonist.

KS: Godard borrows more than the narrative premise of *Contempt* from *A Ghost at Noon*; much of the film's dialogue also comes from that text. But almost everything derivative undergoes a sea-change in the process of being transferred from novel to film. Godard often gives lines to one character which are spoken by another in *A Ghost at Noon*.[2] He also reconceives the relationship between the writer and his wife, and dramatically transforms the semantic field of the narrative.

HF: *Contempt* could be said to offer a cinematic *translation* of *A Ghost at Noon*. In this respect, it mimics the story it tells, within which a book is also transformed into a film. But *Contempt* challenges our usual assumptions about translation. It shows that a translation is not the same text in another language, but rather something entirely new.

KS: The difficulties in adapting a book to the screen are at the forefront of *Contempt*'s narrative. Here, we learn not only that every translation produces a new text, but also that every attempt to identify the *meaning* of the original text is doomed to fail. The producer, director, and writer cannot agree about how *The Odyssey* should be filmed because each has a different idea of what that book is about. As Godard says in a short essay on *Contempt*,[3] that film could be called "In Search of Homer"; *The Odyssey* is for all intents and purposes irrecoverable, disseminated into a cluster of competing translations. *Contempt* ends before the *Odyssey* film has been completed, so we never learn which one finally prevails. But this does not matter, since it is finally *Contempt* itself, rather than the film within the film, which provides Godard's cinematic translation of *The Odyssey*.

HF: *Contempt* begins with an image of a studio compound in Rome. Raoul Coutard is producing a shot. This image tells us: "*Contempt* is a film about the magic of cinema." In the same way, a film opening with a shot of a man waiting in an alley with a revolver proposes: "This is a film about crime." Raoul Coutard moves on his camera dolly slowly

down a vertically placed track, accompanied by a sound-boom opera-
tor and two assistants. To his left are the buildings of the Cinecittà compound, and behind him the hilly suburbs of Rome. Coutard and his
Mitchell camera are filmed from a low angle, much like an approaching
train in a Western. This is a surprising use of *Contempt*'s cinemascope
lens, since it emphasizes the vertical over the horizontal axis.

KS: Coutard shoots Francesca, who walks toward us in a line parallel to
the track, reading aloud from a text. In the English version of the film,
all we hear are the tragic chords of Georges Delarue's music, but in the
French version a male voice-over speaks the credits to *Contempt*.

HF: When read in this way, the credits seem to become part of the
filmic narration, as if a narrator were to say: "This is the story of Camille
and Paul, and how their lives changed when they entered the mag-
netic field of the movie business." Francesca disappears from the frame
as Coutard's camera approaches the extra-diegetic camera; clearly, this
camera is positioned to film not her, but Coutard and his Mitchell. At
the end of the shot, the male voice-over confirms that cinema itself is
the object of this shot: "`The cinema,' said André Bazin, 'substitutes for
our look a world which conforms to our desires.' *Contempt* is the story
of this world."[4]

KS: After coming to a halt, Coutard pans with his camera, which also
has a scope lens, until he is facing us. The extra-diegetic camera
shoots him at this point from a low angle. Coutard then tilts his own
camera down until we seem to be looking directly into the lens. *Contempt* cuts to Camille and Paul in bed (figure 6). They are shot from a
high-angle position, exactly like that assumed by Coutard's camera
in the previous shot. Camille and Paul thus seem to come as the
reverse shot to the shot which ends with a close-up of Coutard's lens,
and with the words promising us a world conforming to our desires.
It is as if the first shot of *Contempt* signifies "camera," and the second
"image." And of course what figures here as "image" is primarily
Camille, in all of her naked beauty. Her reclining body even seems
made to order for the scope format.

HF: To make the equation between Camille and spectacle even more
emphatic, she begins almost immediately drawing visual attention to
the parts of her body. She asks Paul to look at each of these bodily

Fig. 6

parts, either directly or in an out-of-frame mirror, and to tell her if he likes it. The two seem to be repeating a lingual game they have often played before; the words they speak are a mantra proving the existence of their corporeal love. But Camille's body connotes "art" more than "sexuality"; the camera transforms it into a reclining sculpture, and the red and blue light in which the first and last parts of this scene are shot locate Camille in a world apart from our own. The pan also conveys this aura of otherworldliness in the middle, when Camille is displayed in full color, since the illumination in which her body is bathed is so unnaturally brilliant. Godard thereby subverts the demands of the producers, Carlo Ponti and Joseph Levine, who wanted him to make Bardot erotically available to the spectator.[5] Although he shows her nude, he protects her against the overtures of strangers.

KS: This scene, which consists of a single shot, also performs an interesting inversion of a traditional form of praise: the blazon. The blazon has been used by poets for centuries to describe the beauties of the human body. Conventionally, it proceeds through a male anatomization of a woman's charms, and could be said to be territorializing in effect. Here, however, the woman performs the anatomization herself, and orchestrates the praise. And, although the blazon form is generally assumed to be at the service of fragmentation, that is not its function here. Camille anatomizes her body not in order to divide it into a collection of part objects, but rather to establish that it is adored in every detail—as Paul says, "totally, tenderly, tragically." Through her self-blazon, Camille dreams of an Edenic plenitude: of a love adequate to the desire for love, and a language capable of expressing it.

HF: But there is something ambiguous about this paradise. Not only does the adjective "tragically" sound a discordant note, but when Paul touches Camille she also says: "Gently, Paul! Not so hard." In addition, neither Camille nor the camera seems to speak with an unfallen language. Both the words she utters and the images they generate proclaim their insufficiency.

KS: The blazon form is by very definition postlapsarian, since it proceeds through analogy rather than assertion. Before the Fall, language was referential: God spoke, and in speaking created; Adam named, and in naming spoke things in their essence. A rose was a rose was a rose. But in the world we inhabit, it is only possible to talk about things through reference to what they are not (lips through rubies, breasts through snow, teeth through ivory). The blazon form thus articulates the truth about language as we know it: it, too, always works through translation. This is made especially evident here, since the transfer is not from one word to another, but rather from image to word. Since language always carries us away from what it speaks, Camille's dream of a prelapsarian language is just that: a dream.[6]

HF: In the first two shots of *Contempt*, the aesthetic code or pretext is determinative. Every detail in the opening shot signifies "cinema," and seems calculated to violate the imperatives of the scope image. And, in addition to being inspired by sculpture and the blazon form, the second shot is organized through the three colors which will reappear in every subsequent scene: red, yellow, and blue.[7] But *Contempt* also includes shots which could be called "documentary"—shots where life, rather than art, provides the inspiration.

KS: For Godard, "documentary" signifies above all "contingency"— the "unplanned." Contingency occupies a privileged position within his aesthetic; he always hopes, as he himself puts it, to find "the definitive by chance."[8] Hence his insistence upon natural light, his refusal to write a final script before shooting, his reluctance to direct his actors, and—as we saw in the last chapter—his hope that they will bring their "truth" to his fiction. Hence, too, those shots in *My Life to Live* which insist upon the "thingness" of things.

HF: The third shot in *Contempt* dramatizes another way in which documentariness can come into play in Godard's cinema: the narrative can be elaborated on the basis of the options suggested by the location. In this shot, Francesca meets Paul at Cinecittà, the film studio outside Rome, and tells him that the film industry is in bad shape. They move from left to right, in search of Jerry, the camera following them. As they approach the studio, the camera tilts up to the words "Teatro n. 6," which were written at some time in the past above the doors of the studio. Here is the inspiration for everything that follows. Jerry emerges from the building, and begins his declamation about the end of cinema ("Only yesterday, there were kings here, kings and queens, warriors and lovers, all kinds of real human beings . . . now they're going to build five or ten stories of Prisunic. This is my last kingdom!") While delivering these lines, he walks back and forth on the two levels of a ramp, which becomes his impromptu stage. Jerry has a deep voice, which reverberates off the bare stone walls, further helping to create the outdoor theater already suggested by the location.

KS: In this shot, the vertical axis is once again strongly marked. Paul walks down a hill toward Francesca, who comes to greet him on the set of Cinecittà. The street on which he walks extends from the rear center frame to the front center frame. Godard enjoys playing with the scope format in this way, making it accommodate what it would seem to exclude.

HF: But the spaces to the right and left of the street on which Paul and Francesca walk are canceled out by the shadows of Cinecittà buildings. Although he breaks the compositional rules in a literal sense, Godard thus metaphorically obeys them. He diminishes the breadth of the scope image in this way for much the same reason that there are sometimes moments of silence in an opera. The scope image represents a kind of "crescendo," and a crescendo requires the contrast of a diminuendo. A moment after closing the theatre curtains in this way, Godard opens them up again. Jerry walks back and forth on the elevated ramp, deploying the full breadth of the scope image.

KS: Interestingly, Fritz Lang will suggest a few moments later that the scope format is only good for snakes and burials. He thereby puts the second scene of the film, in which the scope format is so splendidly utilized, once again under the sign of the Fall. So far, the world of *Contempt* seems more Christian than Homeric.

HF: The Cinecittà scene contains another reference to the Fall, this time routed through Goethe's *Faust*. Jerry offers Paul a job for which he will have to sell his soul, and he accepts it. For a $10,000 check, he agrees to rewrite Fritz Lang's *Odyssey* script along more commercial lines. Later, Camille will refer to the period before Paul's involvement in the movie business as a lost paradise. Watching this transaction, we should be fortified against temptation. Yet we, too, cannot help but succumb to the seduction of the movie business. We watch enthralled, as Jerry drives his red convertible the few meters from his studio to his screening room, and those same meters magically expand into the little forest through which Paul and Francesca walk.

KS: In the Cinecittà scene, Paul speaks French, Jerry English, and Lang often German. Francesca converts this babble into sense by translating what each man says to the other.[9] But communication often seems based upon misunderstanding, since Francesca's translations can deviate dramatically from the original. "Yesterday I sold this land," says Jerry, and Francesca translates: " *"Hier, il a vendu tout"* ("Yesterday, he sold everything"). Jerry says, "This is my last kingdom!," and Francesca translates: *"C'est la fin du cinéma"* ("It's the end of cinema"). At one point, the translation even anticipates—and perhaps inspires—the original, indicating that the relation between the two can be reciprocally determining.

HF: While at Cinecittà, Paul meets Fritz Lang, and sees the latest rushes from the *Odyssey* film. Even before the screening begins, producer and director are quarreling about the meaning of Homer's text. For Lang, it's about the conflict of individuals against circumstances, and for Jerry, about Penelope's infidelity. After the screening, this quarrel assumes another form. Jerry complains that what he has seen is not "in the script." "Naturally, because in the script, it is written, and on the screen it's pictures, motion picture it's called," responds Lang. Again, Godard insists upon the nonequivalence of words and images.

KS: Later in the film, Lang will make clear that his is an aesthetic of pure mimesis. "The world of Homer is a real world," he tells Paul approvingly, "and the poet belongs to a civilization which is developed in accord and not in opposition to nature." The cinematic adaptation of *The Odyssey* should be guided by the same aesthetic—by "a belief in nature such as it is." Lang, too, seems to think he is living in a prelapsarian world. As we would by now expect, this fantasy of perfect commensurability between cinema and nature is not realized in the rushes. Rather than representations of nature, they provide representations of representations: shots of statues of Penelope, Minerva, Neptune, and other Greek gods. Even the three shots near the end of the rushes sequence, which depict actors instead of statues, are heavily stylized. Lang's flesh-and-blood Penelope, for instance wears heavy eyeshadow around her eyes, and deep red lipstick on her lips. She also stands against a yellow wall, reprising the three primary colors which figure so centrally in the shot where Camille and Paul lie in bed. In his original treatment or *"scénario"* for *Contempt*, Godard wrote that the frame story should be filmed with as much natural light as possible, and the characters in it only lightly made up. The cinematic adaptation of *The Odyssey*, on the other hand, should be full of colors of a much greater brilliance, contrast, and violence. The overall effect should be of a Matisse or Braque painting in the middle of a Fragonard composition, or an Eisenstein shot in a film by Rouch.[10] The end result cannot be described in precisely these terms, since the frame narrative does not always derive its inspiration from "chance." However, Lang's rushes are every bit as artificial as a Matisse painting or a shot from an Eisenstein film.

HF: The shots of the Greek statues could also be read not as a literal quotation of the images of Lang's film, but as Godard's dramatization of the process of making a film from material found in a book or a museum. It is as if Jerry has told Lang, "Make the images in a museum move, give them flesh and blood," and what we are shown is the beginning of that process. In the first image of the rushes, the statue of Penelope is animated through a zoom. In the second, the bust of Minerva is shown turning first to the left, and then back again, as if coming to life. In the third shot of the rushes, the camera zooms into a low-angle close-up of Neptune, again suggestive of motion. The statues are also partially painted, indicating that the marble is beginning to yield to flesh. Eventually the statues are replaced by human figures, as if the transition to life has been successfully effected.

KS: But this reading still underscores the incommensurability of original and translation: whether we translate from life to art, or from art to life, the end result is something new. Your reading also suggests that what passes for the original may itself be a translation.

HF: After the shots of the statues come four of the most "documentary" shots in the whole film: the two shots of the mermaid in the Mediterranean Sea; the shot of Odysseus swimming toward the rock; and the final shot of sea and rocks. Here the camera is subordinated even more fully than in the Teatro n. 6 scene to what it films; the density of the water and the slipperiness of the rocks pose a strong resistance to cinematic control. These four shots differ so much from the stylization and artificiality of the others, that they seem to belong more to a film about the making of Fritz Lang's *Odyssey* than to that film itself.

KS: In the rushes sequence, the characters not only look at representations of the gods, but also talk about them. When seeing the images of Greek gods, Jerry says: "Oh gods, I like gods! I know exactly how they feel." He seems to think that he, as producer, is the twentieth-century equivalent of Zeus.

HF: Lang responds reprovingly, "It's not the gods who have created men, but men who have created the gods." This remark is in part narratively motivated: Lang hopes with it to deprive Jerry of his spurious divinity. But the diegetic director also speaks here for his extra-diegetic counterpart. Godard, too, wants to reverse the creation story.

KS: *Contempt* makes the gods a metaphor for a principle which has been variously interpreted across the ages, and which might perhaps best be characterized as "fatality." For the Greeks, this principle of fatality was in every sense exterior. For Lang, as we learn in the scene where Camille reads in the bathroom, it is both internal and external—"circumstances, " but also "conventions." For Freud and for many others in the twentieth century, fatality is an interior force, which might be called the "drive" or the "unconscious." However, even in this last capacity, fatality retains many of the daemonic attributes of the Greek gods, since it often impels us to act against our own interests.[11] To say that men create the gods which govern them complicates this model. It suggests that we alone are responsible for the destiny to which we are nevertheless fully submitted. But it is not yet clear what this destiny represents in *Contempt*.

HF: Lang, who typically communicates in quotations from great poets, thematizes the gods at one point in this scene through a passage taken from Hölderlin's "Vocation of the Poet."[12] The passage he quotes has three variants. The first suggests that man need have no fear "so long as God isn't there." The second proposes that man will be safe "so long as God is there." In the third and definitive variant, it is the "absence" of God which reassures man.[13] Whatever the gods represent in *Contempt*, it is something that we simultaneously need, and fear. The various references in the film to Athena and Poseidon—the one Odysseus's protectress, the other his enemy—suggest the same.

KS: Paul remains aloof from the discussion of the gods, joining in only to complete a Dante quote. The conversation seems to touch no answering emotional chord. But at the very end of the Cinecittà scene, Godard intercuts a shot of the Poseidon statue into the frame narrative, as if to indicate that the gods also preside over *his* story. The immediately succeeding events make the same point, even more forcefully. After the screening of the rushes, Paul introduces Jerry to Camille, and Jerry invites the two of them to his house for a drink. He claims that there is room only for Camille in his car, and proposes to Paul that he take a taxi. Camille registers her discomfort with this arrangement, but Paul insists that she go with Jerry (figure 7). As the red convertible races out of the image, Camille cries "Paul," and he—with equal but as yet uncomprehending anguish—responds: "Camille." A shot of Poseidon follows, reiterating what their cries also communicate: "This is a fateful moment, the moment when a malign destiny seizes control of Paul and Camille's lives."

HF: It takes Paul half an hour to reach Jerry's house, and by then Camille seems quite estranged from him. Paul says that he is late because of an automobile accident, but he narrates this story so unconvincingly that neither Camille nor Jerry believes it. Paul repeatedly asks Camille what is wrong, but he doesn't really want to know.

KS: Through actions blindly committed, and words half-consciously uttered, Paul seems to have set the fate machine in motion. And, as is often the case, one mistake seems to precipitate others. Knowing—and at the same time not knowing—that Camille is angry with him, Paul nevertheless flirts with Francesca inside Jerry's house. A second infidelity reinscribes the first. Two flashback sequences suggest that the new difficulties between Paul and Camille are compounded by their radically different ways of understanding the events of the last hour.

Fig. 7

HF: In both flashbacks, the image of Camille being helped into Jerry's car by Paul figures centrally. Godard needs to repeat this car image because he films it the first time round so casually. In a Hitchcock film, the importance of such an action is always heavily underscored at the moment it occurs. We see the look of agitation on Scotty's face perhaps five times before Madeleine jumps into the ocean in *Vertigo* (1958). Such shots make that event happen in slow motion, and so give us the time we need to grasp its significance. But in *Contempt*, there is nothing in the original staging of the car scene to tell us that this moment will be the starting point for the rest of the film.

KS: The second flashback is anchored to Paul's point of view, both because it includes memories available to him, but not to Camille, and because it takes place immediately after he has asked Francesca where the bathroom is. In this flashback, the image of Camille entering the car appears only once, and seems of no greater importance than the rest of the memories, which are all from events of the same day.

HF: When Paul recalls this image, he should know that he's not in a low-budget Hollywood film; he won't be able to wake up, as if from a dream, and say: "It was just a B-picture." But once again, he refuses to understand. Instead, he tries to recall everything that has happened since his loving conversation with Camille in the morning, as if to locate the problem elsewhere.

KS: The first flashback, on the other hand, seems to derive from Camille, since it follows directly from a shot of her staring reflectively into space, with her back to us. It refers twice to the car scene, as if to suggest that Camille already imputes heavy significance to it.

In one of these images, Jerry reaches out greedily for Camille, and in the other Paul seems to give her to Jerry, making clear precisely what that event meant to her. The other images do not connect up to anything else in the film. They seem to refer to earlier, idyllic moments with Paul. I say "idyllic," because in each of these images Camille offers herself to the look, just as she does in the second shot of *Contempt*. As if to make the analogy between these images and the second shot of the film more emphatic, in several of them Camille looks into a mirror. Here we have a very classical heterosexual tableau: the man loves the woman, and the woman loves herself through the man's love for her.

HF: During the ensuing quarrel in their apartment, Paul again repeatedly asks Camille what the problem is. And again these questions are really requests to her to provide some explanation other than the salient one.

KS: It is clear to us, if not in the fullest sense to Paul, that Camille thinks that he has used her as a sexual lure to consolidate his business relationship with Jerry. But she is not yet entirely certain what this means for their relationship. What Paul says at any moment of the quarrel can tip the scale unpredictably in one direction or the other. Throughout this scene, both Camille and Paul pick up a book for a while, and read aloud from it at random, without knowing what kind of provocation it will introduce into their dispute. Twice the phone rings, and introduces more contingency into the quarrel. There is even a diversionary incident: Camille's mother calls, and Paul involuntarily reveals that he believes Camille to be having an affair. This man, who so casually leaves his wife alone with a potential rival, nevertheless worries about how she spends her free time. Over the thirty minutes this scene lasts, Camille falls in and out of love again and again, until suddenly the die is decisively cast against the continuation of the relationship. Here, we have a narrative enactment of the emergence of the definitive out of chance.

HF: This scene is more psychological than is usual in a Godard film, but nevertheless it remains true to one typical principle of Godardian composition: a refusal of conventional predication. Godard does not say: "Paul and Camille quarrel for half an hour over his failure to protect her against the sexual advances of a strange man, but neither of them ever articulates the main issue." Instead, he says: "Man in hat. Man in towel. Blond woman. Woman in black wig. Sheets on couch. Sheets off couch. Dishes on table. Dishes off table. Love. Anger. Contempt. Tenderness." This reluctance to "declare" runs counter to the psychological aspects of the scene. It is as if Godard wanted to film all the possible variations on the theme: a man and woman fight.

KS: I think the astonishing array of emotions and modes of interacting which this scene dramatizes is also meant to convey the complexity of a feeling like "love," or "disappointment." Love can modulate for a moment into anger or even contempt without ceasing to be love. And disappointment always secretly harbors the hope that things will somehow turn out differently.

HF: Yes, I agree, but I had something different in mind. It is perhaps better illustrated by what Godard does with the bathroom door. This door has no glass, which multiplies its possibilities. Godard exploits them all, in a kind of declension. Paul first opens the door, goes into the next room, and closes the door. The next time he steps through the opening in the door, without opening or closing it. The third time, he moves the door, but still steps through it. The larger scene works according to the same principle. The architecture of the apartment offers Paul and Camille a certain number of paths for going from one room to another, as well as a certain number of positions from which the camera can see them, and they proceed to exhaust these possibilities.

KS: The door would seem to work, then, something like the "Teatro n. 6" sign in the Cinecittà scene.

HF: The whole apartment provides this kind of documentary provocation. It figures as a nonunderstandable space, one whose topography cannot be cinematically mastered or even deciphered. The characters are always appearing in unexpected places, as if from a labyrinth, so Godard must abandon the tracking shots he uses elsewhere in the film. The apartment is not a stage—it is not subordinate to the author's intentions, but rather dictates what happens and what we see.

KS: This scene seems at first far removed from the project of Lang's film. However, this impression is shown to be dependent upon an implicit identification with Paul, who "sees" without "seeing." In his and Camille's apartment, there is a vaguely neoclassical female statue. At one point during the quarrel, he hits the statue, first on the breasts, and then near the genitals. As he does so, he say inconsequently: "She doesn't sound the same all over." For him, the statue is only a hollow piece of base metal. But because of its neoclassicism, and also because all of the other statues in *Contempt* represent divine figures, the statue cannot help but signify something like "household god." And Paul's violence toward it seems to prefigure and perhaps even predetermine the moment of greatest sexual aggression in his quarrel with Camille, when he slaps her on the face. It appears that in the world of Paul and Camille, as in the world of Odysseus, one must be careful not to anger the gods. With the same indifference, Paul rummages through a book on Roman erotic art. It, too, says nothing to him. But Jerry has given Paul the book to help him write the *Odyssey* script. And unconsciously, Paul has wrapped his bathtowel around himself in the style of a Roman toga. Albeit mediated by other texts, and even other cultures, *The Odyssey* is somehow present.

HF: In the bathtub, Camille reads aloud from a book about Fritz Lang. The passage is one in which Lang argues against crimes of passion; it solves nothing to murder a sexual rival, he maintains. Again, *The Odyssey* speaks through this text. And a moment later we realize that Odysseus is not the only character in *Contempt* who might be said to have a sexual rival, and for whom the question of an adequate response is begged. Again, *The Odyssey* speaks through an apparently unrelated text.

KS: But Paul does not seem to register the relevance of Lang's words to his own life. He continues to think of himself as someone who produces texts, not someone who is produced by them. As if to emphasize this point, Paul at one moment during the quarrel sits down at the typewriter, and begins to compose a passage of a novel. Significantly, part of what he writes comes almost verbatim from the main narrative of *A Ghost at Noon*.[14]

HF: The quarrel scene is one of the longest scenes in the history of cinema. It takes up approximately one-third of *Contempt*, and it is shown in something like real time. Astonishingly, it nevertheless sustains our interest—not only because of the endless variations which it rings on a limited set of themes, but because of its rhythmic modulations. Two shots are particularly significant in this respect. In the middle of telling the story about Martin and the flying carpet, Camille comes in her black wig to the door of the bathroom where Paul is taking a bath. She lifts her hands to her wig, and steps with her left foot forward. The camera films this shot from inside the bathroom. *Contempt* then cuts to a corridor shot of Camille, standing in the same position, and still lifting her hands to her artificial hair. She turns around and walks out of the frame, and, with this movement, immediately quickens the pace of her story. The rhythm of the scene is thereby dramatically altered. We experience this moment as a break, but not an ellipsis; the scene continues uninterruptedly, but there has been a qualitative change.

KS: There is one interruption in the forward movement of the scene—that provided by the fantasy sequence. But like Paul's flashback, this sequence is inserted into a verbal exchange which continues immediately after. Right before that sequence, Paul asks: "Why don't you want to make love any more?" Camille responds, "Very well, come on, but quickly." As she speaks, she throws off the towel she has been wearing. After the fantasy sequence, Paul covers her naked body once again with the towel, while saying: "Don't be like that." Only a few seconds seem to have intervened between Camille's offer and Paul's response.

HF: The fantasy sequence is a "loop" which begins and ends with an image of Camille lying naked on a beige rug. Every one of its other images also shows Camille, sometimes displayed naked on a rug, sometimes fully clothed and drinking a cup of tea, sometimes dressed in outdoor clothes and running through a landscape.

KS: These images indicate to us what Paul and Camille have in common, even as their commonality is lost: her body. Surprisingly, though, they don't always reprise earlier moments in the film. Sometimes they anticipate later moments.

HF: The words spoken by Camille and Paul are subject to the same "loop" structure as the images. Both at the beginning and the end, Paul says: "I had often thought for some time that Camille could leave me, I had thought of that as a possible catastrophe, now I was in the middle of the catastrophe." Camille then adds: "On other occasions, everything had happened as if in a cloud of unconsciousness, of delightful complicity. Everything happened with an unplanned rapidity, mad, enchanted, and when I found myself once again in the arms of Paul I was unable to remember what had happened." This exchange is based upon a passage from *A Ghost at Noon* (pp. 31-32). I think Godard draws upon this passage here because it is so melodramatic. And he uses it during a sequence which, due to its extreme condensation, is also melodramatic. This sequence could be a trailer for a film based on Moravia's *A Ghost at Noon*. It shows that the beauty of characters, situations, and locations can become very concentrated when they are pared down to their essentials.

KS: In this respect, the fantasy sequence is in marked contrast to the scene into which it is inserted. During the quarrel, there are in a way *no* essential images. Every image there has a certain irresoluteness; every image can be undone and often is undone by the next. The black wig Camille dons at one moment and removes at another is a metaphor for this volatility.

HF: Generally, Godard does not distinguish in this way between "essential" and "inessential" images. Unlike most film directors, he doesn't use some images as weak links in a narrative chain leading to strong ones, but only images which, in addition to serving a narrative function, also have independent value. But the quarrel scene is his attempt to dramatize the moment prior to the establishment of "the irrevocable"—the moment when everything still seems possible, when anything could happen.

KS: The fantasy sequence offers not an internal monologue, but an internal dialogue or duet, which—like a unicorn—is literally impossible but imaginarily necessary. This is especially remarkable in that this duet occurs at a moment of estrangement; it is togetherness in separation. The fantasy sequence also dramatizes Paul and Camille's fall out of ostensible immediacy and into self-consciousness. They are no longer punctually "inside" either their relationship or their bodies. As Paul says: "Even under the excitation of the senses, I could examine [Camille's] gestures with a cold observation, just as she, without doubt, could in her turn observe mine."

HF: But as we noted earlier, there is no prior moment in the film when they are fully "present" either to themselves or to each other. Even in the bedroom scene, paradise is less an actuality than something to which Camille aspires.

KS: Curiously, though, although there is no prelapsarian moment in *Contempt*, the Fall is itself subject to a repeated reenactment. Paul sells his soul to Jerry for $10,000, and—as we will see—he betrays Camille not once, but three times. In addition, as I noted a moment ago, the paradise which Paul and Camille lose seems to lie as much in the future as in the past. In some respects, this is a very Christian idea: there can only be original sin if mankind keeps sinning. In order for the Fall to have happened, it must go on happening. What is new in the telling of this story is the idea that that fatal event need not be reconfirmed; it could also be undone. Although Paul's original betrayal of Camille is coded as fatal, Camille gives him two opportunities to rewrite history. Consequently, when he fails to do so, it is as though paradise has been lost all over again.

HF: I find it odd that we are given access to Camille's thoughts in this sequence. In Moravia's novel, we never know what she is thinking. She remains as much an enigma to us as she is to her husband.

KS: *Contempt* is very different in its treatment of Camille from *A Ghost at Noon*. Hers is in many ways the organizing subjectivity of the film. *Contempt* has already declared its allegiance to her by giving such narrative import to the moment when she enters Jerry's car, and by encouraging us to read her subsequent recollection of that moment over and against Paul's. It does so again in this scene not simply on one, but on three separate occasions. When Paul hits Camille in the face, the camera stays with her rather than cutting to him as he justifies his behavior. And when Paul objects to Camille using "dirty language," the camera gives her the opportunity to show that she can make obscenity beautiful by holding on her in close-up as she produces a list of taboo words. Finally, in the fantasy sequence, *Contempt* permits Camille to do what *A Ghost at Noon* does not: to lament the paradise which she never had, but which— through Paul's fatal act—she has nevertheless lost.

HF: Certain shots in this sequence are evocative of the bedroom scene. Camille is several times shown lying on her stomach horizontally, as she does in the earlier scene. But the fantasy sequence also contains two shots in which Camille occupies this position vertically, her face toward the camera. Again, Godard wants to show that he can over-come the constraints of the scope format. Like the condensation of language and image, these exercises in horizontality and verticality dis-tinguish the fantasy sequence from the rest of the apartment scene. They have a legibility which the rest of the scene lacks.

KS: Only at the very end does the camera once again move in such a way as to exploit the rectangularity of the scope format. In this shot, Paul and Camille sit facing each other across a table with a lamp. The camera tracks with an inexorable mechanical precision from one to the other and back again, each time pausing when it reaches its destination. As it does so, Paul turns the lamp on and off.

HF: The starting point for this shot is aesthetic rather than documen-tary—the formal code rather than chance. Although the camera sometimes reveals Paul or Camille while he or she is speaking, its movements are for the most part unmotivated by what transpires in the conversation.

KS: The turning of the light on and off during this shot has some-thing of the drama and significance of the game in which young girls pull petals off a daisy, while saying: "He loves me, he loves me not." The fateful moment of decision is about to arrive, the moment that will set everything in granite. Whether the light is on or off will be decisive in this respect.

HF: Throughout the scene, Paul has been wearing a hat. At the end of the scene, as he leaves the apartment, he takes a gun with him. He is beginning to understand that he is inside rather than outside the world of texts, but he still thinks that he can choose what novel he will inhabit. In his mind, he is Dean Martin in *Some Came Running* (1958).

KS: The next scene, which takes place inside a movie theatre, con-tains another horizontal tracking shot. Here, the camera tracks back and forth from Paul and Jerry, who are sitting to the right of the auditorium corridor, to Lang and Camille, who are sitting to the left. They are all facing a stage, which would normally make a conversation difficult, but the camera's movement puts the characters in communication with each other.

HF: Once again, the 35mm camera is a piece of machinery, like an artillery cannon, a tool machine, or a crane. It does not subordinate itself to what it films, but insists upon its own autonomy. On the stage, a woman sings, while couples wander back and forth. Lang and Jerry are trying to decide if they want her for the *Odyssey* film. Every time one of the main characters speaks, Godard extinguishes the sound of the music. This is another code, like the turning on and off of the light. In addition, it is Godard's way of comically obeying a rule of sound mixing which he almost always breaks: the rule that "background" noises should be lowered during conversations.

KS: The camera also tracks to the right and left in reverse shot, facing the stage. But here it derives its inspiration from contingency. It follows the couples as they drift back and forth on the stage.

HF: In the theatre, Paul reverts to Jerry's interpretation of *The Odyssey*: Odysseus takes so long to return to Penelope after the Trojan War because her infidelity has made him unhappy. Lang asks Camille if this is Jerry's version of Homer's text or his own. The question is more meaningful than it might at first seem. As Paul speaks, he appears for a moment to be reading *The Odyssey* through his own life. Is he not also a man who believes his wife to be unfaithful?

KS: Of course, it is not only wives who can be unfaithful, but translations. In telling the story of Odysseus through his own, Paul might be said to be producing precisely such a translation. And as if in immediate response, Lang now makes his speech on behalf of a pure mimeticism. Just as Homer was faithful to nature, we must be faithful to him. The "form" of *The Odyssey* "cannot be tampered with." We can only "take it or leave it."

HF: Although Lang insists strenuously upon the necessity of remaining true to Homer's *Odyssey*, he is inadvertently the most important spokesman in the film for the impossibility of doing so. In the rushes scene, he is able to give meaning to the Greek notion of fate only by invoking first Dante and then Hölderlin on the subject of man's relation to the divine, and thereby shifting from a pagan to a Christian frame of reference.

KS: In so doing, he suggests that the meaning of one text does not reside within it, but within the world of other texts. Lang also makes clear that the Mediterranean cultural patrimony cannot be separated off from the Anglo-Saxon. We read Genesis through *The Odyssey*, and *The Odyssey* through Genesis.

HF: Jerry asks Camille why she contributes nothing to this story. She responds: "Because I don't have anything to say." Camille is the only one of the four major characters who never offers a verbal interpretation of *The Odyssey*—the only one who makes no claim to stand outside it, to relate to it from a distance.

KS: Instead, she accepts her preassigned role from the start, and simply persists in it. She *is* Penelope, which is to say the wife who expects her husband to slay the rivals. That is her narrative function and *raison d'être*.

HF: That Paul, too, has a narrative function and *raison d'être* becomes more and more evident to us, if not to him. The "Capri" chapter of *Contempt* begins with a shot of Camille sitting on a boat. She is shown in medium close-up, against the blue backdrop of the Mediterranean. The next shot reveals that some meters away from her are two men with the Mitchell camera we saw in the first scene. A shot later, we see Camille once again, now from an overhead vantage. In these three shots, there is an implicit exchange between the woman and the camera technicians, as if both sides were thinking: "Well, here is a woman and a camera, we could get busy." Paul comes into frame, asking: "What are you doing?" The scene is now shot from the position occupied a moment ago by the camera. Paul announces that he has been defending Jerry's theory—the theory that *The Odyssey* is the story of a man who loves his wife, but who is not loved in return. *The Odyssey* is now very close. There has been a virtual condensation both of the diegetic and extra-diegetic cameras, and of the Homeric and Godardian couples. As if to make this yet more evident, Godard, in the guise of Lang's assistant, tells Paul and Camille to move away, since they are "in the shot." They proceed to the back of the ship, while preparations are made to begin shooting Lang's film.

KS: At one moment in this scene, Godard's camera once again asserts its autonomy from Lang's, but only so as to reiterate its devotion to Camille. Sitting in a deck chair with his back to the Mitchell and the crew, Paul asks whether the actresses who have agreed to perform the part of mermaids in the shot for which everyone is preparing will "take off their clothes." When Francesca responds in the affirmative, Paul exclaims: "Marvelous, cinema. [Normally when] one sees women, they are wearing dresses, [but in] cinema, snap, one sees their asses." The diegetic camera finds what it is looking for in the three soon-to-be-naked mermaids, but Godard's camera shows them only in an extreme long-shot, still clothed in tunics, and standing with their backs to us. The extra-diegetic Mitchell remains with Camille.

HF: Paul, of course, does not. A moment later, Jerry glances at Camille, and asks her to join him. Because he speaks in English, and has to wait for the translation and the answer, he has more time for his elegant posing: a man holding onto the ropes of the ship, with the rocks of Capri behind him. From out of frame, Camille responds: "No, I'll return by foot with my husband, in a bit." Jerry repeats his invitation, more forcefully. We then see Bardot in close-up for the first time since she has moved to the stern of the ship. She says "Paul!" This single word is an urgent appeal for help. She bows her head, perhaps ashamed, as Paul responds: "Go, Camille, go! It's fine with me—go, Camille, go! I'll return by foot with Mr. Lang. We're going to speak about *The Odyssey*." After he finishes talking, the camera zooms in on him as he lights his cigarette and closes his eyes for a moment, in a literalization of his metaphoric blindness. When he opens them, the action he has precipitated has already begun. We catch only the last moment of Camille's departure as she grabs the rope which marks access to the other boat, the one in which she will leave. The narration underscores this "leaving her to the producer" much more emphatically than the first time (figure 8).

KS: The first words Lang speaks to Paul after Camille's departure again effect an implicit conflation of their story with *The Odyssey*: "I need to have at the beginning a scene where a council of the gods discusses first the destiny of men in general, and then that of Odysseus in particular." The actor who plays Odysseus moves across the ship, and the camera follows him with a pan. Odysseus and Paul are now overtly in the same narrative space, and the fate of the one

Fig. 8

has become the fate of the other. The pan continues past Odysseus to the ocean, and the rapidly vanishing boat with Camille and Jerry. It is followed by a portentous shot of the Neptune statue.

HF: All of the talking between Paul and Camille has not prevented the repetition of his tragic mistake. It has not even led as yet to a consciousness of error: the camera which pans from Odysseus to the disappearing boat looks not from Paul's point of view, but from a vantage point manifestly exterior to it.

KS: In the two shots that follow the boat pan, the camera asserts its independence even more strongly. In the first, it circles from below around the statue of Neptune, from a position which is never narratively available to Paul. In the second, it cranes up to disclose Paul standing in extreme long shot in a niche at the top of one of Capri's cliffs. The camera seems to want to show us how distant it is from him, in every sense of the word.

HF: Paul advances a new reading of *The Odyssey*. The rivals were already there before Odysseus left for the Trojan War, he tells Lang. Odysseus encouraged Penelope to be cordial to them, and thereby lost her love. When he returned from his long journey, he realized that he must now slay them, or lose Penelope forever.

KS: Paul articulates the reinterpretation of *The Odyssey* which his life has become; the rivals have finally emerged as the central issue, and the narrative is focused upon that fateful moment in which a previous error will either be undone, or reconfirmed. Paul projects as a real possibility the action which would restore to Camille and himself the paradise they have never had. But in the scene that follows, he instead reenacts his initial mistake. He sees Camille kissing Jerry, and once again fails to respond.

HF: It would seem, then, that *Contempt* finally conceptualizes the principle of fatality in textual terms. Because Paul and Camille suddenly find themselves caught up in the cinematic adaptation of *The Odyssey*, they begin to interpret their own lives through that narrative, and in the process embue certain events with an ominous significance. Cultural production is always lying in wait to ambush us in this way—to permeate otherwise inconsequential moments with profound import. But it is generally quite arbitrary which text comes into play in the rendering-significant of our lives. Any two things which are brought together in this way will come to seem related to each other. And, even when the connection is arbitrary, it always comes to seem utterly convincing and inevitable.

KS: I agree with you that *Contempt* makes fatality synonymous with the influence which texts exercise over us. It is in this sense that we could be said to have created the gods which govern us. But it doesn't seem altogether arbitrary to me which texts come into play at moments like those dramatized by *Contempt*. Every culture consists of a range of master texts. These texts provide the overdetermined narratives with which its inhabitants make sense of their lives, and which—in the process—mould, constrain, and coerce them. And none of us can escape this fate. We can no more avoid interpreting our lives through reference to these particular texts than Odysseus can avoid the help and hindrances put in his path by the gods.

HF: But *Contempt* seems to suggest that if texts determine us, we also work transformatively upon them. As we have seen, Paul and Camille do not merely reenact, but also rewrite the story of Odysseus and Penelope.

KS: Yes, *Contempt* makes clear that master texts only maintain their force by being constantly analogized. And each analogy goes away from the term it comments upon, introduces something new. This is what "translation" finally means in *Contempt*. It is Godard's name for that agency through which the binding force of our master narratives is relaxed—that agency whereby we ourselves reconceive the stories which determine us.

Fig. 9

HF: In the scene that takes place on the roof of Jerry's villa, Paul and Camille reenact both of the versions of *The Odyssey* which Paul has put forward. In so doing, they change the form as well as the narrative of Homer's *Odyssey*. The first roof scene is staged less in the guise of an epic poem than a play. The roof is elevated, like a stage; Camille and Paul must climb dozens of steps to reach it. And, like a nature theater, this stage has as its spectacular backdrop the sky, sea, and rocks of Capri. Paul and Camille also behave as if they were on stage. Camille waves with both arms to Paul as he returns from his walk, the oversized scale of her movements suggesting the need to communicate to spectators even in the back row of the theatre that she is Penelope welcoming Odysseus home from his twenty-year journey. Paul enters the stage, and calls loudly for Camille, although he can see that no one is there. A moment later, Camille kisses Jerry in front of one of the villa's windows, and thereby makes Penelope unfaithful to Odysseus (figure 9). As she does so, she displays herself for an implied spectator. The villa window is the inverted equivalent of a balcony on an Elizabethan stage.

KS: In the ensuing scene inside the villa, Paul finally musters the energy to quit his job. However, he cannot bring himself to say why he no longer wants to work for Jerry, and he subsequently indicates that even this decision is less than final. Camille goes again to the rooftop, and Paul joins her a little later.

HF: When Paul arrives, he finds her wearing a metaphoric fig leaf. Covering not her genitals, but rather the buttocks so lovingly photographed by the camera both in the fantasy sequence and the second shot of the film, is an open book (figure 10). When Paul removes this fig leaf, Camille assumes a more ample one: a yellow bathrobe.

Fig. 10

KS: Already during the quarrel scene, Paul felt the need to cover Camille's body, as if it had somehow lost its innocence. Now nudity has assumed a definitively postlapsarian significance. Paul tells Camille that he sees her as if for the first time—that the scales have fallen from his eyes. For the first time, he is also able to articulate to Camille and himself the reason for their estrangement. But it seems that he still sees without seeing. He asks Camille to decide if he should write the *Odysseus* script after all, and he offers to stay on with her at Jerry's villa. With every utterance their estrangement becomes more absolute. The irrevocable is finally made irrevocable, placed beyond the possibility of a redemptive reenactment.

HF: When a misunderstanding becomes so profound that what one person says can find no interpretive commutation within what another person says or thinks, no reconciliation can occur. That is the situation at the end of the roof scene.

KS: Yes, Godard seems to be suggesting that it is not a full and adequate language, but rather translation, which is the condition of love. And faithlessness in the one does not necessarily signify faithlessness in the other.

HF: Does this principle obtain at the level of the enunciation, as well as at the level of the fiction? Is Godard's camera faithful to Camille only by betraying her?

KS: It seems to me that it is. In a way, the film never says "Camille," no matter how the camera lingers on the image of her body. It says: "Eve," "Penelope," "Bardot."

Fig. 11

HF: Paul falls asleep on a rock as Camille swims in the Mediterranean. By the time he wakes up, she has left with Jerry on their fatal journey back to Rome. "*Au revoir,*" she writes in the note she leaves behind. The film does not allow for a literal translation of these words.[15]

KS: Homer's Penelope waits for years for Odysseus to kill her suitors. Camille does not wait so long. She attempts to leave the world of that text, to escape from the "Penelope function." We could say that *Contempt* does not allow her to do so, that it refuses to give her a reality outside this function. Or we could say that her death is the film's dramatization of the closing off of revisionary possibilities. But in either case, the condensation of the frame story with the film inside the film is undone. Without Camille/Penelope, Paul can no longer be Odysseus. He leaves Capri, and *Contempt* ends with the shooting of Lang's version of the return of Odysseus (figure 11). Once again, we are back at the fateful moment of decision. Once again, Odysseus must determine what he is to do with the rivals. But now someone else is playing this part.

HF: *Contempt* is not only the story of Paul and Camille and *The Odyssey*, but also the story of Italy. The theatre marquee in the scene before the Capri "chapter" announces as much: *Voyage in Italy*. Godard can hardly imagine the movement from Rome to Capri without citing this 1953 Rossellini film. The title of that film is narratively significant, as book and film titles are so often in Godard texts. They help us to understand that *Contempt* is set in Italy because that is the country where the past and the present most fully coexist. The reference to the Rossellini film is also significant in another way. In *Voyage in Italy*, a couple rents a house not far from Vesuvius. From their terrace they can see some of the world's most wonderful and culturally charged sights. But Rossellini edits the images of the landscape in short flashes, as if the couple in the film had no eyes for their beauty. Like Paul and Camille, this couple thinks more about separation than Italy.[16]

KS: But perhaps that's the wrong way of approaching this issue. Surely the couples in both films fully inhabit Italy, but not with their eyes.
HF: Yes, maybe their voyages need to be thought about differently than the ones made by nineteenth-century tourists. In the past, people traveling through Palermo, Sorrento, and Capri often painted the land-scape, or made sketches of it. They did so not to produce images, but to understand the region better, just as one understands music better by playing the piano. The couples in *Voyage in Italy* and *Contempt* experience Italy more through their lives; their personal relationships, rather than painting or sketching, connect them to the landscape. Per-haps love is the artwork of today. But if Paul and Camille relate to Italy existentially rather than via painting or sketching, the camera remains a nineteenth-century tourist. It still needs to make images.

KS: Yes, but Godard prevents us from imagining that this nine-teenth-century "tourism" involves a more authentic relation to Italy than that enacted by Paul and Camille by showing us Capri always through the frame of *The Odyssey*. The red plaster building where the final scenes of *Contempt* take place signifies not Malaparte's villa, but the home to which Odysseus will twice return, and find Penelope waiting for him. And the deep blue water of the Mediterranean Sea with which the film ends sings like the sirens about the adventures of Odysseus. *Contempt* teaches us that there can be no Paul and Camille without *A Ghost at Noon*; no words without images; and no twentieth-century Italy without classical Greece. But although par-adise might seem to be lost all over again with each of these transla-tions, something much more important is gained.

three

Words Like Love

Alphaville/Alphaville, une étrange aventure de Lemmy Caution (1965)

Time uses words like love.
    —Paul Eluard, *Capital of Pain*

HF: In *Alphaville* (1965), Eddie Constantine plays Lemmy Caution, as he did in dozens of French films in the 1950s and 1960s. He wears a hat and a trenchcoat, and he loves women, whiskey, and money. But in this film, the man with the pockmarked face also carries a volume of poems by Paul Eluard. Lemmy Caution needs both gun and poetry in his battle against Alpha 60, a computer which has established a totalitarian regime of reason in the city of Alphaville.

KS: He needs another weapon, as well: the love of Natasha (Anna Karina), daughter of Leonard Vonbraun, the scientist who developed Alpha 60. *Alphaville* proves the truth of Susan Sontag's claim that "[in] the landscape of pain, only three . . . responses of real interest are possible; violent action, the probe of 'ideas,' and the transcendence of sudden, arbitrary, romantic love."[1] However, in this film these responses are not "unrelated," as Sontag claims they generally are. Rather, they comprise together what *Alphaville* metaphorizes as "light."

HF: The film begins with a close-up of a round ceiling lamp, which flickers ominously on and off to the sound of what might be called the

Fig. 12

"Alpha 60 theme." This is the first of a series of circular images with which Godard will portray the computer which controls Alphaville. By representing a computer advanced enough to wage atomic war on the world with a simple lamp, *Alphaville* signals its allegiance to those low-budget films in which an ordinary table plate designates a flying saucer.

KS: An identical image follows the credits, accompanied by the same musical theme. Suddenly, the camera pans to the right, across a nocturnal cityscape. Luminous windows in high-rise buildings form beacons in the darkness. As the camera pans, it picks up speed, until it finds what it is looking for: the headlights of a Ford Galaxy. In the next shot, the camera pans to the left, and tilts up and down a skyscraper, as the Galaxy pulls up in front. The voice of Alpha 60 says: "There are times when reality becomes too complex for oral communication. But legend gives it a form by which it pervades the whole world."[2] *Alphaville* cuts to a medium close-up of the driver of the Galaxy. At first, we can see little more than the steering wheel, and the shadowy form of someone sitting behind it. But then Lemmy Caution simultaneously illuminates himself and his cigarette with a cigarette lighter (figure 12). A moment later, in the dim light provided by the cityscape, Caution takes his gun out of the glove compartment, adjusts it, and puts it in his pocket. The legend has made its appearance.

HF: Lemmy Caution is ostensibly a secret agent, but—because he has no apparent institution backing him—he functions more as a private eye. His legend is the legend of the detective hero, created in America in the 1930s and 1940s, when the rackets became a metaphor for political and economic power. The detective is a melancholy figure; he maintains his morality, but it is a morality based on old, doomed ideals. He became a topos for film noir cinema, and here mutates into the old-fashioned hero sent to the city of Alphaville to battle the forces of computer technology. And although *Alphaville* is ostensibly a science fiction film, it is shot with a film noir camera; every light can become a falling star or a planet from the milky way.

KS: Godard claimed in an interview that "Lemmy is a person who carries the light to people who no longer know what it is."[3] At first, this is a surprising claim. Light is very important to the inhabitants of Alphaville. They depend upon electricity for the source of their energy; without it, they cannot live. However, they have forgotten the sacred origins of light. With his cigarette lighter, Lemmy seeks to reignite their memories. He is Prometheus once again carrying fire from the gods to humanity. And it is in the radiance of that legendary flame that the cityscape of Alphaville assumes its extraordinary poetic qualities.

HF: As if to underscore further the mythical value of Lemmy's cigarette lighter, Godard relies upon it almost exclusively to illuminate this shot. In most films, unseen hands switch on a dozen extra-diegetic lamps at the moment that a diegetic lamp is switched off, but Godard is content to let darkness once again descend when Lemmy extinguishes its flame.

KS: For the voice of Alpha 60, Godard used a man whose vocal chords were destroyed in the war, and who subsequently learned to speak from the diaphragm. As Richard Roud suggests, he wanted "not a mechanical voice, but one which [had] been, so to speak, killed."[4] This is because Alpha 60 is at least hypothetically a voice without consciousness. But the computer often says very surprising things. Here, for instance, it attests to the power of the Caution legend, thereby aligning itself with poetry rather than reason. At moments like this, it seems more friend than foe.

HF: When the computer *does* figure unequivocally as Lemmy's adversary, it is always associated with the present tense. In Alphaville, it is altogether forbidden to dwell in the past, and every effort is made to plan for and predict the future in ways which subordinate it to the present. Temporality is banished in the name of the eternal return of the same.

KS: A moment after Alpha 60 speaks for the first time, we hear a second male voice-over—this time that of Lemmy himself. Over another pan of the nocturnal cityscape, which again catches up with the Galaxy, Lemmy says: "It was 24 hours 17 minutes Oceanic Time when I arrived at the suburbs of Alphaville." This remembering voice is drawn from film noir, but here it assumes a new function. It puts the film as a whole under the sign of the past, rather than (as one would expect from its science fiction premise) the future.[5] It also suggests that the battle between Lemmy and Alpha 60 will turn in some central way upon time.

HF: When Lemmy arrives at his Alphaville hotel, Raoul Coutard's hand-held camera follows him through the revolving door, and then enters an adjacent glass elevator as Lemmy makes his ascent to his room. Light is refracted through glass in both of these shots, becoming more expressive than functional. Godard continues his experiment with light as Lemmy follows Beatrice, the Seductress Third Class, down the hall. Here, the only source of illumination is diegetic: ceiling lamps, and—for a moment—Lemmy's lighter. Because the overhead lamps are spaced at distant intervals, Lemmy and Beatrice are manifestly always either approaching a light source, or moving away from one. Illumination gives way to darkness, and darkness once again to illumination. The result is a drama of light and shadows.

KS: Both in the hallway and in Lemmy's hotel room, Beatrice creates a constant flow of words: "This way, sir." "Your case, sir." "You're tired, sir?" "You'd like to take a little rest . . . sir?" Later, Beatrice's replacement will use the same words as she leads Lemmy to his room. The residents of Alphaville engage in a form of utterance composed mostly of endlessly reusable formulas, which attest to the predominance of the type over the individual, and to *langue* over *parole*.[6] Language is rationalized and stabilized to an almost mathematical degree. Alpha-speech also circles back upon itself, eviscerating language of its intersubjectivity. The most frequently repeated formula, "I'm very well, thank you, you're welcome," completely forecloses an answer.

HF: The hotel room is an important location in detective fiction—an anonymous place for love, a drink, a suicide. Lemmy's room is no exception. It is the site, in quick succession, of seduction, violence, and romance. Lemmy has no sooner disposed of an intruder and an unwanted woman than the ravishing Natasha Vonbraun makes her dramatic appearance. But this particular hotel room also has one unusual feature, which Godard will inventively exploit: two different doors lead in and out of the bathroom. As Lemmy enters through one door, another character can unexpectedly appear in the bathroom through the other. After *Alphaville* shows Beatrice and Lemmy entering and exiting the bathroom in every possible combination, it depicts the intruder coming into that room from the left, as Lemmy approaches it from the right. The ensuing fight is shown in a mirror, and the music from the jukebox almost drowns out the sounds of struggle. In this scene, *Alphaville* manages to give back the memory of a Lemmy Caution film. But it offers the gesture, rather than the intrigue, of such a film.

KS: As Lemmy approaches the outskirts of Alphaville, he sees a traffic sign reading "Silence. Logic. Safety. Prudence." Lemmy's own behavior in the first hotel scene is in every respect the opposite of this credo. The first attribute with which the film characterizes him is violence. Lemmy not only dispatches the intruder, but also roughs up Beatrice. A proclivity for violence might seem at odds with Lemmy's role as the savior of mankind, but—as we learn very quickly—his morality has little to do with the traditional virtues. He stands for everything within humanity which is resistant to Alphaville's technocratic vision, whether it is commensurate with what we usually think of as goodness or not: affect, danger, finitude, the unpredictable. And Lemmy's violence is informed by all of these values. It is one of the qualities which most separate him from the narcotized world of Alphaville.

HF: As the moment where he shoots bullets through the breasts of the Vargas nude makes clear, Lemmy's violence is also a trope. He tells Beatrice to hold the poster of the Vargas nude over her head. We then see Lemmy lying on the bed reading Raymond Chandler's *The Big Sleep*. Without putting the book down, he fires at the poster twice. Godard thereby not only pays homage to the detective tradition upon which he draws, but also puts quotes around Lemmy's violence. It is on the same level as his cigarettes, gun, and trench coat.

KS: Like all Vargas girls, the one at which Lemmy shoots has the same tranquilized quality as Beatrice. He could be said to be shooting at the flesh-and-blood woman through her representational counterpart. But in a curious way, this aggression is indicative less of misogyny than sentimentality. It says: "No sensuality without affect." Godard indicates that Lemmy's violence paradoxically signifies tenderness by cutting before and after he fires the gun to a car speeding by outside, accompanied by the beeping sound that often signifies "censorship" in Alphaville. In this world, it is not violence but emotion which is prohibited.

HF: Before Lemmy shoots at the Vargas nude, he takes Beatrice's photograph. The camera with which he does so is as constant a prop as his trench coat and hat, but one without a film noir inspiration. The camera aligns Lemmy with Godard, and thereby reminds us that the passion of the one represents the passion of the other. Lemmy brings sacred light to Alphaville, which knows nothing but electricity. And Godard brings diegetic light to cinema, which has forgotten that there is an alternative to studio lamps.

KS: When Lemmy holds the view finder to his eye, he also draws attention to his look or point of view. His camera is consequently a metaphor of his eye/I: of what the film calls *"conscience."* Although both the English version of the film and the English translation of the script translate *"conscience"* as "conscience," Godard clearly means "consciousness." And it is important that Lemmy's consciousness is once again associated with retrospection. Not only is the camera an apparatus of the nineteenth century, but Lemmy's particular version of this apparatus is also characterized as old-fashioned by one of the Alpha 60 technicians. In addition, the tense with which the camera speaks is the past. It always says "this has been."[7]

HF: After Beatrice leaves, Alpha 60 announces the imminent arrival of Natasha Vonbraun. While Lemmy waits for her, he places his cigarette lighter on the mantle, and lights it by firing at it with his gun. As the camera holds on the cigarette lighter, Natasha asks from out of frame: "Do you have a light?" When the camera cuts to a close-up of her face, Lemmy responds: "I came 9,000 kilometers to give it to you." For the first time, we hear the romantic notes of the "Natasha theme." These two shots further expand the semantic range of the word "light," or—in the French—"*feu*" ("fire").

KS: *Alphaville* provides two different versions of what next transpires. Natasha says, in close-up, "My name is Natasha Vonbraun." From out of frame, Lemmy responds: "Yes, I know." His voice suggests that this knowledge is as old as the universe. It is as if they have been meeting over and over since the beginning of time. "How do you know?" she asks, in response as much to his voice as his words. She, too, seems on the verge of recollection. Then amnesia descends once again. The camera adopts a position showing both Natasha and Lemmy, while he asks: "Miss Vonbraun?" and she responds, routinely, "Yes. I'm very well, thank you, you're welcome."

HF: In Alphaville, people nod when saying "no," and shake their heads when saying "yes." When Natasha engages in these contradictory movements, it always suggests a certain resistance on her part to the words which she speaks. *Alphaville* also communicates a similar self-contradiction through the shot in which the camera holds on Natasha's face while she talks about her plans for the evening. The words could not be less meaningful, but Natasha's voice and demeanor communicate the sadness of the ages.

KS: We often sense that Natasha is psychically "elsewhere." In another text, this "elsewhere" would be the unconscious. Here, it is always designated with the word "consciousness." However, what *Alphaville* calls "consciousness" is structurally analogous to what Freud names the "unconscious." Although subject more to a social than a psychic repression, this consciousness has been "forgotten," and can only be recovered through "recollection." And in *Alphaville*, as in psychoanalysis, this forgetting and remembering is specified in linguistic terms. In both cases, one loses the capacity to recall something when it is denied linguistic expression, and succeeds in recalling it through speech.[8]

HF: As Lemmy and Natasha walk down the hotel corridor on their way to the elevator, Lemmy asks her if no one has ever fallen in love with her. "Love" is the most forbidden word in Alphaville, and therefore the one with the greatest magical power. But here the word only precipitates a misunderstanding. Natasha asks what it means, and Lemmy assumes she's making a fool out of him. With neither able to understand the words of the other, the two lapse into silence. Godard extinguishes all other sounds as well—both the music, and the sound of their footsteps. Lemmie and Natasha are together in their silence in a way that they haven't yet found in language.

KS: *Alphaville* consistently privileges noncomprehension over reason—the "why" which it is forbidden to utter in *Alphaville* over the obligatory "because." The "why" is productive: it can help one to understand that one has forgotten, which is the first step in remembering. But Lemmy is not content on this occasion to surrender himself to bafflement. After a moment, he recalls that he is a character from a detective novel, where not knowing can be fatal. "It's always like that," Lemmy says in voice-over, "One never understands anything. Then suddenly, one evening, you end up dying of it." He writes these words in his notebook, the verbal equivalent of his camera.

HF: As Natasha and Lemmy descend in the elevator to the lobby, the camera once again takes an adjacent elevator. At first, the two glass boxes are parallel. But the one carrying Natasha and Lemmy leaves first, and for a moment the camera and the narrative are disjunctive. Eventually, the second elevator catches up with the first, and the narrative is refound. This drama of loss and recovery is diegetically repeated, as Natasha walks slowly away from Lemmy to the counter, and back again. She leaves room for desire to awaken.

KS: As they walk to Natasha's car, Lemmy says in voice-over, "Her smile and her small pointed teeth reminded me of one of those old vampire films they used to show in the cinerama museums." He thereby suggests that Natasha, too, might be said to represent the past more than the present. Natasha's first name also associates her more with what was than with what is, Lemmy tells her in the car. She responds by articulating the central dogma of Alphaville: "Yes, but you can only know what exists in the present. No one has lived in the past, and no one can live in the future."

HF: Later, we will learn that Natasha's original last name was Nosferatu rather than Vonbraun, which again associates her with vampire films. And, when Lemmy asks how much farther they have to go, Natasha says "Karl?" inquiringly to the driver. "Karl" could be the name of Count Nosferatu's coachman. For a moment we imagine that we are in a horror film, being transported to a hidden castle in a forest. But Karl says only: "You know very well that we must cross the North Zone, Miss."

KS: After trying in vain to reach Henri Dickson (Akim Tamiroff) by telephone, Lemmy goes to the dwelling of the former secret agent, the Red Star Hotel. Inside that hotel, a client reads a passage out loud from a guidebook, reiterating what our visual faculty also tells us: this is a locale from the past, not the present. "In no way can it be compared to our splendid . . . passages, all glittering . . . with luxury and light," he quotes. "It is merely a huge, tall, narrow labyrinth." The single unshaded light bulb which illuminates the staircase where Lemmy and Henri talk attests even more profoundly to the age and squalor of the Red Star Hotel. It is a throwback to a detective novel from the 1930s, or a B-picture from the 1940s. Through a cut-away shot to a large circle of lights, within which a second circle rotates, Godard contrasts it with the official cityscape of Alphaville. But ironically, this futuristic city is also a throwback to the past; Godard conjures it, with metaphoric smoke and mirrors, out of Paris of the mid-1960s.

HF: The money which Lemmy gives Henri not only permits him to pay for his room and a beer, but to buy a dream. Henri invites the resident seductress to his room. Before she arrives, he and Lemmy talk about Alphaville and the computer which governs it. This conversation consists entirely of science fiction clichés: Alphaville is a "pure technocracy," in which there is no room for artists or poets, and Alpha 60 is incomparably advanced compared to our present computers. Godard signifies "technocracy" with close-ups of Einstein's relativity theorem, a formula which we know not only from high school science, but T-shirts and posters.

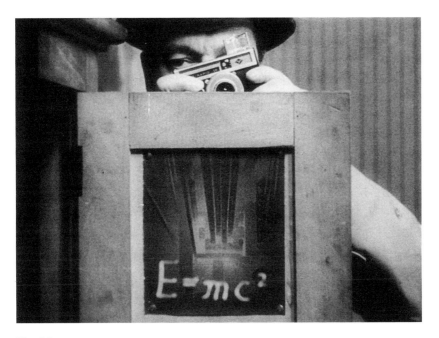

Fig. 13

KS: The science fiction plot is only a premise for a complex meditation upon temporality and affect. What is important about this particular scene is not the exchange which takes place between Henri and Lemmy before the seductress appears, but rather what happens afterward. As she makes her entrance, Henri greets her in the name of the legendary women of yore: "Enter, Madame la Marquise, my cloak, Madame Récamier. . . . Thank you, Madame Pompadour. . . . Ah, Madame Bovary." These retrospective blandishments are the gestures of love; with them Henri transfigures the sordid bedroom, and deifies the Seductress Fourth or Fifth Class.

HF: With the repeated flash of his camera, Lemmy, too, lights up the darkness of the Red Star Hotel (figure 13).

KS: But as Henri embraces the seductress, he is suddenly overtaken by death. Lemmy approaches the bed where Henri lies gasping for breath, hoping to glean information which will aid him in his mission to destroy Alpha 60. He is seemingly unsuccessful. Henri's last words are baffling in their confusion of the political with the affective: "Lemmy

... consciousness ... consciousness ... make Alpha 60 destroy itself
... tenderness ... save those who weep." Equally surprising is what
Lemmy finds under Henri's pillow: Paul Eluard's *Capital of Pain*, one
of the masterpieces of French surrealism.[9]

HF: Lemmy goes to the Institute of General Semantics to meet Natasha.
As he enters the building and looks for the right room, he is shot always
with a great deal of "air" above his head. The framing seems motivated
by more than the desire to communicate anomie; Godard also wants to
show the milky way of ceiling lamps, which is repeated to infinity in the
reflections of the windows. *Alphaville* depicts Lemmy's journey through
the many rooms of the Institute in something approximating real time.
Godard is almost as interested in movement as light, and Eddie Constantine is an actor who knows how to move.

KS: The room where Natasha is listening to the lecture of Alpha 60 is
dark as Lemmy enters. He is guided to his seat by an usherette with a
flashlight. These two figures move gropingly through the darkness,
from time to time illuminating part of a face in an estranging light.
The flashlight becomes a fiery torch, seeking out Natasha; in this vel-
vety night, it is the flame which moves toward the moth, rather
than the moth toward the flame.

HF: After leaving Lemmy, the usherette walks to the wall switch, and
turns on the light. In the electrical illumination, myth recedes, and her
fiery torch becomes once again an ordinary flashlight. Lemmy tries to
speak to Natasha, but she urges silence, and points toward Alpha 60.
Here the computer, which is one hundred and fifty light years ahead of
our own, is represented through the cooling ventilator of a Peugeot or
Renault. Again, Godard shows that high technology can be evoked
through low; by putting a cluster of light bulbs behind the ventilator,
and accompanying the rotation of its fan with the Orphic voice of
Alpha 60, he creates out of an ordinary car part a worthy adversary to
his larger-than-life protagonist.

KS: In the opening shot, the voice of Alpha 60 speaks from an ante-
rior moment to the narrative of *Alphaville*. Like Lemmy's voice, it
inducts us into a world which is no longer. Here, on the other hand,
the computer speaks from the heart of the narrative. But once again

Alpha 60 is a less faithful representative of the ideology of Alphaville than are many of its human inhabitants. It begins conventionally enough: no one has lived in the past and no one will live in the future, because time is an endlessly repeating circle, the constant return of the same. Therefore, "everything has been said." But this last reflection immediately gives way to the anxiety that temporality is inherent in language. Can we really prevent words from changing their meanings, and meanings their words? And is not difference also at the heart of humanity itself, rendering even belief a very individual matter? Is it not obvious "that someone who usually lives at the limit of suffering requires [another] form of religion than someone who normally lives securely?" Alpha 60 reverts to the thought of an eternal present, as if in refuge from these anxieties, but that thought is now also conducive of fear. If no one has ever existed before us, we are "unique, dreadfully unique." Unlike Lemmy Caution, who is in a perpetual dialogue with earlier stories and legends, Alpha 60 hears only the echo of his own voice in the void. And to inhabit only the present means never to be able to think relationally. When one cannot compare what one sees and hears with what one has previously seen and heard, "one isolated word or an isolated detail in a drawing can be understood. But the comprehension of the whole escapes us."

HF: Alpha 60 uses the image of the circle to metaphorize the endless present tense of Alphaville. This is surprising, since the circle signifies "myth" more than "reason." Perhaps this is another way in which Alpha 60 itself exceeds the doctrine it promulgates. The computer cannot live without the ornament of myth.

KS: The circle is a ubiquitous symbol of Alphaville. The major roads are all organized in circles, every image of Alpha 60 is circular, and the endlessly repeated "I'm very well, thank you, you're welcome" could be said to circle back upon itself. Those who inhabit time, on the other hand, will be characterized as going straight ahead. We have become accustomed to thinking of linearity as teleological, as a subordination of means to end. But as we will see, the dissident residents of Alphaville think otherwise. For them, forward movement is redemptive. But this seemingly schematic opposition is not sustained at all points. As you suggest, the circle retains many of its traditional values in *Alphaville*.

HF: The drawings at which we look while Alpha 60 speaks seem to come from nowhere. At one point, we see a white screen, but never the apparatus of projection. Like Alpha 60's words, these drawings are strangely at odds with the ideology of Alphaville. In one striking image, a question mark and an exclamation mark are shown on opposite ends of a seesaw. The seesaw is parallel to the ground, giving priority neither to the question mark nor the exclamation mark. In another image, the abbreviation SOS seems on the verge of drowning in a sea of waves.

KS: Whereas the ideology of Alphaville pushes language in the direction of a mathematical formalization, this scene does the opposite: it attempts to "motivate" the relation between linguistic signifier and signified, and sign and referent.[10] It subjects language to what Freud would call a "primarization," treating words and other linguistic symbols like images, or even things.[11] This move is inimical to reason; it not only renders the meaning of words unstable, but it also puts them at the service of desire. Like Alpha 60's monologue, the images which accompany it suggest that the mega-computer which rules over Alphaville is subject to a profound internal contradiction. This contradiction cannot be resolved; it is integral to the constitution of Alpha 60. To be a computer is to be simultaneously outside of temporality, and made up of memory. It is to be incapable of retrospection, and yet unable to forget.

HF: After the lecture, Natasha walks with a friend down a spiral staircase. The camera depicts her progress down the stairs with its own circling motion. In so doing, it shows the artwork of the staircase. Modern buildings from the 1960's, like the Institute of General Semantics, are predicated on the rectangle. But every so often, the relentless rationalism of the rectangle gives way to the mythos of the circle. By showing us Natasha descending the spiral staircase, Godard suggests once again that even the residents of Alphaville cannot live by functionalism alone. And, as usual, it is the circle which provides the way out of this functionalism.

KS: In the foyer of the Institute of General Semantics, Lemmy tells Natasha that he couldn't understand Alpha 60's lesson. Natasha's response suggests that the inhabitants of Alphaville are so programmed to hear certain pieties from Alpha 60 that they do not register disruptions and deviations. For her, the lesson is simple: life and death exist within the same sphere. Lemmy proves a more attentive listener here than he was in the lecture room. To locate death within the same sphere as life is to refuse finitude; it is to subsume even that most radical of all differences to sameness, to make the Great Unknown into the always-already. To ascertain whether or not he has correctly understood Natasha, Lemmy asks the key question, "Are you afraid of death?" "Of course not," she responds; where there is nothing to challenge certitude, there can be no fear. But, savingly, she asks a moment later: "Why?"

HF: As Natasha and Lemmy's car stops at a red light, Godard finds another opportunity to paint with light. Because *Alphaville* is a black and white film, we register the change in traffic lights not through color, but the relocation of light. And the reflections within the camera lens create a halo effect around the street lights and traffic lights.

KS: Near the end of their journey, we once again hear the voice of Alpha 60. At first, it seems to emanate from the same mysterious location as at the beginning of the film. Here, however, it is unequivocally the voice of reason. "Nor is there in the so-called capitalist world or communist world any malicious intent to suppress men through the power of ideology or materialism, but only the natural aim of all organizations to plan all its actions." As Natasha and Lemmy enter the building of the gala reception, Natasha finishes the speech: "In other words, we minimize the unknown." It is now clear that Alpha 60's voice derives on this occasion from Natasha's psyche. This suggests that the normal mental condition of the residents of Alphaville is nothing more than the repetition within them of its rationalizing pronouncements, a repetition inimical to consciousness. What Alpha 60 says on this occasion is directed more against the threat posed by the future than by that posed by the past, above all that represented by death. Through planification, the technocracy of Alphaville seeks to make the future something which can be controlled from the present, and thereby its simple extension.

HF: The gala reception takes place inside a room filled with an indoor pool. On one side stands a line of dissidents who are to be executed, one after another. Their crime is behaving illogically, or—in a word—affect. One cried when his wife died, and another believes in "love and faith,

Fig. 14

courage and tenderness, generosity and sacrifice." Each is shot in turn
from his perch on the diving board into the swimming pool, where he
is then stabbed to death by women divers (figure 14). There is always
something prisonlike about an indoor swimming pool. Indeed, indoor
swimming pools are evocative in certain respects of a concentration
camp, with their public shower rooms and lack of privacy. Godard
himself underscores this similarity by showing the female executioners
moving choreographically through the water, relics from the strangest
Hollywood genre ever, the Esther Williams film. The button in the elevator leading to the swimming pool also reads "SS."

KS: But this scene is ultimately more committed to another metaphor:
the metaphor of the straight line. And here, again, the venue of the
gala reception is suggestive. The diving board from which the victims fall into the water is an important embodiment of linearity, as
the first victim indicates. "In order to create life, it is merely necessary to advance in a straight line towards all we love," he says as he
walks steadfastly to the end of the diving board. As he does so, he
makes clear that the metaphor of the straight line implies the very

antithesis of progress toward a predetermined goal. It signifies the headlong rush of desire toward its object, and the subject toward its final truth. In neither case can we know where we are going; we move urgently but blindly toward an unknown destiny.

HF: After the gala reception, Lemmy detaches the most distinguished of the spectators, Leonard Vonbraun, from the bodyguards who surround him, and pushes him into the elevator. When they arrive at the fifth floor, the bodyguards are waiting for Lemmy. They shove him back in the elevator, and begin beating him up. *Alphaville* never shows the actual blows, only the interval between them, as the thugs throw Lemmy back and forth. It counts the blows with the downward movement of the floors; "knock-out" is *sous sol.*

KS: When Natasha sees the injured Lemmy, tears well up in her eyes. Like the dissidents, she is now definitively guilty of illogical behavior, which is to say: humanity. A bystander asks if she is crying, and she responds: "No . . . because it is not allowed." As the camera holds on the tears running down her face, Godard resorts to a surprising effect: he extinguishes the illumination around Natasha, so that the light of her face can burn more brightly. As we are thereby given to understand, there is no positive without a negative—no white without black, no stars without the night, no trembling of desire without the certain knowledge of death.

HF: Lemmy is taken to Residents Control, the huge office complex which is the home of Alpha 60, to be interrogated. The computer asks him a series of routine questions, such as his name and age, and then what he calls "test questions." Alpha 60 is represented in part by the automobile cooling ventilator, and in part by a ceiling light. The ceiling light is shot with a changing camera aperture, so that it sometimes seems to suffuse with light until the surrounding darkness bleaches out. The microphones move back and forth while Alpha 60 is speaking, suggesting the gesticulations of a robot.

KS: The test question sequence is evocative of the lecture in the Institute of General Semantics. The exchange turns upon forbidden topics—fear, death, love, poetry—but it seems at times irrelevant who asks the questions, and who answers them. Lemmie and Alpha 60 are becoming more and more alike. At one point, we learn that it is poetry which transforms the night into the day, and at another that there is no mystery in love. The last disclosure seems calculated to elicit in us the prohibited "why?".

HF: Lemmy is shown around the nucleus of Alpha 60. The film sticks close here to the conventions of science fiction. Lemmy discovers that it is a man from his own world, Leonard Nosferatu, who—under the name Leonard Vonbraun—is responsible for the technocracy of Alphaville. The prototypical man of science, he cared more for the development of his theories than for the good of his country. Now amorality has mutated into unqualified evil. Vonbraun's creature, Alpha 60, has declared war on the world as we know it. Only one solitary man can prevent this catastrophe: a man from the older, less technically advanced culture. He alone can muster the weapons sufficient to defeat a machine capable of solving such problems as train and plane schedules, the supply of electrical power, and the logistics of war: love, poetry, and violence.

KS: As Lemmy escapes from the central computer complex, his voice-over rounds out the science fiction parable: Alphaville allows no exceptions to its rule of conformity. Outsiders are quickly assimilated, and dissidents either executed or rehabilitated. But Godard is not so interested in all of this. What is important here is something which seems at first quite marginal to the narrative of totalitarianism and intergalactic warfare: Alpha 60 is suffering a breakdown, and the site of the problem is its memory system. What this means in the case of the computer itself has already been suggested in the scene set in the Institute of General Semantics. What it implies for the inhabitants of Alphaville is indicated in the scene following Lemmy's escape from Residents Control. After a long walk home, he proceeds once again down the hall of his hotel with a Seductress Third Class—this time not Beatrice, but one of her replacements. He asks her if she has ever heard of the Lands Without.[12] When she responds no, he pulls back her hair to look for the tell-tale control number tattoo. After finding it, he tells her to clear off, but his brusqueness turns to tenderness a second later as, in a miraculous return of the repressed, the Seductress asks "why?" In gratitude, Lemmy caresses her thigh.

HF: Natasha is waiting behind the door as Lemmy enters. In a reprise of the earlier scene, in which Lemmy waited in the room as Natasha entered, his entry is given in three variants. The light in the room increases with each repetition. It is unclear which is the authoritative or diegetic version.

KS: *Alphaville* itself might be said to go backwards in time here—to participate in the retrospective turn it consistently equates with consciousness. It also dramatizes the volatility of memory—the constant revisions to which it subjects the past. By giving us three different versions of Lemmy's entry into the hotel room, *Alphaville* reminds us that there is no memory which is not subject to unceasing revision and transformation, and hence resistant to standardization.[13]

HF: Lemmy is not sure whether he is happy to see Natasha or not. While he is deciding, he asks her to bow her head, and he looks to see if she, too, wears a tattoo control number. When he finds the number 508 on the back of her neck, there is a sudden surge of music; the romantic "Natasha theme" suggests that this discovery has precipitated a surprising emotion in Lemmy. Until now, he has assumed such control numbers to be worn only by the most robotic inhabitants of Alphaville.

KS: Already, the Seductress's "why" has disturbed that assumption, suggesting to him that the struggle which lies ahead is not one between human and machine, but rather between human consciousness and what impedes it. With the discovery of the control number on Natasha's neck, it becomes clear that within the psyche of every resident of Alphaville, a human being is struggling to emerge. Lemmy falls in love with that human being, which has the face of Natasha Vonbraun.

HF: Lemmy asks Natasha if she has heard of Eluard's *Capital of Pain*. Some passages are underlined, he says meaningfully, as he hands the book to Natasha. She begins reading these passages aloud: "We live in the void of our metamorphoses./But the echo that runs through the day. . . . The echo beyond time, despair and the caress. . . . Are we close to, or far away from, our consciousness."[14] A moment later, Lemmy asks Natasha if she has heard of a secret message. That is precisely what he takes the Eluard book to be: a message, in code, about Alphaville. Like a good secret agent, he seeks to break the code.

KS: Natasha broods upon the word *"conscience,"* a word which she does not yet remember. In so doing, she makes the words of the Eluard text available to us in another form. They *do* offer the key to the destruction of Alphaville, but not in the guise in which Lemmy expects to find it. The echo which "runs through all the day," and is beyond time and affect, is the voice of Alpha 60, which has seized possession of the psyches of the inhabitants of Alphaville, and rendered "consciousness" unconscious. If Alphaville is to be defeated, this metamorphosis must be reversed; what is unconscious must be made once again conscious. But Lemmy continues to look for a more conventional code. "Death in conversation," he says portentously, "To be trapped by trying to trap." He has not yet understood that *Capital of Pain* will yield its secret only to the one who reads it poetically. As is true of many profound truths, it must be learned by the teacher from his student.

HF: Natasha begins frantically searching for the "Bible." In Alphaville, the holy script is a dictionary; in it are all the words which the inhabitants of that city are allowed to know. When words are excised from it, as happens every day, they are soon forgotten. Natasha recalls some of the words that have been eliminated in recent months. They are all affectively charged: "robin redbreast," "to weep," "autumn light," "tenderness."

KS: As Natasha cites these words, Lemmy looks at the page in his notebook in which he wrote Henri Dickson's final utterances: "Make Alpha 60 destroy itself. . . . tenderness . . . save those able to weep." The cross-references between the two lists make clear to us, if not yet to Lemmy, that love is the secret message Dickson tried to convey with the Eluard book and his final words.

HF: Lemmy and Natasha eat breakfast in front of a television set, which reflects back the contents of the table as a twentieth-century still life. For a while, all that we can see of the two of them is their fingers, engaged in a miniature courtship dance. Like a good hard-boiled detective, Lemmy pours whiskey into his breakfast cup. But now he plays psychoanalyst as well, prompting Natasha to remember the land of her birth. Eventually, she utters the incantatory words "Nuevo York . . . where the winter . . . Broadway . . . sparkles under the snow, as soft and gentle as mink."

Fig. 15

KS: Godard wants us to understand that no one is ever born in Alphaville. Alphaville is less another planet than a state of mind, a "place" where people find themselves when reason has succeeded in driving out affect. Everyone begins life somewhere else. There are many names for this "elsewhere"—Tokyrama, Florence, Nuevo York—but they all signify "consciousness," or "being within temporality." What Lemmy says to Natasha after explaining to her how she came to be in Alphaville—"you don't belong here"—is thus true of everyone who lives there.

HF: Natasha asks Lemmy what love is. He tries to show her with a caress, but his touch is not sufficient. "No, that's something I know all about—that's sensuality," responds Natasha. Lemmy then gives voice to his erotic credo: "No, sensuality is the result; it cannot exist without love." But even this is inadequate to the task at hand. The coming of Natasha to an understanding of the word "love" is dramatized instead through a sequence with its own musical theme. In this sequence, Natasha speaks the following words over a lyrical series of images of herself, sometimes with Lemmy (figure 15), and sometimes without:

Your voice, your eyes, our silences, our words . . . Light that goes, light that returns. One single smile between us both. From needing to know, I watched the night create the day. O, Beloved of one alone . . . In silence your mouth promised to be happy . . . Further and further, hate says, nearer and nearer, love says . . . The heart has but a single mouth. Everything by chance. Everything said without thinking. Sentiments drift away . . . One need only advance to live, to go straightforward towards all that you love. I was going toward you, I was perpetually moving toward the light . . .

KS: Significantly, it is through language rather than touch that Natasha recalls the meaning of the word "love." But it seems that not just any language will do. The only language capable of renewing this knowledge is a language capable of evoking or "performing" love in those who speak or hear it.[15] Here the psychoanalytic analogy which often seems at work in this scene reaches the limits of its usefulness. For Freud, therapeutic speech tames or subdues affect;[16] poetry is the illness, and rationalized speech the cure. For Godard, on the other hand, therapeutic speech produces affect; reason is the illness, and love the cure. The words Natasha speaks make clear that it is finally less the teachings of psychoanalysis than those of surrealism, with their valorization of chance, drift, and unconscious thought processes, which are at the heart of this film.

HF: In this sequence, the straight line is once again an important metaphor, and once again it turns into a circle. As Natasha says "One need only advance to live, to go/Straightforward towards all that you love," she walks directly ahead, but as she adds "I was going towards you,/I was perpetually moving towards the light," she walks around a table with an illuminated lamp. Perhaps Godard is suggesting that only those who not only renounce the attempt to control the future by planning for it rationally, but also surrender themselves to its uncertainty by running headlong toward what they love, will finally enter the circle of myth.

KS: Light is also a privileged trope in Natasha's monologue. The light about which she speaks constantly evolves out of darkness, and returns once more to it. It is not only in a dialectical relationship with its opposite, but is actually generated out of it. The night creates the day, we learn. Once again, the positive is born out of the negative.

HF: The light also comes and goes in the images which accompany this text. Most of this sequence is given over to shots in which there is alternately illumination and darkness, often in quick succession, and sometimes even within the two halves of the frame. The effect is a more evocative version of Lemmy's flash. We now recall that this device was designed precisely for creating the day out of the night.

KS: Four policemen break into the room to take Lemmy to Residents Control. They know that legends cannot be defeated by ordinary means, so they resort to cunning. They order Natasha to tell story number 842, one with a failproof punch line for those who still know how to laugh or cry. The policemen wait until Lemmy doubles up with laughter, and then make their attack.

HF: At Residents Control, Lemmy is questioned one last time by the computer. During this exchange, Alpha 60 proclaims once again the triumph of the certitudes of the present over the uncertainty of the future. In its war with the earth, Alphaville is certain to win, since Alpha 60 will "calculate . . . so that failure . . . is impossible." "Everything I plan will be accomplished," it tells Lemmy.

KS: But if Lemmy Caution has an Achilles heel, so does Alpha 60; presented with a riddle, it cannot *not* solve it. Lemmy provides the computer with a riddle whose solution will disarm it by rendering it human—by making it, as Lemmy says, "*mon semblable, mon frère.*" Rather than destruction, this, too, might be called the "cure by love."[17] Now there can be no further doubt: the two terms which *Alphaville* pits against each other, whether we call them "technology" and "poetry," "materialism" and "spirit," or "reason" and "emotion," can be no more neatly mapped onto the opposition of Alpha 60 and Lemmy than it can onto "residents of Alphaville" and "residents of the earth." We are dealing here with something like different psychic states, to which Alpha 60, the inhabitants of Alphaville, and Lemmy all have equal access.

HF: The riddle Lemmy tells Alpha 60 features once again the paradox of the straight line turning into a circle. It is "something that never changes with the night or the day, as long as the past represents the future, towards which it will advance in a straight line, but which, at the end, has closed in on itself in a circle." As Lemmy speaks with the computer, the light once again comes and goes, in a proleptic asser-tion of its fraternity with Lemmy. We realize now that the lamps desig-nating Alpha 60 have had this volatile luminescence from the very beginning of the film.

KS: The key to solving this riddle is understanding in what sense the past can be said to represent the future. *Alphaville* gives us plenty of help in answering this question. The future which is Alphaville is depicted through images of Paris of the past. The secret agent into whose semblant Alpha 60 evolves is a throwback to detective fiction of the 1930s and film noir of the 1940s. And the future into which Lemmy and Natasha head at the end of the film is made possible through a transformative act of recollection; Natasha remembers the meaning of love transferentially, by falling in love with Lemmy.[18] In advancing into the future, the characters in *Alphaville* could thus be said to circle back to the past. The answer to Lemmy's riddle is now evident: it is temporality, that overarching category to which every privileged trope in the film is finally subsumed.

HF: The final words Alpha 60 speaks in this exchange are: "You will not leave; the door is locked." Lemmy immediately disproves this predic-tion. He smashes through the door, and dispatches the bodyguards waiting on the other side with his legendary gun. One must choose one's weapon well; some foes can only be defeated with love, others only with firepower.

KS: Lemmy eliminates several more obstacles in the same manner, before making his way to the office of Leonard Vonbraun. The moment has come for the confrontation between the two men from earth: the one who seeks to destroy it, and the one who alone can save it. "Haven't you noticed that Reporter and Revenger start with the same letter?" Lemmy asks one of Vonbraun's assistants. We are back in the world of hats and trench coats and secret agents.

HF: Each of the two antagonists attempts to persuade the other to join his side. Vonbraun promises women and money, and stresses the tech-nical advancement of Alpha 60. Vonbraun's computer network is rep-resented by an industrial heating system, which emits primitive light signals and the sound of electrical currents as manifestations of intel-lectual activity. Lemmie responds: "You are opposing my moral and even supernatural sense of vocation with nothing more than a physical and mental existence created and dictated by technocracy." Now, more than ever, it is clear that this is a battle not so much of man against machine, as of spirit against what can perhaps best be characterized as a rational materialism. Vonbraun warns Lemmy that "men of your kind will soon no longer exist. You'll become something worse than death; you'll become a legend . . . " From the perspective of Alphaville, to be a legend is to be doubly dead—to be not merely extinct, but also banished to the past.

KS: It does not become a legend to speak of his legendary status. Instead, Lemmy responds only to the threat of death. He does so by simultaneously affirming his mortality, and confessing to the fear which it induces in him. In *Alphaville*, fear of death is finally as definitive as love is of humanity. "Yes, I'm afraid of death," Lemmy says, " . . . but for a humble secret agent, fear of death is a cliché . . . like drinking whiskey, and I've been drinking it all my life." During this conversation, Lemmy is plunged into a deeper and deeper darkness, suggestive of the night which will finally swallow him up. After he shoots Vonbraun with his pistol, the camera cuts to the flashing panel of the heating system, and then back to Lemmy, who sits in total darkness. Lemmy then once again illuminates his cigarette and his face with the cigarette lighter, in a repetition of the gesture with which he earlier laid claim to his mythical status. This light burns brightly in the shadow of death.

HF: The legend then assumes once again a more familiar form, as Lemmy escapes from Vonbraun's office complex, and makes his way to Residents Control, where Natasha is held hostage: gunshots, a taxi holdup, a dramatic car chase. Filmed from above, the cars make 180-degree turns, as if they were revue girls or circus elephants. Lemmy shows that the man of poetry can also be a man of action.

KS: He looks in room after room of Residents Control, until he finds Natasha, who—like the other inhabitants of Alphaville—is suffering from electricity deprivation due to the breakdown of Alpha 60. We hear the computer's voice one last time: "The present is terrifying because it is irreversible . . . because it is shackled, fixed like steel. . . . Time is the material of which I am made. . . . Time is a stream which carries me along . . . but I am Time . . . it is a tiger which tears me apart . . . yet I, too, am the tiger." In solving the riddle posed by Lemmy, Alpha 60 has for the first time grasped its own contradictory status. All of the words which we have for memory—recollection, remembrance, retrospection—stress its backward turn. There can be no act of memory that is not a reversion to the past. Alpha 60 is consequently inside rather than outside temporality. Indeed, time is its very heart and soul. Yet for the computer to understand that is to be riven by conflict. It is to be torn apart by the incommensurate imperatives of computation, calculation, and prediction, which grip Alpha 60 like "steel," and the unpredictable tigers of past and future, desire and death.

HF: Lemmy's plan is brilliant. It is to destroy Alpha 60 merely by letting it find out who it is. The computer is defeated through self-consciousness. This is a strange rewriting of the story of Oedipus and the Sphinx. In that story, the Sphinx is destroyed when Oedipus is able to answer the riddle it poses: when he is able to name what he himself is: man. But the answer is finally the same in Godard's film. In grasping its essentially temporal nature, Alpha 60 understands itself to be Lemmy's "brother" or "double," i.e., to be a man.[19]

KS: At the end of *Alphaville*, Lemmy and Natasha travel through the night in the Ford Galaxy. Significantly, they never reach the geographical border where Alphaville ends, and our world begins. That is because the border is psychic rather than terrestrial —because the earth is a state of mind, rather than a place. Natasha definitively achieves that state of mind only when she says the magic words: "I love you." These are the most performative words in *Alphaville*. Only those who can utter them are saved. All others are forever lost.

HF: Natasha does not find these crucial words at once. She claims that she does not know what to say, and twice, like Orpheus with Eurydice, she even begins to turn around to see what she and Lemmy are leaving behind. But finally the woman with the name from the past makes that simple declaration which, no matter how many times it is repeated, brings light to those who hear it, and humanity to those who utter it. Although Lemmy and Natasha still have many miles to drive, they have already reached their destination.

four

Anal Capitalism

Weekend/Le Week-End (1967)

KS: *Weekend* (1967) opens on a sunny day in a luxurious Parisian apartment. The inhabitants of that apartment, Roland (Jean Yanne) and Corinne (Mireille Darc) are having drinks on the balcony with a friend.[1] Roland is called to the phone, and the fiction of bourgeois propriety is quickly shattered. Within seconds, we learn that the friend is in fact Corinne's lover, and that she and Roland are both scheming to kill each other. At the same time, the couple is working together to dispose of Corinne's father, who stands between them and a substantial fortune.

HF: A day or two later, on an unspecified Saturday, this couple sets off for a small town in the provinces, where Corinne's family lives. They hope to arrive before the death of her father, so as to prevent him from writing a new will. But weekend traffic is today's battlefield, as the film dramatically shows. Cars and corpses pile up on the road as a blood offering to the god of highways.

KS: Corinne and Roland ultimately arrive at their destination, but they are too late, in every sense of the word. They also never make it back to Paris. Instead, they get lost in a fiery apocalypse, which is the

83

end of "our world," if not of "the world."[2] But their affect in the face of this vision of doom is strangely muted.

HF: They stroll past the debris as if they were window shopping. They are no more touched by the modernist sculptures into which Godard shapes the piles of twisted steel than they are by the mangled bodies. The burning wrecks by the side of the road are heart-breakingly beautiful, but the hearts of our heroes are not broken.

KS: The opening scene suggests that in the world of *Weekend* only material goods are capable of eliciting passions. In this scene, the camera crosscuts from the Parisian apartment, where Corinne talks matter-of-factly with her lover about how she might dispose of Roland, and Roland unemotionally with his mistress about his attempts to kill Corinne, to an animated scene on the street below. From the vantage point of an extreme overheard shot, we watch as the drivers of a Matra and a Mini come to furious blows over the damage done by one to the automobile of the other. The pride of possession, which is so conspicuously absent not only from married but also from adulterous relationships in this film, still seems fierce when it comes to cars.

HF: This scene begins even before the first of two subtitles has left the screen, through a sound bleed. As we look at the words "A Film Adrift in the Cosmos," we hear the sounds of traffic and murmured conversation. The phone rings, and Corinne calls out to Roland: "It's for you."[3] A moment later, as Roland speaks on the telephone in the bedroom, and Corinne and her lover on the balcony, Godard interrupts the scene with a second subtitle: "A Film Found on a Scrap Heap." With both subtitles, he suggests that *Weekend* belongs to the same world as Corinne and Roland.

KS: The first subtitle creates the narrative fiction that *Weekend* is a relic from the apocalypse, perhaps blown into space through some final conflagration. The second subtitle consigns the film to the place to which all the burning auto heaps are destined. It characterizes *Weekend* as something like "trash."

HF: In later Godard films, this kind of self-hatred will precipitate extreme forms of auto destruction, but *Weekend* has been created in a very different spirit. Although narratively attenuated, and at times given over to extreme spectatorial provocations, it is constructed with the care of the artisan. Godard provides smooth transitions from one scene to the next, and enough exposition to motivate, if not all events, then at least the primary ones. And *Weekend* even provides a great deal of pleasure, something which Godard will withhold in later, more politically programmatic films. Only by relegating famous actors to supporting roles, and by mustering all of the production devices of a commercial film for the purpose of shooting nonevents, does he "undo" *Weekend*.

KS: But perhaps the film is relegated to the wastebasket less through the process of production, than through that of consumption. Perhaps Godard is anticipating what *Weekend* will be when we have finished watching it, not when he has finished making it: when it is "used up," psychically speaking. Perhaps, in other words, he is inviting us to understand it as a commodity. As Georg Simmel pointed out almost a century ago, a commodity has value only so long as it hasn't been enjoyed.[4] The act of enjoyment "consumes" the value conferred upon it by economic and semiotic exchange, and reduces it to metaphoric waste (p. 66). *Weekend* could be said to be a text made to be enjoyed, in both meanings of the word: an object which gives us pleasure only at its own expense.

HF: In a way, Godard *hopes* that *Weekend* will be quickly consumed. He does not want it to be passed from generation to generation, like a Biedermeier chair, but rather to be digested on a warm evening in the late sixties, by people with flowers in their hair. But like Dylan's "The Times They Are A-Changin'," *Weekend* has nevertheless become a classic.

KS: That is yet another reason to relegate it to the scrap heap. With *Weekend*, Godard hoped to make a film which could be digested, but not consumed—which would be a marijuana brownie, rather than a three-course bourgeois meal. But, like many members of our generation, he came to understand that nothing that we take within ourselves, whether literally or metaphorically, can remain untouched by commodification. It is no wonder that he would try so often in the years immediately following to make "undigestible" films.

HF: The opening scene of *Weekend* ends with another sound bleed. Roland says to his mistress "See you Monday," and these words are

Fig. 16

repeated two more times over the black onto which the final image fades. "When did it happen?" asks Corinne's lover at the beginning of the next scene. "Tuesday," she responds, " . . . I'm sure it was Tuesday because I stopped taking the pill on Wednesday." *Weekend* obsessively tabulates the day of the week, and sometimes the hour of the day.

KS: In this scene, Corinne sits in panties and a bra on a desk, recounting a story to her lover, who occupies a chair behind her. The camera moves continuously toward and away from these figures, but we never seem to get any closer to them (figure 16).

HF: Shot against the brilliant illumination of a window, both figures are dark silhouettes. Silhouette photography usually beautifies, but that is not the case here. Nothing solicits the look. The seduction of the scene resides not in the image, but in the words Corinne speaks.

KS: Both the visual treatment of Corinne and her lover and the subordination of the image to the word could be characterized as "sublimating." Each effects an abstraction away from sensory particularity—the image by making the lovers "generic," and the word by substituting the mental for the visual image.

HF: The two human figures in this scene are less persons than position-alities, into which a multitude of characters could be slotted.

KS: The notion of equivalence is also central to the story Corinne tells. It is the account of an orgy with three participants: Corinne, Paul, and Paul's wife, Monique. Corinne and Monique occupy more or less interchangeable positions vis-à-vis both Paul and each other. And the story is meant to excite Corinne's lover by putting him in an identificatory relation to Paul. Finally, like the opening scene, which stresses the symmetry of Roland and Corinne by positioning both in adulterous relationships, and showing that each is plotting against the other, this scene works to establish the reversibility of the categories of "man" and "woman."

HF: But Corinne's lover still seems to have the upper hand. Corinne tells her erotic story at his prompting. It could even be said to proceed as if from his fantasy. There's a long tradition of men standing apart from a scene of sexual congress which they at the same time orchestrate, which is "for" them. You don't lose power when you let others sleep with your mistress, as Corinne's lover does—you gain it. It is a kind of entrepreneurial position.

KS: This scene undoes gender not because it puts Corinne's lover in a subordinate position, but rather because the thematics of the story she tells work to decenter the key term upon which gender rests: the phallus. At a key moment, Godard punctuates the scene with the title "Anal Ysis," thereby underscoring what is by then fully evident. Although Paul at one point proudly displays his erection in Corinne's fantasy, virtually every significant erotic transaction in that fantasy centers on the anus. Paul admires Corinne's buttocks, and pours whiskey down them; Monique puts her finger in Corinne's anus; Paul sodomizes Monique, with the "help" of Corinne; Monique sits in a bowl of milk; and Paul inserts an egg in Corinne's anus. As Guy Hoc-quenghem has argued, the anus is the one sexual organ which does not recognize gender.[5] Where the penis and vagina affirm difference, it asserts similitude. That gender is under siege here in some larger sense becomes particularly manifest at one of the climactic moments of the orgy, when all three participants are described as engaging in identical behavior: masturbating while looking at the others doing the same.

HF: But Corinne's lover still acts as if his supremacy remains unquestioned. At the end of the scene, he tells Corinne to come and excite him, as if the pleasures of foreplay were a male prerogative. And throughout the film, Paul's attitude is uncompromisingly one of "me first."

KS: This is a case of what might be called "anachronistic consciousness"—of the uneven development of the social field and the masculine psyche. Although *Weekend* insists ever more fully upon the equivalence of "male" and "female," Corinne's lover and Roland cling to their illusions of mastery. Of course these illusions have real effects: Corinne must not only service her lover, but later carry her husband when he gets tired of walking. But both male characters are shown to have no real power in the world of the film.

HF: There's something very strange about the way in which Corinne relates her story. She doesn't address either her lover or the camera. Nor does she seem to be speaking to herself. The conditions for verbal exchange—the "I" and the "you"—seem to be missing.

KS: Perhaps that's because the characters in *Weekend* aren't exactly subjects, in the usual meaning of that word. To be a subject in our culture signifies to be the one who exchanges (language, women, money, etc.), rather than what is exchanged. A woman's claim to this position is often felt to be weaker than a man's, because in some cultures she circulates like a commodity, and because even in our own she is passed from father to husband.[6] But *Weekend* makes commodities out of its male as well as its female characters. It does so precisely by stressing their commensurability. As Simmel emphasizes, equivalence and exchangeability are "reciprocal notions" (p. 93).

HF: Perhaps Godard is trying to show that goods have ever more variety and distinction, but the consumers ever less. More and more people speak the same languages, inhabit the same mode of production, listen to the same records.

KS: I think that he's also suggesting that late capitalism has effected a reduction in the number of terms which can function as standards of value. The phallus has traditionally enjoyed an analogous status within the erotic domain to that of gold within the domain of commodities:[7] it was the "general equivalent" to which the particularity of all other bodily parts was subsumed.[8] But if we are to take *Weekend* at its word, the phallus has lost its privileged status. In the seduction scene, Godard shows the male sexual organ to be only one in a series of three objects capable of being inserted into the anus, a series which also includes an egg and a finger. It seems that as gold exercises its "Lordship" over a larger and larger domain, it is stripping other general equivalents of their prerogatives.[9]

HF: Ironically, then, it seems as if capital is unconsciously accomplishing what all of the conscious strategies of feminism have been unable to achieve: it is bringing patriarchy to an end.

KS: So Godard would have us believe. But we should not be too hasty in celebrating the dethronement of the phallic signifier. *Weekend* makes clear that the gain within the domain of gender which capitalism effects is more than offset by the ever greater semantic reduction to which it subjects the social field.

HF: "*Gleich geltend*" and "*gleich gültig*" are related words in German: "equivalent" and "indifferent." They have the same linguistic roots. This etymology suggests that what we're talking about here is a kind of flattening out, the reduction of human existence to the horizontal dimension. Where equivalence reigns, there is a loss of the sacred.

KS: Yes, there is what Max Weber calls a "disenchantment of the world."[10]

HF: But how, precisely, does anality fit into this disenchantment of the world? Is it simply a signifier at the level of sexuality of what we might call an "unrestricted market," one in which everything can be bought and sold?

KS: As we will see when the camera hits the road, where cars are transformed from treasured commodities to worthless junk, *Weekend* gives anality a central place not only because it is a signifier of equivalence, but also because it is a signifier of excrement. In late capitalism, the commodity quickly gives way to "waste." The supremacy of economic over other forms of value leads to a dramatic diminution in the *kinds* of value any thing can have. It also leads to a decrease in the *amount* of value a thing can have. The value of the commodity must never be increased beyond the capacity of many to pay for it, financially or libidinally, nor leave that many without the reserves for the next purchase. There can no longer be absolute value, only objects for which substitutes can quickly be found.[11] With this serialization of the exchange process, the moment of enjoyment of each new commodity also becomes briefer and briefer, so that it passes for this reason as well much more quickly into the category of "shit." Anality would thus seem much closer than the phallus to the "truth" of late capitalism.[12]

HF: But surely sexuality is not simply reflective in this respect. I don't feel that the seduction scene in *Weekend* proves "economics in the last instance." There's too much perversity, too much idiosyncratic elaboration: sitting in milk, pouring whiskey over buttocks, etc.

KS: In a certain sense, one could as legitimately speak here of "sexuality in the last instance" as "economics in the last instance." As the seduction scene indicates, with its insistence upon unconventional erotic transactions, sexuality is as resistant as late capitalism to the priority of the phallus. It is initially polymorphous or "anarchic." The phallic phase implies the ruthless subordination of this anarchy to a kind of central government, and many subjects simply refuse this erotic colonization.[13] Even in the most normative psyche, according to Freud, the unconscious treats shit, money, gift, penis, and child as interchangeable terms.[14] Capital has only tipped the balance in favor of the first of these terms.

HF: It seems to me that there is more at issue in the seduction scene even than sexual perversity, or the reign of money. In the story recounted by Corinne, there is an almost ceremonial use of the primordial substances of milk and eggs. It would seem that at the very moment in which the rule of equivalence most fully triumphs, the desire for magic will inevitably resurface.

KS: Human beings cannot manage for very long without some recourse to the sacred, and *Weekend* helps us to understand why. The scene where Corinne arouses her lover suggests that in an unrestricted market, as you have called it, the human commodity is perhaps the quickest to lose its value. Corinne remarks that Paul and

Monique have been married for only two months, yet Paul is already prepared to treat her as interchangeable with Corinne, and Monique to go off on a vacation with another man. The following scene, on the other hand, echoes that played out on the street below Roland and Corinne's apartment in attributing to car ownership a more lasting value. Roland backs his car into someone else's, and a frenzied free-for-all ensues between the two sets of owners. Where economic value reigns supreme, the human being cannot hold its own against the humblest object. Perhaps the only kind of value such a being *can* have is absolute value.

HF: The two car scenes introduce another of *Weekend's* constitutive elements, and one which mitigates the darkness of its general vision: slapstick. Both car struggles are playfully shot, as if they occurred within a circus. The protagonists behave more "choreographically" than realistically, and the passions motivating their struggle seem assumed rather than organic; it is as if they display rage less because they experience it than because their roles call for it. But there is the suggestion that under the thin veneer of this "civilization" beats the heart of a more affectively vital "barbarism." The father of the family with whom Corinne and Roland struggle brings out his gun and starts shooting, and the son wears Indian feathers, and plays with a bow and arrow. There is also a pop-art aesthetic at work in the two car scenes. Things from many different categories are placed side by side: gun, spray paint, bow and arrow, Chez Dolores dress. This principle is pushed much further in the famous tracking shot of the traffic jam: tropical animals, people playing cards, dead bodies. The tracking shot is like one of those television shows in which a dazzling array of merchandise passes before our eyes. We are always bored by what we see, but still we anticipate the next revelation.

KS: As with so much consumerism, the pleasure inheres only in the prospect of an enjoyment which never punctually arrives. This is serial consumption at its most profound.

HF: Like Andy Warhol's silkscreens, the happenings of the 1960s were an aestheticization of this phenomenon, an attempt to make the moment of boredom perversely fascinating. The shot outside the moving car, much favored in experimental films from the same period, was part of the same impulse: you turn on the radio, and submit yourself to the flow of people and things passing by, which in their very meaning-lessness become once again meaningful. Godard's tracking shot of the traffic jam operates very much within this conceptual framework.

KS: This shot also offers an ironic commentary on the cult of individualism at the heart of late capital. No two cars in the traffic jam are alike, and in many other respects as well the drivers assert their difference from each other: what they have in their vehicles, how they are dressed, how they spend their time. But all of these drivers presumably headed out onto the French highway at the same moment, and all of them are now stuck in the same traffic jam. It seems that the more equivalent subjects are to each other, the more they will assert their uniqueness.

HF: The character who insists most fully upon his individuality is of course Roland, who forces his way through the mass of cars until he is once again on the open highway, free from the "masses." As if to dramatize the absurdity of this ambition, Godard will later reduce him to an indistinguishable component of an outdoor barbeque. But although *Weekend* does not sustain Roland in his delusion of individuality, it is not totalizing. It suggests that there *is* a world apart from the one it critiques. In this scene, as in later scenes, *Weekend* maps this "elsewhere" onto the French countryside, presumably because it has not yet been fully commodified. At first, we are so fully engrossed in the surprising spectacle of the traffic jam that we don't see anything else. But then we notice that behind the stalled cars and trucks lies not an urban or industrial landscape, or even one which might be displayed on a poster or a postcard, but a yellow, freshly-harvested field. This field frustrates all of our attempts to incorporate it into what is happening in the foreground, or even into the categories through which we determine what is visually "interesting." It is without narrative, thematic, or photographic significance. [15]

KS: As Roland and Corinne extricate themselves from the traffic jam, they discover what caused it: an accident, which has strewn mangled bodies by the side of the road. Our protagonists drive unconcerned past this spectacle. Death is something that happens only to the other.

HF: Almost immediately, Roland and Corinne find themselves in the midst of another accident, this time one involving a farmer on a tractor, and a rich boy and girl in a Triumph. As the farmer (Georges Staquet) drives into frame, prior to the accident, he is singing the "International," the theme song of socialism. "You bastard of a peasant," shouts Juliet (Juliet Berto), the girl, after she has discovered her boyfriend's death. "Little bourgeois cunt," he responds, and *Weekend* cuts to the intertitle "The Class Struggle."

KS: This sets the terms for what follows. "You fucking bastard!" shrieks Juliet, with the courage of her bourgeois convictions, "It makes you sick that we've got money and you haven't, doesn't it?" "If it weren't for me and my tractor, the French would have nothing to eat," is the farmer's version of the same argument.

HF: Juliet appeals to the bystanders to validate her claims, but the days of class solidarity are over. The local onlookers refuse to take sides, and when Juliet appeals to Roland and Corinne, they immediately drive away. It is everyone for him- or herself on the commodity market.

KS: But Godard cannot resist fantasizing for a moment about the possibility of the goods getting together.[16] Both the farmer and Juliet protest as Roland and Corinne drive away; both feel stripped of value by the couple's refusal to take sides, and in their misery they seek company. The farmer puts his arm comfortingly around Juliet, and they walk away together.

HF: Of course this identification across class lines, which signifies at least a vague awareness on the part of Juliet and the farmer that they are in the same boat, is facilitated by relegating Corinne and Roland to the category of "filthy, rotten, stinking Jews." One opposition gives way only when the two sides can be united against a third. Ironically, this racial insult follows close on the heels of the farmer's appeal to inclusivity, "Aren't we all brothers, as Marx said?"

KS: But Godard is not content to end this episode here. After a fade-out, he gives it an alternate conclusion. *Weekend* cuts to an intertitle with the words "Phony Graph," and then to a group portrait mapping (or graphing) the relations which the characters have themselves been unwilling to acknowledge. It films Roland, Juliet, the farmer, and the various onlookers standing against a wall plastered with political posters, in an unwilling collectivity (figure 17).

Fig. 17

The Marseillaise provides the only commentary, but the conclusion we are meant to draw is clear. The class war at the heart of *Weekend* is not that between workers and capital, but rather that between gold and commodities. It is the war between the general equivalent and the many whom it dooms to having only a relative value.

HF: As Roland and Corinne drive away, she complains that his short cuts "do nothing but lose us time." And time, she adds, "means money." As *Weekend*'s relentless division of weeks into days and days into hours has already begun to make clear, this is a world where even temporality has been commodified. But unlike Roland, Corinne is given to occasional bursts of lucidity. A moment later, she looks at the countryside and asks: "When did civilization begin?" For a split second, she imagines a time before or outside market time. When Roland asks her why such a question should interest her, she answers cryptically: "it's in the landscape." We look inquiringly at the green fields, but they are as enigmatic as the freshly harvested countryside behind the traffic jam. Once again, the landscape functions as something like a site of resistance to that process of rationalization which makes everything "mean" money.

KS: Corinne mulls over the words spoken a moment before by the farmer: "Aren't we all brothers, like Marx said?" Roland responds that these words were spoken by Jesus, not Marx. This becomes the starting point for an inspired "riff," which begins with the notion of the son of God, but circles back to Marx. Corinne and Roland are highjacked by two hitchhikers: Joseph Balsamo (Daniel Pommereulle), a twentieth-century Jesus, and his consort Marie-Madeleine (Virginie Vignon), a twentieth-century Mary Magdalene. Balsamo owes his divine lineage to a most unimmaculate conception: the sodomy of Alexandre Dumas by God.

HF: "Balsamo" is the name of the magician Cagliostro, who appears in Balzac's *Sarrasine*. But here it means "erotic lubricator"—or, since the lubricator is of divine origin, something like Genet's holy vaseline.[17]

KS: Balsamo almost immediately calls into question the rule of the father, something which his status as anal product or shit ideally qualifies him to do. He asks Corinne what her name is, and—as she provides first her married name and then her birth name—points out that these are paternal names, not hers. "You see, you don't even know who you are," he protests.

HF: Balsamo is not only the son of God, but also the son of Marx. In this capacity he again functions to subvert the law of the father; like his historical predecessor, Paul Lafargue, he stands not for labor power, but for laziness.[18] In keeping with the slapstick logic of this scene, Balsamo obliges Roland to turn his car around so as to drive him and Marie-Madeleine to Mont-Saint-Gely by shooting his gun wildly. He brandishes it like a circus master's whip. Again, this sequence is intensely choreographic. Balsamo does not so much act as improvise around a set of elements: a trilby hat, a branch of greenery, a flock of sheep, the rabbit he pulls out of the glove compartment.

KS: He proposes to Corinne and Roland an unconventional exchange, of the sort that we find in fairy tales: if they drive him to London, he will give them whatever they want. Here is an opportunity to dream about absolute value. But Corinne and Roland are unable to desire outside the parameters of the market. They can only fantasize having a Mercedes, Yves St. Laurent evening dresses, and a weekend with James Bond. Significantly, Corinne also slips at a key moment in this conversation out of wanting to *have* desirable goods, into wanting to *be* one. She asks Balsamo if he could make her a "real" blonde. In so doing, she hopes to approximate the gold standard of womanhood. Appalled, Balsamo rescinds his offer.

HF: Near the end of this scene, Balsamo proclaims the end of the "grammatical era and the beginning of an age of flamboyance in every field, especially that of the cinema." Of course, everyone was ungrammatical in the late 1960s. And cinema, because it has no grammar, was a privileged playing field for such experiments. Straub, Pasolini, and the German avant-garde all used it in this way. The idea here is: grammar comes from school, so therefore it's like the police. But grammar is not at issue in *Weekend*; it is not in rebellion against the constraints of the pregiven codes. One could even go so far as to say it is saturated with references to Hollywood genres. It is not only a road movie, but a musical, with autonomous "numbers."

KS: Perhaps "ungrammatical" means something other here than "aesthetically transgressive." Maybe it signifies less "rebellion against the usual rules of construction" than "resistance to the restricted range of linguistic categories through which we colonize the world." The word could be said to perform an analogous semantic reduction within the domain of things to that performed by the name of the father within the domain of subjects, or gold within the domain of commodities. This sequence launches an extended assault upon all forms of abstraction.

HF: Understood in that way, Balsamo's proclamation could be said to represent one of the governing aesthetic principles of *Weekend*, one which is at work not only in all of the slapstick scenes in that film, but in all of the sixties' art-forms upon which it draws at other times—happenings, pop art, improvisation. Insofar as money is the word of commodities, these art forms are "ungrammatical."

KS: A moment after Corinne wonders whether all men aren't in fact brothers, *Weekend* shows her and Roland engaging once again in very unbrotherly behavior: biting the hands of what are presumably other drivers, who seem to be attacking them. Here we have something like a literal consumption, one which makes evident that activity's lethal effects.

HF: This is shown in a very reduced and enigmatic way, in two non-contextualized shots. We don't know where these scenes occur, who the other people are, or why they are attacking. This is something like "pure aggressivity," stripped of narrative pretext. Such indeterminacy makes the precision of the intertitles all the more striking: "Saturday/Saturday/Saturday 4p.m." On this occasion, time seems to mean something like "the hour of social conflict."

KS: In effect, the motorists are fighting over the delay each is costing the other. And no one wants to pay.

HF: The same motivation compels Roland to drive at breakneck speed down a narrow road after he and Corinne have finally extricated themselves from Balsamo and Madeleine. He ruthlessly mows down the vehicles which stand in his way, whether they are bicycles or cars. After all, he has already lost too much time! But the camera refuses to travel so fast. Several times it stays behind to look at what Roland has no eyes for: the verdant green of trees and grass.

KS: The next scene helps us to understand better what *Weekend* poses as the alternative to commodification. St. Just (Jean-Pierre Léaud), the first of a series of allegorical figures, walks in historical costume in a lush meadow, reading aloud from a book. "Can one believe that man created society in order to be happy and reasonable therein? No! One is led to assume that, weary of the restfulness and wisdom of Nature, he wishes to be unhappy and mad!" Corinne and Roland carry on their own conversation, oblivious to St. Just. Whereas the passage which St. Just reads is retrospective, full of a sense of regret, their conversation is anticipatory, oriented toward the future in which they will dispatch Corinne's parents with a knife or an axe. His is the time of loss, theirs of hoped-for gain.

HF: That Corinne and Roland are still fully engrossed in their fantasy of future wealth is all the more astonishing given that Roland's reckless driving has just landed them in a fiery crash. Roland extracts himself cooly from the wreckage, and Corinne's cries of anguish concern only her lost Hermès bag (figure 18).

KS: Even such a vivid dramatization of fatality as their car accident does not reorient Roland and Corinne toward the past, or put them in a new relation to sacrifice. On the contrary, they soon begin dramatizing the ultimate dream at the heart of late capitalism—acquisition

Fig. 18

without payment. They embark on what might be called a "bargain-basement" shopping spree, peeling designer clothes from the corpses of other accident victims.

HF: Immediately before the St. Just scene comes an intertitle reading "From the French Revolution to U N R Weekends."[19] References to the French Revolution will be numerous from this point forward. They provide an invitation to think critically about the legacy of the French Revolution. This becomes especially evident in the meadow scene, which calls into question one of that legacy's central terms. St. Just suggests there that "liberty" can be a dangerous rallying cry, since one person's freedom can imply another person's servitude. "Freedom, like crime, is born of violence," he said. "It is as though it were the virtue which springs from vice fighting in desperation against slavery. The struggle will be long and freedom will kill freedom."

KS: *Weekend* also provides an extended meditation on the last of the three terms at the heart of the French Revolution — equality. The world of the film is one where the dream of equality has been realized, but in a nightmare form: every character in the film is on a par with every other, because commodification has leveled all distinctions. Not surprisingly, the inhabitants of this world do not welcome and Roland taking an interest in his car. He then becomes a medieval knight defending his steed, with a tire as his shield, and a wrench as his dagger. Most storytellers would be content to let one car battle stand in for many, but Godard insists upon the details which make each one different from the others. The extreme animation of Léaud's acting works especially well with this kind of slapstick. In his boyish desire to please he even has the inspired idea of leaping over the car.

KS: Corinne and Roland are obliged to continue their journey on foot. Before long, they enter a forest, where they meet two more allegorical figures: Tom Thumb (Yves Afonso) and Emily Brontë (Blandine Jeanson), both again in historical garb. Tom Thumb reads aloud from pieces of paper which have been attached to his clothing, onto which passages from a range of books have been written. Each time he does so, Emily Brontë gives him a stone. She also reads passages aloud, but from a book.

HF: Godard can be very didactic in his insistence upon making us listen to long passages from great books. But here he shows that he has a sense of humor about didacticism. The pieces of paper attached to Tom Thumb's clothing remind us of the crib notes children use in school. With them, Godard says: "It's really hard to remember the old texts. We need help." And the stones Emily Brontë gives Tom Thumb when he produces these passages show that culture doesn't pay.

KS: In this scene, Godard tries to conceptualize exchange outside the parameters within which it generally occurs in *Weekend*. The exchange of words for stones is a direct exchange, unmediated by a general equivalent. And because words and stones are, from a semiotic view, not only disjunctive, but mutually exclusive, it is two manifestly incommensurate things which are here exchanged. This is finally the hidden truth of all exchange: no two things can ever be equivalent to each other. Godard makes the same point via another example. Emily Brontë and Tom Thumb hold up a stone and a tree branch to Corinne and Roland, and ask them what they are. Both times our protagonists provide the linguistic category into which we are accustomed to slotting those objects, a category which works to suppress their diversity. Emily Brontë responds with two quotations from Lewis Carroll, quotations which fracture the categories of "cat" and "fish" into a multiplicity for which there can no longer be any

their equality. But rather than forming a "fraternity"
hood" through which they might collectively contest t
general equivalence, as the Phony Graph shot encoura
do, the characters in *Weekend* waste their energies
attempt to differentiate themselves from each other. T
precisely the situation decried by St. Just. One characte
his or her liberty only by denying it to another. Goda
how complicated the French Revolutionary legacy can l
crucial it is that all three of its values be simultaneously a

HF: Ironically, although Godard could be said to offer the
tique of car culture in *Weekend*, he also inadvertently pror
often puts the camera on a crane, and the crane on tracks.
say that in doing so he manifests the same class consc
Roland and Corinne. The St. Just scene is a good example
the characters walk right, across the meadow, the camera
them. The distance covered is enormous. Godard must have
almost as many tracks as he did for the traffic jam. Then,
reaches the climax of his speech, the camera cranes up, a
Corinne and Roland disappearing in the distance. The upwa
the camera is rhetorical; it mimics the elevated style of
speech. And although the next scene begins with a
avant-garde trope, the "loop back" to the beginning of
which is repeatedly shown, it, too, ends with a crane up, wl
us an overhead view of the struggle over the young man's
Because there is no rhetorical pretext here, the crane is more
kind of status symbol, a way of separating *Weekend* from und
filmmaking. It says: "Look, we have a Mercedes. We're not
with a Deux Chevaux."

KS: The Porsche scene provides an occasion for the demonstr
that feeling which seems most out of place in the world of V
romantic love. The young man (again Jean-Pierre Léaud) sta
glassless phone booth at the beginning of this scene, singing
tive song to a faraway mistress.

HF: But he is, as he himself puts it, "calling out in the emptiness'
is no response from the other end of the line, and perhaps non
wanted. There is something solipsistic about the way the youn
sings, and he quickly abandons the telephone when he sees C

common denominator (kittens without tails, kittens who are ready to play with a gorilla, kittens who like fish and can be educated; fish who cannot dance the minuet, fish who have three rows of teeth, corpulent fish).

HF: Emily Brontë also provides a meditation upon a stone which helps to make clear how it is that nature can at times escape commodification in *Weekend*. She represents the stone as an object which has been ignored by "architecture, sculpture, mosaic, jewelry," and which—because it has never been incorporated into human art or industry—remains outside our systems of intelligibility.

KS: The stone is consequently irreducibly singular, without either exchange value or use value.[20] It is also associated with a different temporality, one which predates commodified time, and will in all likelihood outlive it. The stone perpetuates "nothing but its own memory."

HF: Irritated by the refusal of Emily Brontë to provide them with directions to Oinville, Corinne and Roland set fire to her. As she burns to death, Tom Thumb underscores once again that the late capitalist is one who exteriorizes sacrifice. "What's the use of talking to them," he asks of Corinne and Roland, "They only buy knowledge to sell it again. All they're looking for is cheap knowledge they can sell for a high price."

KS: Corinne and Roland hit the road again, and are before long picked up by a traveling musician (Paul Gegauff), who sets up his grand piano in the courtyard of a farmhouse, and plays Mozart for the farmers. The camera tracks twice around the courtyard in one direction, and then once in the other.

HF: Godard dubs the scene "Musical Action," and indeed the only things which really happen in it are the playing of the Mozart piece, and the recital of some off-the-cuff facts and opinions about Mozart and musical history. Like the traffic jam, the Musical Action is very much a happening. Again, there is the bringing together of things that don't belong together (a grand piano and a farmyard, Corinne and Roland and the peasants), and the drama of slight permutations within a limited set of elements. This scene also makes an important contribution to *Weekend's* meditation on time. The piano player suggests that all contemporary popular music builds upon Mozart's harmonies. This notion of a going forward which is really a going back is reiterated by the tracking shot.

KS: The piano player distinguishes between two kinds of music—the kind we listen to, and the kind we don't. This is really a distinction between the sort of music we are willing to pay for, and the sort we aren't. Mozart represents the prototype for the first variety of music; he is the gold of composers. Modernist composers did not grasp this principle, and so failed to secure a foothold in the music market. But somehow Godard manages to decommodify Mozart in this scene.

HF: *Weekend* is shot in 35mm, which is the equivalent of oil painting in art. But it is shot in a sketchlike way. The film takes things back easily, as if they were only written on a blackboard. The Mozart is played in the same way. So rendered, it's not yet a finished artwork, and so can't be "sold." Perhaps we also hear the Mozart differently because the location where it is played is suggestive once again of a place "apart."[21] The farm hands seem oblivious to the clock-tick of capitalism. The clothes they wear make no concessions to fashion, and they do not market themselves in the way they stand or move. Some drift purposelessly in and out of the camera's range, while others remain motionless, almost hidden from view by the recesses within which they stand. The shadows thrown by people and objects grow ever longer, with the progress of the sun, and no one but Roland and Corinne registers any impatience.

KS: The peasants and the farmyard are devoid of narrative significance. They also escape the category of the "picturesque," which is the primary one through which the countryside is commodified. They are simply allowed to "be," in their irreducible particularity. This "being" does not preexist the film; rather, the film makes it possible. It does so precisely through the affirmation of a going forward which is really a going backward. This is the temporality of sacrifice, a temporality which reaffirms what has been in what is, and—in so doing—is paradoxically able to disclose people and things in their radiant singularity. Only by assuming the past can we know what, in the present, exceeds it. And only by allowing the present to conjure forth in a new form all that we have ever loved and lost can it assume an absolute value.

HF: The camera operates here in a way which is dramatically at odds with the behavior of Corinne and Roland, who are shown yawning in boredom. It dissociates itself from them even more dramatically in the scene where Roland permits a stranger to rape Corinne. It suddenly tracks to the left, without narrative motivation, as Corinne begins to climb out of the ditch she has been lying in, and walk toward Roland, who is seated on the ground. The camera seems to want to be somewhere other than in the company of a man who would refuse to share the light of his cigarette with another man, but abandon his wife to sexual abuse.

KS: Shortly afterwards, Corinne and Roland are picked up by two immigrant garbage men, who put the pair to work in their place. Throughout this scene, the garbage men stand eating a loaf of bread in front of their yellow truck. At a certain point, each in turn reads aloud a lengthy text while the camera holds in close-up on the other.

HF: In this scene, Godard tries hard to provoke us. The actors, one an African and the other an Algerian, deliver their lines in a rapid monotone, calculated not so much to instruct as to insult. And Corinne and Roland, who are less than enthusiastic about the situation in which they find themselves, provide us with an unappealing image of ourselves.

KS: The text offers an impassioned appeal for and justification of black violence in the face of white oppression. As the two men speak, *Weekend* provides a series of flashbacks to earlier moments in the narrative—Balsamo shooting at Corinne and Roland's car, traffic carnage, St. Just exclaiming against freedom. These intercut images have the effect of repositioning the principle of violence from the future to the present tense of the film, and of suggesting that the threat to Western civilization which ostensibly comes from outside, from the Third World, actually comes from within.

HF: At a certain point, the paradigm shifts. The camera starts cutting back and forth between earlier images of carnage and violence and the shots of Corinne and Roland sitting on the ground under a tree, pretending to listen. Another text is read off-frame, this time addressed to the topic of class. We are told that the history of mankind until now has been the development of a class society, and that the more primitive stages in our own history can be seen in the organization of certain other cultures, such as the Inca, Mayan, and Aztec.

KS: But *Weekend* works to trouble the notions both that Western history represents a development away from something more primitive, and that, insofar as this primitivism still manifests itself, it does so elsewhere. At the moment that the voice-off begins to speak about Indian tribes, Godard gives us a flashforward to the cannibalistic culture with which the film will end. We see three figures in hippie dress wearing Indian headbands. Later, the film will insist even more strenuously upon the "primitive" as something which lies not in the past but the present, and not without, but within.

HF: In the second off-frame text, we can hear very clearly the operations of what might be called a "general equivalent" view of history. Every moment in history and every culture in the world is made to tell only one, repetitive story: the story of class struggle. Every trace of alterity, contingency, and particularity is expunged.

KS: Race performs a similar homogenizing role in the first text. Every detail seemingly testifies to an uninterrupted history of the oppression of blacks by whites. But the rhetorical strategy to which the first speaker has obsessive recourse belies the binarism upon which he insists. He argues his case by drawing a series of parallels between black and white: "I maintain that a black man's freedom is as valuable as that of a white man. I maintain that, in order to win his freedom, a black man is entitled to do whatever other men have had to do to win theirs."

HF: The scene itself is organized through the same rhetorical trope. When Roland asks the African for a piece of bread, the latter gives him one equal to the Congo's percentage of the annual American budget. And when Corinne tells the Arab that she is hungry, he subjects her to the law which the large Western oil companies subject Algeria: the law of "the kiss and the kick in the arse."

KS: Again, *Weekend* suggests that the differences through which we are accustomed to conceptualizing human relations may mask some more profound affinity, and that the antagonism which most profoundly structures the social field may lie elsewhere altogether.

HF: *Weekend* does not dramatize the moment at which Corinne and Roland finally arrive at their longed-for destination. Instead, a single, stationary shot of Corinne enjoying her first bath after her extended journey signals to us that they are at her parents' house. But again Godard provides the exposition necessary to paper over this discontinuity; we learn through an exchange between Corinne and Roland that her father died before they arrived, and that her mother is now unwilling to share the inheritance with them.

KS: On the wall to the right of Corinne hangs a painting depicting a woman engaged in a culturally idealized female activity: washing herself. Corinne is careful to match her movements to those of her model.

HF: From off-screen, Roland reads a long story about a hippopotamus. This creature is characterized as "the most ungainly beast of all" because of its challenge to our notions of form. It has a "gigantic mouth," "misshapen body," "absurdly short legs," and "grotesque tail." It would seem to represent the antithesis of the woman bather. Like Emily Brontë's stones, the hippopotamus remains outside use value and exchange value. As Roland continues to read, the camera cuts to "scenes of provincial life." One—an image of a gas advertisement—indicates that we are not so far from the beginning of the film. But the other suggests once again that the landscape has not yet succumbed completely to commodification. Three times the camera focuses upon a road leading into a village—presumably Oinville. But the church steeple does not occupy the usual pride of place. It has been relegated instead to an inconspicuous spot in the right rear of the frame. In the center of the image, rendering it finally unintelligible, is the formless green mass of a tree.

KS: *Weekend* narrates the mother's murder in two economical shots. The first shot shows Roland following her toward the house, proposing to her various ways in which they might divide up the father's inheritance. She rejects every one, and in retaliation Roland begins to strangle her with his scarf, as Corinne approaches with an oversized knife. In the second shot, the skinned rabbit which the mother has been carrying is shown lying on the terrace, as blood pours onto it from out of frame (figure 19). Although the mother's screams can still be heard, she is represented as already dead, through her implicit equation with the rabbit. This shot prepares the way for the

Fig. 19

next scene, which will push much further the thematization of human flesh as meat.

HF: The old law that you should inherit money from your family still exists, but the basis for this arrangement does not. We have forgotten that inheritance was once part of an exchange: children were expected to care for their aging parents, and were then reimbursed for doing so. These days, it's a crime to inherit. As *Weekend* shows, others pay with their lives so that we may profit, while we offer nothing in return.

KS: At the end of *Weekend*, as Roland and Corinne set off for Paris with their ill-gotten gains, they are attacked by a group of marauders in hippie dress. They are seemingly transported from their bourgeois world to one which is in every respect opposed to it. The hippies are cannibals who live in a forest, next to a lake. They show no interest in money, and they have no cars, or other private property.

HF: But the way they look and dance is not so far removed from the society they oppose: the women wear mini skirts, and dance the latest dances. The hippies could be said to represent nothing more dramatically countercultural than a preference for the fashions of London over those of Paris.

Fig. 20

KS: The desire for a resacralization of a flat or desacralized world which surfaces from time to time in *Weekend* finds its fullest expression in the forest scenes. At a key moment, Kalifon (Jean-Pierre Kalifon), one of the cannibals, sits in front of the river, beating his hippie drums and declaiming, as if to an aquatic god: "Ancient Sea, I greet you."

HF: This is not the only appeal to the divine. Elaborate cultic ceremonies surround the eating of human flesh. The hippies paint their victims before killing them, in the manner of Yves Klein, and insert magical substances—eggs, fish—in their orifices (figure 20). Again, such events have the quality of a sixties happening.

KS: This ritual consumption of human flesh might appear to be the very antithesis of the kinds of consumption dramatized elsewhere in *Weekend*. However, commodification has not always and in all places implied desacralization. Marx argues in perhaps the most famous passage of *Capital* that the commodity is sometimes capable of assuming an auratic value, of becoming "suprasensible," an "autonomous" figure endowed with a life of its own. Marx himself compares this process of commodity fetishism to what happens in "the misty realm of religion."[22]

HF: And Marx is not describing a state of affairs operative only in early capitalism. We, too, might be said to climb the holy mount every time we look at an advertisement for Absolut vodka or a Cartier watch.

KS: But because its luster is second-hand, no commodity can shine forever. As soon as the source of light is removed, its metal dims. *Weekend* suggests that capitalism has also developed in ways which make commodity fetishism ever more difficult and fleeting. The subordination of more and more people and things to the general equivalent of gold has effected a profound leveling out of value. At the end of *Weekend*, Godard dramatizes the perhaps inevitable reactive gesture: the attempt to restore auratic value to that commodity which has been most thoroughly divested of its value, the human being. But because it is conducted within the parameters of capitalism, which ineluctably decrees equivalent value, this is a doomed undertaking.

HF: Interestingly, it is only women whom the hippies seek to refetishize in this way. No religious rituals surround the ingestion of the men. The hippies also at one point effect an exchange of women with a rival cannibal group. In both ways, they could be said to hyperbolize traditional gender divisions.

KS: Godard perhaps ritualizes the eating of female flesh not to reassert gender difference, but rather to distinguish *Weekend* from Freud's *Totem and Taboo*. In the latter text, to which the closing minutes of *Weekend* make several references, it is male rather than female flesh which is ceremonially eaten, and this action inaugurates patriarchy.[23] A primal horde of brothers murder the father who rules over them and keeps all of the women for himself. Afterwards, they cannibalize him, and vow never to repeat this act of patricide. They incorporate the father not only literally, but also symbolically, which is to say that they identify with him as law, constitute him as the general equivalent of subjects. Crucially, they then decree that this action is never to be repeated. If the father had been murdered and eaten a second time, he would have been denied this privileged status. He would have become merely one in a potentially infinite series of "meals."

HF: In the hippie culture in *Weekend*, on the other hand, we see precisely the same principle of serial consumption at work as in the world of Corinne and Roland. The sacrificial fires are kept ever burning, and

Fig. 21

must be constantly fed. The hippies attempt to reassert male privilege, but—as in the larger film—it is undone by this seriality. *Weekend* ends with a barbecue in which pieces of Roland's body are indistinguishably mixed with those of British tourists, and a slaughtered pig. Not only does this meal have no sacral value, it is not even particularly meaningful. "Not bad," says Corinne with measured enthusiasm, as she takes another bite (figure 21).

KS: It could be said that because Roland has throughout the film refused to make a sacrifice, he ultimately becomes the sacrifice. However, those who eat him remain true to his ethic: it is always others who must pay. They do not understand that the world of absolute values for which they are nostalgic can only be produced through the acceptance of loss. Only that which costs us everything can be infinitely valuable.

HF: Intertitles refer throughout this section of the film to the French Revolutionary calendar, seemingly proclaiming the end of one world and the beginning of another. But by now we know that history in *Weekend* is not about endings or beginnings, or regress or progress, but rather about a relentless rationalization which paradoxically produces the desire for magic.

KS: The film also shows us that capitalism provides a frame of reference within which to articulate the yearning for the sacred to which it gives rise, but that it is powerless to satisfy that yearning.

HF: *Weekend* does not propose any alternative vehicle for the reenchantment of the world, but it does take very seriously the desire for absolute value. In the scene where Kalifon addresses the river, the film communicates to us the euphoria of that exalted state in which one believes oneself moving along a vertical rather than a horizontal axis. For a second, we can believe that the river is the domain of gods, and not a little watering hole where families go to swim.

KS: There is also a moment, near the end of *Weekend*, when the death of one character is registered on the part of another as personal loss, an affect which could in fact be the starting point for something new. After Kalifon exchanges Corinne for Valérie (Valérie Lagrange), Valérie is shot by the rival hippies, and dies in his arms. He holds her tenderly as she sings her dying song. But the fact that Kalifon has exchanged Corinne for Valérie means that Valérie can now be exchanged for Corinne. He does just that after the death of his mistress, his wounds immediately healed.

HF: The close-up of Valérie singing is mismatched with the shots which precede and follow it. Godard acknowledges the mistake with an intertitle: "*Faux Raccord.*" These words mean "false connection," but also— more profoundly—"false union." The mismatch underscores the emotional value of the close-up of Valérie; it says: "We have to interrupt our narration for this dramatic moment." But it also suggests that there can be no lasting union of the hippie general and the dying soldier in the civil war of late capitalism.

KS: In the final section of *Weekend*, one of the hippies tells a story which takes us back to the beginning of the film. It is an allegory for that anachronistic consciousness which can continue to see the phallus where there is only shit. "It was 1964," narrates Louis to whomever will listen, "We were under the Trocadéro bridge. It was hellish cold, d'you remember? It was the famous winter of '64. . . . And Alphonsine was so cold that she'd taken my prick in her hands to warm them. And Alphonsine was saying: 'Wow, Louis, what a big prick you've got!' And I said to her, 'That's not my prick, you idiot, it's just me shitting.'" This story again makes clear that wherever commodification reigns supreme, whether in the bourgeois culture of Paris or the counterculture at the end of *Weekend*, the phallus will give way to the anus. This is not the utopian sexual liberation hailed by Hocquenghem thirty years ago, but the catastrophic end of all singularity. What we might call "anal capitalism" decrees the commensurability of "male" and "female," but only by consigning both, along with *Weekend* itself, to the cosmic scrap heap.

five

I Speak, Therefore I'm Not

Gay Knowledge/Le Gai Savoir (1968)

HF: After his success with *Breathless* (1959), Godard was probably the most successful auteur filmmaker. Although his films transgressed the market rules, often two or three of them every year found world distribution. But Godard became increasingly discontent with such half-measures. *Gay Knowledge* (1968) was his attempt to make a film which would break so dramatically with the existing system of production and distribution that he would never be able to use it again. Like the many people in those days who tried hard to lose their jobs or be thrown out of school, Godard hoped that this break would lead to something new. Not surprisingly, then, *Gay Knowledge* was never shown by the French television station which commissioned it.[1]

KS: *Gay Knowledge* was the beginning of a curious chapter in Godard's filmmaking career. Most filmmakers hope to produce "good objects"—films that will "please."[2] Starting with *Gay Knowledge*, and continuing through the Dziga Vertov period,[3] Godard was motivated by a directly contrary wish—the wish to produce "bad objects." During this period, he set out to make films which would frustrate the expectations of spectators as well as producers, and thereby generate unpleasure. But at least in the case of *Gay Knowledge*, some viewers proved surprisingly resilient; they discovered that there can be more than one way of having fun.

HF: In 1968, university students began asking: "What does my work mean politically? What purposes does it serve?" Once in the air, such questions sowed seeds of self-doubt everywhere; even bureaucrats began to ask questions about the companies for which they were working. Godard was then ten years older than the student generation, but he participated in this reflexive turn. "What is cinema?," he asks in *Gay Knowledge*. He poses this question not only with the discourse of his film, but also with its form.

KS: This film, which was shot before the French student uprising of May 1968,[4] but edited afterward, is the product of its historical moment in another sense, as well. It stages as sweeping a cultural revolution as that carried out by Chairman Mao, the hero of many French students. In *Gay Knowledge*, two young people, Patricia Lumumba and Emile Rousseau (Juliet Berto and Jean-Pierre Léaud), meet for seven nights in a darkened television studio to implement a new representational regime. On the first night, they articulate a three-year plan to be carried out over the next six nights. The first year, they hope to collect sounds and images. The second year, they expect to critique these sounds and images—to "reduce" them, "decompose" them, subject them to "substitut[ions]" and "recompose" them. The third year, they propose to build some alternative textual paradigms.

HF: This is an undertaking of which only surrealism could make literal sense. But in fact, Emile and Patricia's project breaks down neatly neither into six nights, nor three years. It consists, rather, of a series of "chapters," within which the activities of collecting, critiquing, and model building are not always sharply differentiated, but often converge.

KS: *Gay Knowledge*'s interrogation of the signifying and representational bases of cinema is effected within the context not of a return to the origins of cinema, but rather of that fresh beginning which the protagonists of the French student movement believed May 1968 to represent. This was not a new idea in France. Already the revolutionaries of 1789 had imagined they could begin again from year one. But the clock which *Gay Knowledge* seeks to reset is epistemological rather than temporal. The May 1968 which takes place here is less the one enacted on the streets of Paris than that staged in the pages of Althusser's *For Marx*, Foucault's *Archaeology of Knowledge*, and Derrida's *Of Grammatology*.[5] Godard borrows the title of

Fig. 22

the film from Nietzsche,[6] and Emile and Patricia are above all students.[7] To be a student in this film means to participate in the critique of the university, as well as the political system in which it is embedded. But more radically, it implies undoing our received ways of knowing.

HF: *Gay Knowledge* does not offer anything like a conventional narrative. Instead, it crosscuts between studio scenes and montage sequences. The montage sequences bring together documentary footage of Paris in 1968 with cartoons, newspapers, the covers of contemporaneous theoretical books, political posters, drawings, and photographs. In those days, many cameras were turned in this way on the "people," in the belief that in them lay the true sources of the revolution whose avant-garde the student movement represented. That May 1968 is nowhere to be seen in *Gay Knowledge*'s documentary footage may seem to give the lie to this principle. But if you stare at a chemical solution in a laboratory, you also do not see the energies which make possible a chain reaction.[8]

KS: The studio images are uncompromisingly minimalist: they show only Patricia and Emile, with an occasional prop (a transparent

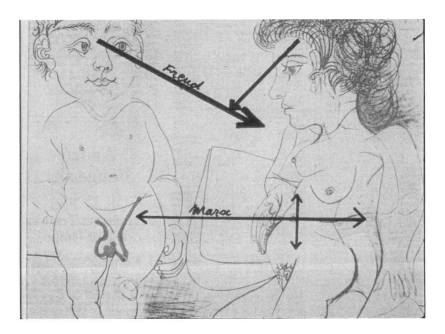

Fig. 23

umbrella, a bicycle, a book). But these two characters always wear at least one garment in a bright color, which glows warmly against the surrounding darkness (figure 22). And with the removal of a sweater or a change of bodily position, a differently colored item of clothing is revealed, and the scene is magically changed.

HF: As we know from other films with only one location, it is difficult to vary the scene metaphorically without doing so literally. Claustrophobia and tedium are the almost unavoidable result of remaining always in the same place. Prison films and films dramatizing a state of siege do not fight against such responses; rather, they internalize them, build them into the narrative itself. But Godard does not free the spectator from claustrophobia and tedium by delegating those sentiments to the characters. Rather, like Andy Warhol in *Sleep,* he seeks to maximize the spectatorial effects of the film's minimalism.

KS: The found images which intervene between the studio scenes are handled very differently from either the documentary footage or the studio shots. They have mostly been written upon (figure 23), and often have an accompanying auditory text. Godard deploys the screen like a blackboard, a practice which he associated with militant filmmaking a year later.[9] But whereas the blackboard usually offers a relatively durable and intelligible image, here one image replaces another with lightning rapidity, and even within individual images meaning is volatilized through the juxtaposition of visual and verbal signifiers. In a 1980 interview, Godard was to characterize his practice of writing on images as an inoculation against naming—against the "this is."[10] In *Gay Knowledge*, this homeopathic project is very much in evidence.

HF: Because cinematography lacks an equivalent to words in language, it needs a strong structure to work. *Gay Knowledge* lacks such a structure both visually and linguistically. It generates too much information, and does not provide enough repetition in the verbal text and montage sequences to facilitate the process of recollection. A good film is a mnemotechnic building, whose various "rooms" allow words and images to be memorized. But *Gay Knowledge* does not want to be "well-made"; its provisionality says: "Events are moving too fast to worry about lasting aesthetic construction." And it may in any case be less a film than a sketch for a film.[11]

KS: As their names indicate, Patricia and Emile are the "children" of the revolution. They are given generic histories and attributes: Emile is a cinéaste who militates for an open university, while Patricia is fired from her job for giving tape recorders to factory workers. Emile ostensibly represents revolutionary praxis, and Patricia revolutionary theory. But even these distinctions are not rigorously enforced. The primary functions of both characters are speaking, listening, and watching.

HF: In his early films, Godard never works with "types." He always insists upon the personal obsessions of his characters, even at the risk of obscuring the political issues. In *The Little Soldier* (1960), for instance, he depicts a character who chooses sides in the Franco-Algerian War strictly according to biographical disposition. In *Gay Knowledge*, we have the reverse situation: the subsumption of biography to politics. This leaves the actors very exposed.

KS: But this deindividualization serves a vital purpose. Godard makes Patricia and Emile children of the revolution and reduces them to the activities of speaking, listening, and seeing as a way of emptying them of their apparent substance. Later, it will become evident why it is so important for him to do so.

HF: On the first of *Gay Knowledge*'s seven nights, Patricia and Emile articulate the revolutionary task to which they intend to devote themselves for the remaining six: to learn, to teach, and to "turn against the enemy the weapon with which he most fundamentally attacks us: language."

KS: Knowledge is the goal which takes precedence over all others for Emile and Patricia: "First to know, and then we will see what follows." Four times, as if it were a mantra, they repeat that magical verb. But *Gay Knowledge* shows that knowledge is a complex affair. Unlike English, French differentiates between "*savoir*," which designates knowledge of the objective or impersonal sort; and "*connaissance*," which signifies knowledge of the subjective or personal kind, based upon familiarity. Godard makes much of this distinction. In this opening scene, Emile and Patricia use "*savoir*," but over the course of the film they work their way toward "*connaissance*."

HF: Television is to be the vehicle of Patricia and Emile's learning, but not in the usual sense. Rather than looking at the images and listening to the sounds which proceed from the monitor, they look at the images and listen to the sounds of those into whose houses they, as television, are beamed. "Let's go into the homes of people and ask them in order to know more," Emile says.

KS: With the words, "Right, knowledge," Emile reaches outward, toward the television spectators who have now themselves become the spectacle. His gesture underscores the exteriority of the object of study. The camera pans with Emile's gestures, and a montage sequence follows, in which moving images of contemporary Paris alternate with a variety of still images. With an image of a group of men struggling together to erect a giant razor blade onto one of its tips, the first discernible chapter or section begins (figure 24). The word "Revolution" has been written on the image, and—as we attempt to make sense of it—the voice of an old man says: "A society reduced . . . " Together, the three components of this shot thematize revolution as a reduction or cutting away of what is.

HF: The image resembles those we find in children's alphabet books. Such books guide their readers from image to language. But here the ambiguity of the image persists. Is the big razor blade a weapon or a

Fig. 24

monument? A signifier of a present or a past revolution, one which is an agency of destruction, or one which has itself now become the status quo? When writing on images, Godard also breaks the words down into their constituent parts, revealing other, normally concealed words. In so doing, he further underscores the notion of reduction. But again this cutting away is ambiguous: it does not so much undo language, as produce other words. Through it, Godard creates imaginary etymologies.[12]

KS: The sentence which begins "a society reduced" is completed several images later with the words "to its most simple expression." "Zero" is written on the last image in the sequence, which consists of a photograph of Godard with a book. The "o" is underlined three times, turning it into a numerical zero within the verbal zero, further foregrounding the notion of "nothingness."[13] A second montage sequence follows almost immediately, and links the concept of reduction with the return to origins. Over still images of Edward Sapir's *Language*, and Derrida's *Of Grammatology*, the second of which provides much of the inspiration for this chapter of *Gay*

Knowledge, we are offered a more complete account of this return: "I went to the end of the world in search of what Rousseau called the imperceptible progress of beginnings, and I searched for a society reduced to its simplest expression." The word *"savoir"* is written across two of the images in this sequence.

HF: As if in response to these sounds and images, Emile enthusiastically characterizes his and Patricia's project as one of starting from zero. But Patricia cautions: "No, before making a fresh beginning we must [first] return *to* zero." And when she and Emile arrive at zero, they should "look around to see if there are traces."

KS: The concept of traces is of course radically incommensurate with the idea of nothingness; it calls into question Emile's belief that it is possible to find a zero state of sounds and images.[14]

HF: Traces of something else are also always present at those moments when the film offers its most programmatic political statements. There is always a lot of "noise" around the images of revolutionary figures. They derive from newspapers or magazines, where they rub shoulders with very different kinds of material: advertisements, comics, text. The ostensibly new is always shown to be embedded in the old. Revolutions sometimes even legitimate themselves by referring to the past: Christianity to the prophets, and the French Revolution to the Roman Republic.

KS: Although Rousseau is the most frequently invoked name in this chapter of *Gay Knowledge*, another philosopher is even more central to the notion of returning to zero: Descartes. In the *Discourse on Method*, Descartes records his attempt to dispense with all the "reasons . . . formerly accepted . . . as demonstrations," and build the edifice of the true from the foundations up, so that, at the end, not one of its tenets would be unverified. But he exempts himself from this interrogation, insists upon his exteriority to the epistemological project. Descartes assumes as irrefutable proof of his existence his very capacity to doubt the reality of everything else: he thinks, therefore he is.[15] That he is from this starting point quickly able to reconfirm everything else that he has always believed suggests that the *cogito* is somehow the lynchpin of the world as we know it. *Gay Knowledge* will ultimately call into question not only the belief that it is possible to dismantle all preconceived assumptions, but also this notion of a transcendental subject, who thinks from a position outside language.

HF: In this respect, *Gay Knowledge* goes beyond Marx. Marx, too, could be said to challenge the *cogito*. He emphasizes that the one who is within the class struggle, and so history as such, has no access to transcendental knowledge. Even assuming that this subject can avoid looking through the distorting prism of dominant ideology, what he or she can know will have class limitations.[16] What is impossible for the individual however, is possible for the collectivity. As a group subject, the proletariat of industrial capitalism *can* gain access to a position of authoritative knowledge.[17] It is perhaps significant that *Gay Knowledge* so seldom mentions Marx, since it seems hostile to the notion even of a collective *savoir*.

KS: *Gay Knowledge* also implicitly distinguishes itself from Marx on a second point. It seeks not merely to rethink man, but to undo him altogether. Emile says at one point, "For the human sciences, it's not a matter of constituting man, but of dissolving him." Foucault's *The Order of Things* is the source of the notion that the human sciences do not so much make as unmake man. In that text, Foucault maintains that man as such appeared only with the elision of the signifier—with the "disappearance of Discourse."[18] When, as a result of the combined activities of linguistics, anthropology, and psychoanalysis, we are able to grasp the linguistic bases of human subjectivity, man will be "erased," like "a face drawn in sand at the edge of the sea" (pp. 385–87). This fundamentally anti-Cartesian project is at the heart of *Gay Knowledge*, and is in a profound tension with the notion of objective knowledge.[19]

HF: Significantly, for your reading, the second chapter of *Gay Knowledge* focuses precisely upon language. But Godard is working here with an expanded notion of that category; he wants to show that it includes images as well as words. Through a series of syntagmatic clusters, we learn that images, too, derive much of their meaning through their relations to other images. In this chapter, we also learn that images represent a form of enunciation. "In each image, one must know who speaks," Patricia tells Emile. Godard loves such transsensory catachreses. Writing on images is perhaps his way of helping us to "hear" them.

KS: To say that in every image someone speaks is to suggest that vision is at least partially productive of what is seen. We look, and in so doing help to create the visual domain. A few moments later, *Gay Knowledge* will make this principle more explicit. "If you want to see the world, close your eyes," says Patricia, as the camera holds on her. She then does just that, and the film shows us what she sees: Paris street scenes, precisely that category of footage which has until now enjoyed the greatest claim to objectivity. In asserting that "in each image, we must know who speaks," Patricia also suggests that it makes a difference who looks—that we cannot really understand what an image is communicating until we know from which pair of eyes it proceeds.

HF: As Patricia says these words, Godard cuts to a black-and-white photograph of Stalin, in which the black has been colored red. How are we to read this image? Is Godard suggesting that Stalin himself speaks through his image? Or has the image been put to someone else's discursive purposes? A bit later, *Gay Knowledge* will give us an image of Mao, in which *his* scarf is colored red. Does the same subject also speak through this image?

KS: Godard seems to be suggesting just that. But the subject who speaks through both images escapes biographical localization. It is not so much Stalin or Mao, as what they represent: the subject who says he knows.[20] The French student movement championed Chinese over Soviet communism, but *Gay Knowledge* proposes that, at least in this respect, the one cannot finally be distinguished from the other.

HF: During the period extending from the end of the war to the late sixties, the project of the Russian Revolution was thoroughly discredited—first by Stalin's dictatorship of the party, then by the new class from which his followers came. Mao's cultural revolution seemed to offer a more authentic revolutionary model. Like Trotsky's permanent revolution, it seemed to say: "We must fight against the aging of the revolution, and the establishment of new classes. We must carry the revolution into ever new domains." Mao's cultural revolution appeared to encourage not only societal critique, but also self-critique. But none of these assumptions is to be found in Mao's *Little Red Book*. That book speaks only of the difference between the "right" and the "wrong" party line.[21] And Mao actually provides a much easier access than classical Marxism to a position of untroubled knowledge. Marx warns with every word: "Don't dare to engage with this issue before you have studied the entire intellectual history." Mao, on the other hand, promises precisely the return to zero about which Emile dreams. He says: "We can start again, go back to 1917. The social revolution can be done again, and done better."

KS: Mao would seem to stand in some way for *savoir*—to be a representative of the belief in scientific knowledge. At a certain point in this chapter, the camera even holds on a poster with the words: "Mao sait tout [Mao knows everything]."[22]

HF: Ironically, Mao's simplifications have a primarily poetic appeal. They interpellate us into politics through their artistic radicality. You don't have to become a Protestant just because you love Bach, but May '68 activists began by admiring Mao's prose and ended up by becoming Maoists. This shows that Maoism finally appealed less to conscious knowledge than unconscious desire.

KS: Perhaps it is finally more important to ask than to answer the question, "Who speaks in this image?" since to do so is immediately to challenge the notion of a transcendental perspective, unconstrained by time or place. It is to remind us that every image is the product of a finite optic.

HF: Another exchange in the language chapter encourages us to think about the exclusionary role which each sound and image plays in relation to other sounds and images. Again, Stalin figures in a surprising way. Patricia tells Emile to articulate two seemingly unrelated sounds: "O," and "Stalin." She then suggests that the crucial question here is what separates them, what keeps them from being an ensemble.

KS: Patricia characterizes the activity of determining what these hidden words are first as *"savoir"* and then as *"connaître."* She thereby implies that knowledge of the exclusionary operations of language is perhaps better gained subjectively than objectively. After all, does not the psyche work as relentlessly as a police state to isolate certain terms from each other by censoring what links them? But almost immediately the will to truth asserts itself once again. Patricia says: "We must search for the truth in facts." When Emile asks Patricia what facts are, she responds: "They are things and phenomena, as they exist objectively."

HF: Patricia produces her little speech about facts in a tone of voice calculated to provoke assent in the listener, as if she were making a political speech. She pauses after each word, so that Emile may repeat it, and he complies. This is an indoctrination session, in which Patricia attempts to reproduce Emile in her own image. It demonstrates precisely the way in which words can silence other words, and prevent new linguistic connections from being made.

KS: Another montage sequence, accompanied by a Cuban revolutionary song, introduces a new chapter. The words "Let me tell you, at the risk of being ridiculous, that a revolutionary is accompanied by a very great love," are written across a group of images which, like a rebus, spell out the same words. The first image, which seems to show Ché Guevara addressing a crowd, signifies "revolutionary telling." "Risk" is communicated through a cartoon of a woman plying a frail craft in high seas. "Appear" is connoted through a newspaper photograph of a student demonstration. Here again we have images speaking.

HF: Two images do more than contribute to the rebus effect; they also push the word "love" in a carnal direction. The first is an ad from a magazine. It shows a preposterously dressed man, the visual equivalent of the word "ridiculous," which is written across it. On the same page, a woman suggestively pulls up her sweater, and the word "ridiculous" has been subjected to a corresponding dismemberment. *"Cul"* ("ass") has been written across her body. The last image in this sequence, representing "a very great love," shows a naked man and woman embracing. This is the beginning of what might be called the "libidinal politics chapter" of *Gay Knowledge*—a chapter devoted to the articulation of some of the relations between the political and the sexual.

KS: The ultimate inspiration for the first part of this sequence would seem to be Wilhelm Reich's *The Mass Psychology of Fascism*, a book which was widely read in the late sixties. Reich argues there that sexual repression is the precondition for fascism. Sexual liberation, on the other hand, leads to political freedom.[23] For Reich, sexual liberation assumes a necessarily heterosexual form. That same presumption is operative in the final image of this sequence.

HF: The next installment of the libidinal politics chapter is introduced with the voice-off of a woman demonstrator uttering the words: "Unwanted in France." *Gay Knowledge* cuts immediately to a photograph of a nude woman reclining against white pillows and sheets, across which has been written *"dis cours du soir."* The division of the word *"discours"* into two permits it to signify simultaneously "discourse of the evening," and "something running counter to the usual idea of an evening course"—a kind of alternative or transgressive university. Now the sexual is posited over and against the conventional university curriculum.

KS: But this image is followed by a sequence stressing more the negativity than the subversiveness or revolutionary potential of the sexual—its alliance with death. Lit from overhead, so that her eyes and the hollows of her face are dark sockets, Patricia utters the words "The erotic is the affirmation of life even unto death." Sexuality is represented as the site at which life reaches its maximum intensity, and in so doing passes over into its opposite. This shot gives way to three images suggestive of a dark *jouissance*—one showing a car seemingly moving at breakneck speed; one showing a nude woman's back and buttocks; and one showing Dylan's face, transected by shadows.

HF: The second image works especially well in this respect. In another context, it would be poster-kitsch, but here it connotes mortality. The photo has been enlarged to the point where the grain is more prominent than the shape of the woman's body, an effect which is compounded by the drops of water covering the latter. The body has been derealized.

KS: The next installment of the libidinal politics chapter surprises and provokes. As the camera focuses in close-up on Emile, Godard's voice-off offers a paraphrase of a sentence from Marcuse's *Eros and Civilization*: "The history of man is the history of his repression, and the return of what has been repressed constitutes the subterranean and taboo history of civilization."[24] The simplistic equation of sexual repression with fascism thus gives way to a much more complex account of that psychic operation. Repression is depicted as the only condition under which man *can have a history*, whether normative or transgressive. What *Gay Knowledge* calls the "subterranean" or "taboo" is thus shown to be profoundly implicated in the law which it opposes. It is becoming harder and harder to believe in the possibility of a clean break.

HF: At one moment in the first chapter of *Gay Knowledge*, Godard himself makes an appearance. In an aggressive voice-off, representing something like the political super-ego of the student movement, he asserts the good of that movement for the entire French nation. Once again, just before the libidinal politics chapter, we are obliged to listen for an extended period to Godard's hortatory voice. And during that chapter itself, we are exposed for an extended period to similar voices mysteriously emanating from the environment of May '68—first Godard's, and then that of a French student leader. Over the course of the film, Godard's voice will become ever more dominant and invasive. Its bullying attitude is intolerable. Although Godard whispers, he might be said to do so in a shout. Perhaps it is not only Emile and Patricia, and Stalin and Mao, but also Godard himself who at times represents the subject who says he knows.

KS: But during the libidinal politics chapter, *Gay Knowledge* itself comments ironically upon the aggressive nature of these voices. As the student leader speaks, his voice swollen with epistemological self-importance, a montage sequence characterizes a slap in the face as an "irrefutable philosophical argument." Like all analogies, this one is reversible: an irrefutable philosophical argument—one which asserts its absolute truth value—is also like a slap in the face. And as the film progresses, Godard's voice is stripped of its pretense to rationality, and becomes more and more free-associative. Significantly, free association is the linguistic form with which psychoanalysis was born.

HF: As part of their project of learning from the television spectators into whose houses they are beamed, Patricia and Emile "interview" a little boy and an old bum. Because the aim of these interviews is to show in a very dramatic way the relations and connections which link words apparently brought randomly together, free association is also the chosen form here. The little boy proves to be a much more skillful participant in this verbal exchange than the old bum. He produces "Papa" in response to the prompt word "sexual," "October" in response to the prompt word "revolution," and "magician" in response to the prompt word "revolutionary." The *clochard*, on the other hand, often seems at a loss for words.

KS: The interview with the old man is spread over two of the seven nights in which Patricia and Emile talk in the darkened studio. Between the two parts of this interview comes a sequence devoted once again to the fantasy of returning to zero, this time by undoing not sounds and images, but rather unexamined assumptions. This sequence consists of a series of images drawn from newspapers and cartoons. Across these images are written the words: "We no longer accept any self-evident truths. We don't believe that there are self-evident truths. Self-evident truths belong to bourgeois philosophy."

HF: One of the early images shows two cartoon policemen standing on either side of a television set, on which "self-evident truths" is inscribed. Others show revolutionary figures with guns. The sequence suggests that the masses are not aware that washing the car or mending clothes are bourgeois activities, and that in participating in these activities they are submitting to consumerism. The masses also do not realize that the images they pleasurably imbibe from television every night are under police protection. They accept as "reality" an ideological construction backed up by a repressive state apparatus. We should declare war on this state of affairs.[25]

KS: Interestingly, this sequence itself can now be seen to promote its own self-evident truths. Thirty years since the film was made, we are no longer so certain that washing cars and mending clothes are ipso facto bourgeois activities, or that the masses are duped by the media.

HF: We are also no longer so sure that it is bad by very definition to be a member of the middle class.

KS: We are consequently able to see that this sequence itself inadvertently works with a number of unexamined class assumptions. Once again, *Gay Knowledge* shows that there can be no starting from scratch. It also demonstrates the pitfalls implicit in any critique which does not at the same time include the one who makes the critique.

HF: Finally, Godard's voice-over, which resumes again a moment later, reminds us that the revolutionary subject also often uses psychic—if not physical—violence to enforce his or her self-evident truths.

KS: The next clearly recognizable chapter of *Gay Knowledge* proceeds from a much more overtly psychoanalytic premise even than the two free association sequences. Like the second chapter, it is centrally concerned with images. But the focus here is less upon how we "speak" images, than upon how we are "spoken" by them. In the first shot of this chapter, Patricia looks at an image of herself which she holds in her hand, as if it were a mirror. This image is manifestly a representation: rather than a mirror reflection, it offers a black-and-white still photograph. Emile says, from off-screen: "The child's conflicts . . . are not conflicts with the real, but are born from the difficulty experienced by the subject in identifying." "Then what's at stake is one's image of oneself," responds Patricia, turning toward the camera. Godard is drawing here upon one of the key texts of May '68, Lacan's essay on the mirror stage.[26] In that text, Lacan explains that we acquire a sense of self only by identifying with images of one sort or another. But this identification is impossible to sustain, because the images within which we attempt to find ourselves remain stubbornly exterior, and irreducibly fictive. The words which Godard puts into Emile's mouth refer precisely to this "love affair/despair"[27] which every subject has with the mirror, and which makes the world of images one from which we can never have anything like an objective or disinterested distance. As Patricia suggests, when it comes to this domain, every image is a potential image of self.

HF: But the list of different kinds of images which follows—"nylon image[s]," "reflex image[s]," "virtual images," "book images"—seems to have nothing to do with the self.

KS: I think that is in a way the point. After encouraging us to focus upon the image's subjective effects, *Gay Knowledge* invites us to think about it in its materiality. To think about an image in its materiality is to allow it to appear as such, distinct from ourselves; it is to grasp the image as a signifier. And, as in Foucault's *The Order of Things*, the appearance of the signifier means the disappearance of man.

HF: As if to emphasize this point, Godard has Patricia describe herself in ways which the image shows to be false. We automatically impute subjective reality to the image. But at the moment that we do so, she begins to speak from off-screen. The image is drained of its illusory reality, shown to be a representation.

KS: Immediately prior to this little demonstration, Patricia proposes a radically new reading of the categories of truth and falsehood. She asks, "What is a false image?" and answers, "There, where the image and sound [seem] true."[28] She thereby suggests that an image or sound is false not when it misrepresents reality, but when it seems adequate to reality—when we are able to assimilate it to ourselves. An image or sound is true, on the other hand, when it manifestly fails to represent us.[29]

HF: But there is a problem with this sequence. In order to establish that the mirror does not faithfully reflect Patricia, Godard must impute reality to her off-screen voice. And he doesn't subsequently derealize this voice in the way he does the images of Patricia. He allows it to preserve its illusory power, something which is all the more disturbing because he himself also consistently speaks from off-screen.

KS: I think that what we're confronting here is once again the impossibility of ever achieving a full and complete deconstruction. There will always be sounds and images which we fail to apprehend as signifiers. By not discrediting Patricia's voice-off, Godard suggests as much. But by then, he has given us the means to strip that voice of its apparent truthfulness. This is no longer work which the film needs to perform.

HF: Perhaps Godard is not finally suggesting that images and sounds always give us a false sense of who we are, but is rather proposing that no image and no sound *always* provides a true mirror. Emile proposes a moment later that "In this image and this sound of you, we must find what is, and the moment when it is."

KS: In the sequence which begins with the mirror, *Gay Knowledge* pits image against sound, and sound against image. But elsewhere in the film, Godard suggests that every image has an auditory complement, and every sound its visual correlative. At one point, Emile proposes taking guerrilla action against spectators who watch dubbed films, since they have never heard a talking film actually "talk."

HF: *Gay Knowledge* also includes another sequence deploring the mismatch of sound and image, thereby again suggesting the converse possibility of a correct match. In this sequence, Emile stands behind

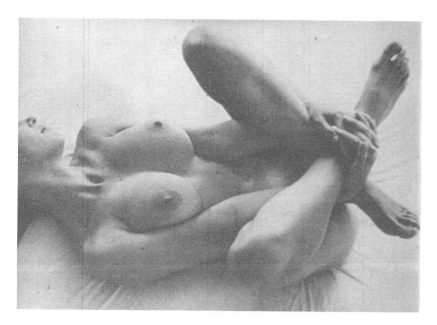

Fig. 25

Patricia, so that we can't see him, while uttering the words: "Man is what he has done and what has been made of him." Patricia mouths the words which he speaks, as if Emile is articulating them through her. Her image takes the place which should be occupied by his.

KS: This sequence, which comes shortly after that involving the mirror, is part of a chapter devoted to images whose sounds have been censored, and sounds whose images have been censored. To illustrate the latter, Godard uses black film. He is working his way toward the notion that just as there is "sound-silence," so there can be "image-silence." Patricia could be said to "silence" Emile's image in the sequence you just described.

HF: Again, we are reminded that in every image someone speaks.

KS: But no one can really be said to speak, whether in word or image, unless someone else hears. And hearing is more than a physiological activity; it also implies understanding, in the most profound sense of that word. "We've heard a statement when we've become part of it," Emile says.

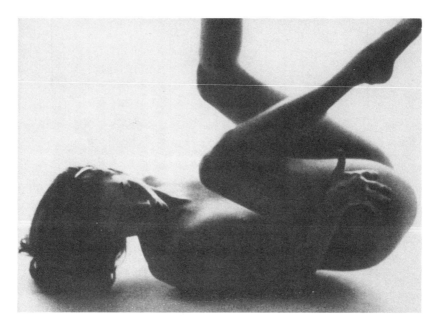

Fig. 26

HF: *Gay Knowledge* then invites us to become part of a particular state-ment. Patricia twice articulates the words "A woman's freedom begins with her belly." Godard cuts quickly back and forth between two images, both showing women on their backs (figures 25 and 26). In one image, a woman wraps her hands around her crossed legs, block-ing access to her genitals. There is perhaps a reference here to Man Ray's *Prayer*, in which a woman folds her hands over her buttocks. The second shows a woman on her back with her legs slightly extended in the air. This could be an image from a peep show. The montage is so rapid-fire that we can never see what I have just described. It is impos-sible to determine whether we are looking at a woman who is protect-ing herself against sexual aggression, or a woman who is opening herself to sexual pleasure. There is a constant oscillation between the terms "refusal" and "invitation." A woman's freedom is apparently to be found in neither image, but rather in the interval between them.

KS: In this sequence, "hearing" seems to require both looking and listening; the words which Patricia speaks are not enough by them-selves to induce understanding, but require the two images of women on their backs. Again, Godard suggests that every sound has its visual correlative, and every image its acoustic complement. But word and image do not match up here in a one-to-one way. It seems that the visual and the verbal do not have to replicate each other to belong together.

HF: There are several more major chapters in *Gay Knowledge* before the building of alternative cinematic models begins in earnest. One is devoted to a study of the relations between language and money. Over an abstract image with the words "meaning plays" (*"sens joue"*), Patricia says: "given word" (*"parole donnée"*). This is an example of the play or slippage of the signifier from one domain (that of economics, of giving or exchange) to another (language). It points to the profound connectedness of those two domains.

KS: This chapter next encourages us to consider the monetary crisis in London in tandem with the linguistic crisis in Paris. At first, this proposal is baffling, but then we realize that language, like money, is subject at moments of crisis to a *revaluation*, with as dramatic consequences. May 1968 entailed precisely such a revaluation of the linguistic signifier. The importance of the linguistic signifier increased dramatically, and the world has been different ever since.[30]

HF: As Patricia sits on a stool, turning the pages of a children's alphabet book (figure 27), Emile again demonstrates the interrelationship of the economic and the linguistic. He cites examples of the words with which the French educational system illustrates the letters of the alphabet, arguing that in each case there is an implicit defence of economic privilege, and the repression of opposing values.

KS: The first example Emile gives, "a brioche is better [*'meilleur'*] than bread," comes directly out of the mouth of Marie Antoinette. But for the most part, the alphabet book speaks the values of bourgeois culture: "Letter A: to buy [*acheter*], not art. . . . Letter F: not fascism, but family and cheese [*fromage*]."

HF: Emile responds with a more complex formulation of the relation between language and money: "Banks exist to lend bills, and dictionaries to lend words, but what can't be borrowed is the distinction between this and that bill, and this and that word." Dictionaries

Fig. 27

make available all the words, just as banks do all the denominations of bills—"fascism" as well as "family" and "cheese," "art" as well as "to buy." But they don't teach us to understand the differences between them. We can't learn the hierarchies and relations of exclusion between words there. All words seem equal, like citizens in a democracy.

KS: Sitting with their backs to us, and with her arm around him, Emile and Patrica meditate upon one of the rules governing sounds and images which dictionaries don't make clear to us: the rule of "one after another." Because of this rule, we can't affirm two words or images at the same time, or make evident the repressive role that one word or image plays in relation to others. But as soon as we have sounds *and* images, both of these limitations can be overcome. By putting them "on top of each other," we can communicate two things at the same time, or make apparent what a word or image excludes. In articulating this principle here, Emile helps to clarify many of *Gay Knowledge*'s experiments with sound and image.[31]

HF: Emile and Patricia turn their attention next to the acoustic dimensions of language. Certain languages are inaccessible to us not because of their alien grammar or syntax, they muse, but simply because we can't hear them. Dolphins, for instance, communicate on a much higher frequency than we do.

KS: Emile and Patricia then try to approximate the "Oh yes," with which a female friend responded to the proposal that they go play the clown at the Pentagon. They are unable to do so; the sound is inimitable. A person's voice is a distillate of a very particular education, in the broadest sense of that word. The two words which Emile and Patricia try to duplicate contain all of the Beatles' albums, and the novels of André Gide. The voice emerges here as the most individual thing about speech—as that which has never been before, and will never be again.

HF: Significantly, Emile refers in this context to the cry of the new-born baby, which for Hannah Arendt represents the introduction into the world of the absolutely new.[32] But this sequence emphasizes not only the singularity of the voice, but also its capacity to communicate. When Emile expresses his regret that he and Patricia didn't record the "oh yes," Patricia responds that words weren't meant to be recorded by a machine, but rather transmitted to someone else. Patricia thereby isolates a crucial feature of sonorousness: its capacity to convey a feeling, or—better yet—an attitude toward the world, from one person to another.

KS: The sonorousness chapter leads logically to the time chapter; in both cases, what is at issue is that which is unique within an utterance.

HF: "Time," Patricia says, " . . . one doesn't know (*sait*) what it is." Emile tries to prove her wrong by offering a definition of time drawn from physics: a scientific definition. Patricia rejects this clarification. She puts in its place one which can be understood only through the subjective experience of reading a text.

KS: The text with which Patricia tries to communicate this concept of time is Descartes' *Meditations on First Philosophy*, the companion volume to the *Discourse on Method*. The time which is her concern is not the period which it took Descartes to write *Meditations on First Philosophy*, nor the hours it took her to read it, but rather the time of that book itself. Emile struggles with this concept, and then says, as an apparent nonsequitur: "Suddenly I think that there is something infamous about time." Patricia responds, "Yes, eternity and infamy are born together." After a moment, the seeming nonsequitur yields a certain sense. Emile and Patricia are trying to understand the time which is specific to a text through an attribute which it doesn't have: infinitude. The time of the *Meditations on First Philosophy* is absolutely particular to it; it is coterminous with the words and silences out of which it is constructed. The notion of infinity is infamous because it denies this specificity.

HF: But Godard is not arguing here for a kind of historical relativism; he's not saying that Freud's *Interpretation of Dreams* was true in 1900, but not for us today. The time of a great text is something which we can experience all over again two hundred years later. It's a "zone" into which we can enter at any subsequent moment. In this sense, reading is a kind of time travel.

KS: Nevertheless, Godard does seem to be suggesting that the words of a text are true only so long as we are within that "zone." This means that those words are not subject to a subsequent invalidation: they remain forever after the irreducible expression of their time. But it also means that they cannot be universalized, assumed to be forever true. The text from which Patricia is reading is one to which we have attributed such universality—one which has succeeded in commanding our belief long after its moment has past. Patricia and Emile attempt to combat the apparent infinitude of *Meditations on First Philosophy* by finding the time to which it belongs. Shortly after this chapter, *Gay Knowledge* makes much more evident its critical relationship to the Cartesian project. Emile asks Patricia how many levels of discourse there are, and—over an image of a young woman seemingly lost in reverie—Patricia offers the following declension: "She thinks. She is thought. She unthinks. She is unthought." With these words, *Gay Knowledge* undoes the definition of man offered by Descartes in the *Meditations* and *Discourse on Method*. It "unthinks" woman—and, by implication, man—by proposing that what defines her is less thinking than being thought. At the same time,

Gay Knowledge references its own project of returning to zero. But the zero point now has a radically new meaning: it signifies not a site of epistemological stability, a place where we can be sure that we are no longer in any way deluded, but the nullity disclosed through the unthinking of the thinker.

HF: In the first of its cinematic models, the amateur film, *Gay Knowledge* offers a metaphor through which to conceptualize this theoretical project: Patricia rides her bicycle in circles around Emile, while he says: "in making a circular journey, one returns to one's point of departure, but asymmetrical to what one was at the beginning."

KS: With the next cinematic model, the education film, *Gay Knowledge* begins its reconceptualization of relationality, something which follows logically from its reconceptualization of subjectivity. Love, Emile and Patricia suggest at the beginning of this sequence, is typically a discourse "in which each tells the other what he is"—a nominalizing or substantializing exchange. But Patricia and Emile speculate that "in searching for a zero degree of images and sounds," they are perhaps in the process of discovering "the zero degree of love," a love presumably beyond such nominalization.

HF: The education film seemingly proposes the end of sexual repression as the mechanism for achieving a genuine relationality. The camera tracks from Emile to Patricia and then to Emile again as they say: "We know, since the discoveries of psychoanalysis, that the perversions arise and are developed through the negation of sexuality." A line drawing of the police raping a woman with the Croix Lorraine makes sadism representative of the perversions.[33]

KS: But this simplistic account of the erotic quickly gives way to a much darker vision, suggesting the need to find another way of conceptualizing the relational. Patricia asks Emile what sexuality is, and he responds "a divine and magnificent activity." Patricia retorts that "It's a murderous activity," in which people "assassinate" each other in bed. Shamefacedly, Emile agrees.

HF: Although various little experiments with image and sound follow, the next clearly defined cinematic model would seem to be the historical film. In this sequence, Patricia, in a period costume, stands before a wall with three giant cartoon characters on it. She reads aloud from a book, but the words are mostly unintelligible. Perhaps she is speaking a private, woman's language. Or perhaps Godard is indicating that the historical film is no longer possible: that it has become unintelligible, or should be so rendered.

KS: Your second idea is closer to my sense of what this sequence is doing than the first. As Patricia reads, Emile also begins to speak from off-frame. He produces clichés from Alfred de Musset about the treachery of women: "always playing a role, lying, weak and violent," etc. This might be said to be the historical text, over and against which Patricia's text must be read. In this latter text, language manifests itself in the form of pure sonorousness, and thereby inhibits the movement from signifier to misogynist signified. Significantly, one of the few intelligible words is "language." Language might be said to appear, and woman as we have long known her to disappear. The cartoon figures are all masculine heroes. They dramatize that idealizing rendition of masculinity which is the complement to Musset's de-idealizing account of femininity.

HF: The following film model is called the "imperialist film," but in fact offers more a critical allegory of imperialism. Standing with her back to us, but facing Emile, Patricia sings a little song to the letter "O." Emile counters with the letter "A." He bullies her until she substitutes the "A" for the "O." Here the hidden connection between "O" and "Stalin" is finally demonstrated.[34]

KS: The novel film also foregrounds the voice. In it, a stationary camera focuses on Emile as he reads aloud from a text by Isidore Sollers. At first we don't hear what he says. We listen, rather, to a conversation about the text which goes on off-screen between Emile and Patricia. This sequence recalls the one about self-images; again, the voice takes up residence elsewhere, and discredits the image.

HF: We see here how much cinema's character system is tied to speech, even in as experimental a film as this. But on this occasion, off-screen sound eventually loses its primacy. Emile begins reading again from the Sollers book, and this time we hear what he says: a collection of sentences drawn from other books. This cut-up principle is also at the heart of *Gay Knowledge*. It, too, is stitched together out of elements drawn from a range of other texts. And Godard is a little like Isidore Sollers, who worked in a bookstore, and only ever had time to read the first sentence of the books he sold. Godard, too, doesn't have to read all of the texts from which he quotes to make something out of them.

KS: In a long sequence of what might be called "image-silence" near the end of the film, Emile and Patricia sit in the darkened studio listening to two voices which claim to know. At first, the voice of a student leader talks about the aims of the student movement, and Godard about the plight of French workers. Then, the student leader begins to speak about the workers, and Godard about the students. This sound montage seems calculated to bring the concerns of these two groups together. At a certain point, they are unified; the topic becomes the need to educate the workers.

HF: On paper, this text in two voices would have at least a documentary value; it would provide a record of some of the central concerns of May 1968. But in the film itself, it is not really possible to follow the argument. What the two voices say is unassimilable.

KS: The primary effect of this sequence is unpleasure. This unpleasure derives not only from the shutting down of the visual access, but also from the fact that the voices speak less to us than *at* us.

HF: But in this sequence, Godard seems finally to purge himself of what you call his Cartesianism. Like a stormy night, after which the weather can be especially beautiful, this makes possible a new lyricism. The experimental film sequence follows immediately afterwards, and has the virtuosity of the New American Cinema. In it, Godard plays with a device similar to the magic writing pad, which translates the user's movements into rectangular patterns. He also "squiggles" with a Mozart piece, which he plays on a tape recorder with a loose electrical connection. The sound fades in and out.

KS: At first glance, this sequence has nothing to do with politics. It seems a purely formal exercise. However, upon closer scrutiny, it could be said to be a dramatization of Marx's claim that men make their own history, but not just as they please.[35] In the experimental film, the filmmaker does not lay claim to an absolute autonomy, an *ex nihilo* production. Rather, he manifestly works within certain con-

Fig. 28

straints. The filmmaker is free only to intervene within the pregiven structure of the Mozart piece in disruptive ways, and to produce visual patterns of the sort that the magic writing pad allows. He does not start from zero.

HF: The most beautiful of the cinematic models is the psychological film, which comes near the end of *Gay Knowledge*. In it, Patricia stands with her head on Emile's shoulder (figure 28). Her hair falls like a thick carpet across his body, and both of their faces are also subject to a certain disfiguration; the human is rendered abstract, figural. As the film cuts back and forth from Patricia's face to Emile's, those two characters talk not about the bourgeois present, nor the revolutionary future, but about that most psychoanalytic of all temporalities, the past.

KS: The conversation turns upon the darkness or void at the heart of subjectivity. Patricia speaks of finding herself before an imageless mirror, and of feeling herself to be the shadow of an absent being. This experience of self-dissolution coincides with an apprehension of the linguistic bases of subjectivity—of what *Gay Knowledge* calls "this long speech which is me."

HF: Significantly, there is no appeal to objective knowledge here. Emile and Patricia grope their way toward their inner night only via fear and memory.

KS: At the end of the psychological film, the possibility of the relational, and so of the political, is broached once more, but with a difference. Emile and Patricia speak of that "false plural" which is generally assumed to mean "us," and which we have experienced firsthand at all of those moments when Godard's voice seems to demand our consent. They suggest that this "false plural" exists only "through the extension of me." To it, they oppose that "us" which is only available on the other side of the empty mirror, an "us" which signifies not just the long speech which is "me," but also the long speech which is "you"—in short, a genuine conversation.

HF: The last cinematic model is the guerrilla film. As the camera holds on Patricia, Emile's voice provides instructions for making a molotov cocktail. Surprisingly, he anthropomorphizes the molotov cocktail; the bottle is a face, the cork the eyes, the wick the hair. All the time we are looking at Patricia's face. We cannot help but see the molotov cocktail in her image. At the end, Emile proposes to the listener that he or she throw the completed molotov cocktail at the enemy. He again uses the metaphor of the face: the enemy is "the face of repression." The camera continues to hold in closeup on Patricia, as if she were somehow the distillate of "faceness."

KS: To immolate the enemy is thus simultaneously to immolate the self. This is not surprising, since the primary weapon which *Gay Knowledge* invites us to turn against the enemy is language.[36]

HF: At the end of *Gay Knowledge*, Emile and Patricia part for the last time. Emile is off to make another film. He asks Patricia what she will do. She answers "je ne sais pas." Here, at last, is a voice which says it doesn't know. Patricia laments all the shots which they have failed to produce. Emile responds that other filmmakers will shoot them. Bertolucci will make the film showing that there is no situation that can't be analyzed in Marxist or Freudian terms, and Straub the one showing that an honorable family is one where everything is forbidden. No film by itself can be complete, say "everything."

KS: A moment later, Patricia remarks: "Even so, it's a bit of nothingness that we've discovered." Emile's initial response is to declare *Gay Knowledge* to be a failure. But almost immediately, he corrects himself: "No, not really, not at all. Listen: what better ideal could we propose to people today, than to reconquer nothingness through the knowledge of it which they themselves have discovered?" Emile here uses *connaissance* rather than *savoir* to designate the kind of knowledge he has in mind; he thereby suggests that our exemplary relation to the zero is one of familiarity. And the French word which I have translated as "to reconquer," "*reconquérir*" also means "to regain"— to recover something that has been lost, stolen, or (in this context) forgotten. Emile suggests that what *Gay Knowledge* has finally made possible is not an objective knowledge of "the workers," or "the bourgeoisie," or even sounds and images, but rather a subjective knowledge of the void which grounds us. In the place of the "I think, therefore I am," it proposes something like: "I speak, therefore I'm not."[37]

HF: After Emile and Patricia bid each other farewell, Godard's voice whispers a kind of postscript. In it, he turns *Le Gai Savoir* back upon itself, in a gesture of self-dissolution: "This film is not the film which must be made, but rather an indication of some of the paths which one must follow, if one is to make a film."

KS: With these words, Godard makes clear that *Gay Knowledge* is no more self-identical than Patricia and Emile. He subjects the film to what Marc Cerisuelo calls a *désœuvrement*, undoes it as a "work." What is *Gay Knowledge*, then, if not an *œuvre*? The answer is "language," and it is already available in the opening words of the film, words which Godard himself once again utters: "444,000 images [speaking about themselves] . . . the same with 127,000 sounds . . ."

six

In Her Place

Number Two/Numéro deux (1975)

HF: *Number Two* (1975) depicts the domestic life of three generations of a proletarian family living in a social housing apartment. Usually, when we see working-class people in a film, they are somehow exceptional. They win in a lottery, fight a revolution, or marry someone rich, and thereby earn our interest. But in *Number Two*, Godard focuses relentlessly on the ordinary. He shows a wife masturbating, her husband painting a chair, the family watching television. The result is not a conceptual minimalism, but rather an explosion of meaning. Godard allows us to see that even the most routine household activities and bodily functions are semantically dense.

KS: The film's images are unlike any we have seen before. Most of them were shot in video, then reshot in 35mm as they played on video monitors. Often two monitors are shown together. Because the 35mm image is always larger than the video images, those images swim in a pool of blackness. But at the beginning and end of *Number Two*, the full 35mm image is deployed for the purposes of sketching out another "scene," one which is usually foreclosed from the cinematic text: the site of production. It shows us Godard at work in his studio, surrounded by the tools of his trade, and the material he is in the process of weaving into a film. The 35mm image also depicts

141

something even more remarkable: a filmmaker interrogating and attempting to transform the relationship between himself and the film he is in the process of making.

HF: The idea of doubling the image must have come to Godard from working in video. Video editing is usually done while sitting in front of two monitors. One monitor shows the already edited material, and the other monitor raw material, which the videomaker may or may not add to the work-in-progress. He or she becomes accustomed to thinking of two images at the same time, rather than sequentially.

KS: In an interview, Godard remarked that whereas film is better than video for image quality and purposes of dissemination, video permits something which film disallows: simultaneity.[1] In film, one image comes *after* another, and implicitly negates everything which it isn't. As Stephen Heath once wrote, it says: "This but not that."[2] Video permits "this" and "that" at the same time. This principle of simultaneity is at the heart of *Number Two*, and one of the primary references of the title. Godard insists upon it not only by doubling the image, but by sometimes splitting the video screen into two further images, or superimposing one image on another. *Number Two* also gives us film and video at the same time.

HF: When Godard shows two monitors, he makes one comment upon the other in a soft montage. I say "soft montage" since what is at issue is a general relatedness, rather than a strict opposition or equation. *Number Two* does not predetermine how the two images are to be connected; we must build up the associations ourselves in an ongoing way as the film unfolds. There's another sense in which the film seems to have been conceptualized more within the parameters of video than within those of cinema. It would be difficult to shoot a work this intimate and physically confined in 35mm from the beginning, since 35mm usually requires a large crew. With video, Godard needed only a crew of three, and could ask the actors to do things which would otherwise have been intolerably invasive. This way, he was able to produce something very close to a home movie.

KS: Every shot in the film is stationary. Godard claims that he stopped moving his camera around this point in time because he couldn't think of a good reason to pan or track.[3]

HF: The decision not to move the camera, like the black around the video images, creates a great deal of off-screen space, which adds mystery to the everyday activities which are depicted. The apartment also gains dignity from this decision. Most cheap apartments look terrible in film; the filmmaker denounces the characters by shooting them there. By not moving the camera to show rooms in their entirety, Godard avoids this discrimination against his proletarian characters. The fragmentary details of the apartment that are shown are made abstract, elevated to the status of ideas. But with the sound, the misery of social housing is back. A kiss sounds like a shot from a child's pistol because it reverberates off the concrete walls. The sounds are too "pointed."

KS: The film begins with two video monitors showing a series of shots of family members, either individually or in tandem. Since we haven't yet been introduced to any of them, these images remain very enigmatic. A lengthy preface follows, consisting of a single very long take. It shows Godard standing in a darkened workroom smoking and talking. He is adjacent to a blue video screen, which shows his face as he talks, filmed by an unseen camera. In the left of the image, videotape runs from one reel to another on a large video recorder. This monologue proceeds in a way that is difficult to characterize. Godard talks mostly about his workroom, and about himself as filmmaker. He specifies both through a series of metaphors which he no sooner introduces than he qualifies. The qualifications, however, are never absolute. Aspects of each metaphor are always carried over to the next stage of the monologue.

HF: The effect is vertiginous. The speech goes like this: "Mac, machine. No Mac, only machine. We are printing, printing paper, as the bank says, so we are a printshop. No, we are reading books, we are a library. This room is a factory, I am the boss. I am also a worker . . . " As Godard speaks, we admire the wonderful low-key lighting that is possible when shooting in 35mm, and contrast it with the video monitor in the middle of the image. Because the video camera has better night eyes than the 35mm camera, what the video monitor shows is utterly without romance.

KS: Godard uses the video image of himself to demystify the 35mm image. Ever since the formation of the Dziga Vertov collective, he had been struggling to divest himself of authorship.[4] "In order to film in a politically just manner," he wrote in a text from 1969, " . . . [one must abandon] the notion of the author . . . [This notion] is completely reactionary."[5] *Number Two* represents a limit-text in this respect. Godard claims to have "invented" nothing in it.[6] It was made, as he put it, "under the influence of [Anne-Marie] Miéville."[7] The grandmother's long voice-over monologue was taken from Germaine Greer,[8] and Godard for the most part coaxed the actors into creating their own lines.[9] Even what you called the film's "soft montage" indicates Godard's desire to avoid being the one to produce meaning. In the preface, he pushes this process one step further. First, he turns the 35mm camera on himself, and in so doing renounces the most definitive attribute of traditional authorship: transcendence. He becomes embodied, localizable, and visible. But that by itself would not be enough, since he is still exterior to the video monitor, which, much more emphatically than the workroom, signifies the "textual frame." He also shows himself with his video equipment, in what he calls his "factory," and is therefore associated with the enunciation. Consequently, he must put himself where his characters are: inside the video image.[10]

HF: After this shot ends, there is a brief interlude consisting primarily of images from later in the film, shown on two monitors. Godard continues speaking: "And about 300,000 kilometers from here, what am I saying, 20,000 kilometers from here the Vietcong already thought about Saigon." The mistake is telling: 300,000 kilometers per second is the speed of light. Godard is saying that Vietnam is light years away from this film. *Number Two* represents a dramatic turn away from the Dziga Vertov films and the films of the late sixties in its notion of "the political." At the same time, by naming Vietnam, Godard continues his practice of invoking the war in every film he makes.

KS: In *Number Two*, Godard is concerned with sexual difference and the family, rather than with the Maoist and Marxist concerns of the years immediately before. Not surprisingly, then, his attempts at authorial divestiture effect some important gender displacements. The names of two women even work their way into the primary credits for the film.

HF: After the video interlude, there is a second prologue, again consisting of a sustained long take, and again showing Godard's workroom. It is interrupted from time to time by titles against black, and—toward the end—by a single video monitor with a scene of anal sex. This time the main image shows two video monitors in left frame, one above the other. The upper monitor displays excerpts from a wide variety of feature and pornographic films; it signifies "fiction." The lower monitor shows television news footage, mostly pertaining to a May Day demonstration; it signifies "documentary." *Number Two* thereby signals its unwillingness to choose documentary over fiction, or fiction over documentary; like many other Godard films, it wants to be both at the same time.

KS: The video machine from the first prologue unspools continuously behind these monitors. In the left front frame a tape recorder plays a song, stops, rewinds, and begins again. Godard sits in the shadow in front of it, almost invisible, and is seemingly responsible for nothing more than its manipulation. He figures here less as "author" than as "worker." During this shot, the words "A film written and directed . . . " appear on the screen, but no name is attached to either of these activities. Some time later, the voice of Sandrine Battistella, who plays the central character in the film, provides a very different version of the credits to the film, this time in a complete form. Significantly, the categories "direction" and "writing" are now absent, and have been replaced by the much more labor-significant "production," which is credited not to one, but four names: "*Number Two*: a film produced by A.-M. Miéville and J.-L. Godard, with S. Battistella, P. Oudry and others." Pierre Oudry is the other primary actor in the film, and the "others" added at the end of the credits presumably include—at the very least—the other actors.

HF: Surprisingly, the factory metaphor is still a positive one for Godard, and over and over again he puts it at the heart of this film. It is not only that he characterizes his workroom as a factory, and represents *Number Two* as a film which has been "produced" rather than "written" or "directed," but also that later in the same shot Sandrine will query: "Ever ask yourself whether papa was a factory or a landscape? And what about mom?" She then answers her question in a way that runs counter to the history of representations of the feminine, again giving primacy to the metaphor of production: "I say she's a factory. I guess maybe an electrical plant: charge and discharge." This metaphor is one of the points of continuity between Godard's earlier, more Maoist and Marxist films, and *Number Two*.

KS: Godard does not talk in the second prologue. Rather, it is Sandrine's voice which occupies a metacritical position, and which speaks from outside the story proper. We will later understand how crucial it is that it be her voice rather than Godard's that occupies the enunciatory position.

HF: But the two prefaces in *Number Two* work against this self-effacement. Their inclusion indicates that Godard is anxious that what follows might be misunderstood, and this manifest anxiety makes him more authorially present than he would be were he simply to list himself as the director of *Number Two*.

KS: Total authorial erasure is perhaps an impossible goal, but in this case a necessary impossibility. We can learn a lot from the attempt, even if it is ultimately unsuccessful.

HF: Sandrine emphasizes that this film does not fit easily within traditional political categories, and that it brings together things which are normally kept apart ("the film's not left or right, but before and behind . . . In front are children. Behind is government"). The "before" and "behind" are central signifiers throughout the film; through them Godard elaborates a new signification of the body.

KS: Sandrine also characterizes *Number Two* as a film which is simultaneously political and pornographic: "A political film? it's not political, it's pornographic. No, it's not pornographic, it's political. So, is it about pornography or politics? Why is it either/or? It can be both sometimes . . . " Since to affirm both terms in a binary opposition simultaneously is to undo that opposition, we can now begin to see that this principle of "both at the same time" might also be put to transformative uses within the domain of "difference."

HF: At the end of the second prologue, Sandrine asks: "Have you ever looked at your sex? Did anyone see you look at it?" She thereby introduces one of the most central topics of the film: the seeing and showing of sexuality. Astonishingly, every character but the son exposes his genitals at some point in the film.[11]

KS: But in spite of this repeated literal exposure of genitals, the seeing and showing of sexuality is heavily metaphoric. In *Number Two*, the body always expresses itself "hysterically," i.e. as a displaced signifier for psychic, social, and economic relations.[12] Near the end of the second prologue, Sandrine asks: "Why do you listen to music?" She then answers her question in a way which transforms what it means to "look"—which lifts that activity out of the sensory domain and into the conceptual and affective: "To see with wonder. What's wonder? What you don't see." It is in this sense that *Number Two* encourages us to look at sex. We are encouraged to see what is literally unseeable.

HF: In the first episode of the film "proper," Sandrine wears a white bathrobe, which—because it is unfastened in the front—exposes her breasts and pubic hair to our view. Here we have a very literal showing of sexuality. Vanessa walks around her mother, who is ironing, and then stoops down to go between her legs. Again, sexuality seems emphatically corporeal. As she emerges in front of Sandrine, who faces us as she irons, Vanessa asks: "Will I bleed between my legs when I'm big?" Sandrine answers in the affirmative, but immediately translates menstrual blood into a metaphor for the danger of heterosexual relations. "Yes," she answers, "but be careful of guys. They're hard to handle."

KS: In the next episode, we see two images mixed together on a video monitor: one showing Pierre anally penetrating Sandrine, and one of Vanessa facing an off-screen interlocutor while saying: "Sometimes I think it's pretty, mama and papa, sometimes I think it's poopy." Once again, sexuality seems insistently material. Vanessa, as we later learn, has witnessed this scene, and thinks: "Daddy's penis in mommy's anus: that's where shit comes out." But we will later learn that Sandrine thinks the same thing, and that this precipitates in her psyche a complicated metaphorics which is capable of invading her bodily functions, and completely denaturing them.

HF: In the third episode, the camera holds tightly on Vanessa as she bathes, Sandrine reaching into the frame to help her (figure 29). As she touches her genitals, Vanessa asks: "Do all little girls have a hole?" After her mother answers in the affirmative, she queries: "Is that where memories come out?" Sandrine responds, "Of course." Finally, Vanessa asks: "Where do [the memories] go?" and is given the response: "Into the landscape." In this episode, the vagina becomes a metaphoric receptacle for memories.

Fig. 29

KS: In all of the first three episodes of the story proper, the camera shows only one video monitor. But in the three in which the son, Nicolas, is introduced, a second is added. In the first of these, he does his homework, sitting alone at his desk. This image is depicted on both monitors, as if to suggest that Nicolas resists putting himself in relation to others. Between this episode and the next, we see the word "factory" mutate against a black screen into the word "solitude." In the second episode, Nicolas sits in center frame at the kitchen table, eating. Sandrine decides to play a political song, and she and Vanessa dance together to it, mostly in the room behind the one in which Nicolas sits. They attempt to involve him in their dance, but he brushes them irritably away.

HF: A second song, with the theme "solitude," and sung by Leo Ferré, keeps intruding. It is clearly Nicolas's "theme song," and it ultimately takes over the soundtrack completely. However, for a while we hear both songs at the same time, in another demonstration of the "both at the same time" principle.

KS: After this episode we see the word "solitude" mutate against black into the words "number one." The film here makes explicit for the first time that the categories "number one" and "number two" have a gender significance. It also puts masculinity under the sign of solitude, a characterization which it will consistently maintain.

HF: Nicolas seems to find his solitude more heroic than oppressive.

KS: I think that is because of the "solitude" song, which proceeds as if from his imagination. Ferré's music is consistently used in *Number Two* as an emotional magnifier, much as Legrand's is in *My Life to Live* (1962). At various moments in the film, we see the characters reaching out through this music to a more expansive space, a "larger" life. This is particularly true in the scene where the grandfather, Sandrine, and Vanessa listen to another Ferré song with Pierre's earphones. We, too, experience an affective expansion every time the song cuts into the soundtrack, and the lyrics of that song make explicit the utopian function of music in *Number Two*: "I live elsewhere, in dimension 4 with cosmic GMC2," sings Ferré. Through his solitude, Nicolas tries to inhabit this heroic "elsewhere."

HF: In this episode, there is again only one monitor, but the open doorway behind Nicolas which leads to a second room creates a frame inside the frame, and so doubles the image. In the last of the sequence of episodes introducing Nicolas, he sits across the table from Vanessa, and they tell stories—or perhaps two variants of the same story—to each other. Nicolas faces us, and Vanessa away from us, but we nevertheless see Vanessa's face through an unusual variant of the shot/reverse shot: Godard superimposes an image of her face over the image of the two children. This double camera coverage is another example of simultaneity, but it also tells us that the micro-world of the family is as important as the macro-world of more conventional politics—so significant that it must be filmed from every direction, like a major public event.

KS: The story or stories the children narrate are about "big" topics—love, betrayal, murder, prison—and are melodramatically recounted. Again, we see this aspiration to a "larger" life. But the stories involve an anonymous "he" and "she," rather than the children themselves; it is as if Vanessa and Nicolas are too young as yet to have narratives of their own to recount. Although they are equal in this respect, sexual difference intrudes even here: Nicolas at one point puts himself in the story, as if he knows already that he will later have one. Vanessa does not, suggesting that her access to the world of action is more uncertain.

HF: Yet the film privileges the little girl over the little boy, just as it will later privilege Sandrine over Pierre. In *Number Two*, Godard creates a story about those who are generally left out of narrative, whether one construes that category historiographically or cinematically: not only women, but also children and old people. The episodes involving the grandmother and the grandfather emphasize that those two figures are marginal even within the family. In the scene in which Nicolas watches soccer on television, and the grandfather asks him to change the channel so that he can watch a Soviet movie, the grandfather is shown to have absolutely no authority within the home. Nicolas refuses, and Pierre tells him to buy his own television. And the grandmother seems completely isolated from the other members of the family; we never see her even exchange a word with anyone else.

KS: Yes, the grandmother is the most marginal figure in the film. Once again, *Number Two* suggests that even within a dispossessed category like that of children or the aged, gender can make a big difference. Storytelling is an important function in the film, an index to who a character is, but the grandmother—unlike all of the other family members—has no story to tell. The grandfather, on the other hand, tells more stories than any other character.

HF: While preparing something to eat in the kitchen, he narrates a story about working in a munitions factory . He recounts a story about his former marriage and his time in a concentration camp on a tape to which the family listens one night. And he relates a story about a trip to Singapore while sitting at his desk on the balcony. His stories are full of intrigue and high adventure: world travel, strikes, organizing workers, a politically motivated marriage, surviving the unimaginable. The grandfather also represents a form of political action which no longer seems possible within the present tense of the film. He tells stories from a time in which there was a worldwide proletarian network—a time when a worker traveled on behalf of the Communist Party as if he had to serve and help maintain an empire.

KS: There seems to be a cause-and-effect relation between the fact that the grandfather has so many heroic narratives to recite, and the fact that the grandmother has none. As the grandmother says, the grandfather "jerks off" with his storytelling. The grandmother objects to the grandfather's stories not only because the grandfather derives a solitary and almost erotic pleasure in retelling them, but also because they are so phallic—because there is no room for a female protagonist within the virile leftism they purvey. As the grandfather acknowledges at one point, everything "comes out of [his] cock."

HF: But the film distances itself from the grandfather's stories. It is not on the side of these *grands récits*. The scene in which the family listens to the grandfather's voice is staged a bit ironically, as if the family is being obliged to listen to an "oral history" program on the radio. It is not really possible to digest his stories.

KS: The grandfather's stories are also definitively in the past. The film makes this explicit in the wonderful scene with the head-phones. Vanessa, who is sitting beside the grandfather on the couch, tells him that he shouldn't use her father's possessions. He says *"pas d'histoires,"* which means in this context something like: "Don't give me any trouble." However, the word *"histoire"* also means "story" in French, and prompts him to say, meditatively, about himself: "There's no story. No music." It's as if he no longer has access either to narrative or affect. Vanessa asks, poignantly, "How do you manage?" as if life without such forms of sustenance would be intolerable.

HF: The grandmother is depicted very differently from the grandfather, in keeping with her greater marginality. The long sequence which introduces her is the only one consisting of a series of successive shots. She is shown peeling vegetables, making her bed, washing the floor, ironing, and cleaning herself. In the case of the last of these activities, there is only one video monitor, but with all of the others there are two. When there are two monitors, Godard shows the main action on the left, larger screen, while reprising the one that came before it on the right, smaller screen. He thereby makes succession yield to simul-taneity, and obliges us to think each new image in relation to those which preceded it.

Fig. 30

KS: As in the rest of the film, the grandmother does not speak about herself here. Indeed, she makes not a single use of the first-person pronoun, as if she is incapable of inscribing herself either in language or narrative. But although she performs all of her household work silently, her voice-over accompanies the images shown in this sequence with a paraphrase of two passages from Germaine Greer's *The Female Eunuch*.[13] For most of the sequence, the topic of this commentary is the sexual subordination of women, which it attributes not only to male violence, but also to female passivity ("The male perversion of violence is the cause of women's degradation. . . . Men are tired of bearing the sexual responsibility alone, and it's time to release them. Woman's sex must grasp its right . . . "). As the grandmother utters the last words, she sits down on the side of the bed, and spreads her legs. Her unfastened bathrobe opens, exposing her genitals (figure 30). The gesture is ambiguous; although it lacks the militancy of the commentary, it nevertheless represents something of a demand. But its effect is more to remind us that "postmenopausal" does not exactly signify the end of sexuality than to dramatize woman's assumption of erotic responsibility.

HF: During the last part of this sequence, when the grandmother is washing herself, the topic of the voice-over text is rather the idealization than the passivity of woman, along with the abuse of nature on her behalf ("She's the masterpiece of creation. The ocean is plundered to give her pearls and coral. Seals are clubbed, lambs torn from mothers. . . . Men risk death hunting leopards and crocodiles for bags and shoes. Bit by bit Venus asserts herself"). With the final words, the grandmother looks ironically at the camera, in an overt acknowledgment of its presence.

KS: She does so because the words Godard puts in her mouth entertain such a complicated interrelationship with the images he produces of her. The grandmother has just uttered words which do not have her as their referent, and she wants to signal as much to us. She asserts herself here, like the protagonist described by the voice-over, but only to remind us that she is not Venus—that her class affiliation, and, more emphatically, her age, prevent her from being characterized as "the masterpiece of creation." Whereas the attractive woman of a certain age, class, and race is subject not only to oppression, but also to idealization, the grandmother (like countless others who do not belong to that category) is not so fortunate. No men die in order to wrap her in furs. *Number Two* reminds us how inadequately feminism has traditionally dealt with the many disparities that transect sexual difference.

HF: Yes, it is startling to have these two paraphrases of passages from *The Female Eunuch* spoken by the grandmother; it problematizes them in important ways. But I have the impression that this is another situation analogous to Godard's speech in the first prologue: the words are qualified by the grandmother's look, but not entirely canceled out.

KS: That is because feminism is badly needed here, in spite of all of its limitations. The grandmother has no way of speaking about herself in the first person, since not only bourgeois culture, but also traditional leftism has failed to provide her with the narrative resources to tell her story. Feminism must therefore represent her, however inadequately. *Number Two* needs not just feminism in general at this point, but Germaine Greer in particular. It is part of the film's deconstruction of binary opposition to remind us that women can be complicit in their oppression, especially when oppression brings with it certain compensatory privileges. *Number Two* works very hard in this scene to prevent the easy characterization of women as victims, and men as their victimizers.

HF: That is also the case in the first scene devoted to Pierre and Sandrine. In this scene, Pierre is shown in the left monitor in a medium close-up, smoking. Sandrine enters through the door behind him, and asks him what he does at work. He explains that he tests microphones, and checks texts for his company's magazine. Sandrine flips impatiently through an issue of the magazine, and says dismissively: "I don't understand." "I know," Pierre says with resignation, as she leaves the room. On the right monitor a double image comes and goes, showing Pierre on his way to an antinuclear demonstration in the upper half, and Sandrine in the lower half, sleeping. Since she faces the camera, and he walks away from it, the impression is created that they have their backs to each other. In every detail of this episode, we learn about Sandrine's willful ignorance of what Pierre does when he leaves the apartment. Her ignorance is willful because she refuses to concern herself with a world where she could only play a subordinate role. However, it leaves her without any relation to society or paid labor, or any way of talking to her husband about his work.

KS: This places Pierre, like Nicolas and the grandfather—who is at one point shown preparing his dinner alone, and at another drinking by himself on the porch—under the sign of "solitude." *Number Two* also shows that although Pierre occupies the privileged position within the domain of gender, he occupies a subordinate position at work. And what happens within the socioeconomic sphere finds displaced expression within the home. "I fuck my wife," says Pierre, after Sandrine has left the room, "but it's all wrong. Thanks, boss." The next scene clarifies in what sense it's "all wrong" between Sandrine and Pierre. We look from the corridor into the bathroom while Pierre complains about the broken toilet, and pees in the sink. Sandrine, who is brushing her teeth from a hidden position, asks if they will have sex in the evening. He answers, evasively: "We'll see." She responds with the same words Pierre uses in the preceding scene: "Thanks, boss." Pierre then explains that at the end of a day of work, he is often impotent. *Number Two* thereby establishes that the male body can function as hysterically as the female.

HF: The next episode dramatizes yet another failed exchange between Sandrine and Pierre. She finds him painting a chair on the balcony, and offers to help. This time it is Pierre who rebuffs Sandrine's overture. Sandrine angrily responds: "You know, there are other guys." Through this episode, which is shown on the left monitor, the right monitor flickers unintelligibly, as if to suggest an aborted communication.

KS: This episode also shows the most frequently reproduced image in the film, on a single, large monitor: the image of Pierre anally penetrating Sandrine. Vanessa's distressed face bleeds into and out of this image. Pierre says in voice-over: "Something terrible happened. She fucked another guy. Never said who. I wanted to rape her. She let me, so I ass-fucked her. She began screaming. Then we saw Vanessa watching us. Family affairs, I guess." It is important to keep in mind, when attempting to understand the entirely negative metaphoric network which *Number Two* weaves around anal sexuality, that this particular act of sodomy is a rape. Although Sandrine "allows" Pierre to take her violently, she screams when he enters her anally, suggesting that this is not what she agreed to. Vanessa's distress further underscores the violence of this scene. Second, Pierre means to punish Sandrine for her infidelity by sodomizing her. He means, that is, to insist upon her "shitlike" status, and he chooses his orifice accordingly.

HF: Finally, reading this episode through the prism of the rest of the film, it is clear that, by sodomizing Sandrine, Pierre also seeks to situate himself sexually in relation to the man she slept with.[14] Indeed, he seeks to use her as if she were his rival. Prison novels would have us believe that certain men, when in prison, use the anus of other men as a substitute for the missing vagina. These particular men—as opposed to those for whom the rectum is the preferred orifice—are not gay. Rather, they sleep with other men as if they were women. Conversely, Pierre here treats Sandrine as if she were a man.

KS: Several episodes later, Pierre is shown lying in bed, with the back of his head facing the camera. Sandrine, at his request, sits on his chest with her buttocks toward him. She says: "Why always like this?", making clear that she is often asked to sit on Pierre in this way, and thereby indicating his general interest in her posterior region. He answers: "I see parts you never do." A moment later, she complains "you, you, you," suggesting that his tastes do not correspond to hers. This is hardly surprising, since he has just defined her viewing position as one of manifest exclusion. Ironically, Pierre says at the end of this scene that when Sandrine assumes this position he is able to see *her* violence.

HF: Pierre compares the mass of her body to a river, and its outline to the banks which enclose the river. "They talk of the river's overflowing violence," he adds, "never of the bank's violence to the river." When Sandrine sits on him, he can see the bank's violence, which is the violence of an articulation or a formal "cutting out," of the imposition of an identity upon an otherwise shapeless mass. Again, we have a very metaphoric treatment of sexuality. It is also clear from this scene that the same part of Sandrine's body—her buttocks—can mean very different things to her and her husband. Signification is never stable in this film—never a matter of matching up a signifier with a single signified.

KS: The next episode follows very closely from those which precede it. Sandrine and Pierre lie in bed together, she in center frame, and he semidiagonally across the lower frame. She throws back the blankets to reveal his body, asking: "Can I look, too?" Then, as if in direct response to Pierre's river and bank metaphor, she says: "See, Pierre, I look facing you. Mornings you leave. You walk out. I don't criticize, no. I've got no work. I see your ass go out the door. Your ass is off to work. That's a part you never see of yourself. So evenings I have to look at you. Facing you when you come in. Facing me is your cock. Not your ass." In this extraordinary resemanticization of the body, buttocks come to represent work and separation, the division and asymmetry of man's and woman's spheres, and nonreciprocity. The front of the body, on the other hand, means home, reunion, and reciprocity.

HF: The notion that sexuality was a liberatory force was very much in the intellectual air in the late 1960s and early 1970s, but Godard seems to have a more complex view. He suggests that sexuality can represent *every* human relation, negative as well as positive.

KS: *Number Two* shows that sexuality is the site at which all forms of repression are most fully felt, and where they become most legible. At the same time, the new politics the film puts forward is routed through the sexual. Sandrine will come to at least a rudimentary feminism via her bodily relations with her husband.

HF: The workers of the present tense of *Number Two* have access to the media in a way in which their predecessors did not, but they are very isolated from each other. Except for one neighbor, there is not a single nonfamily member in the film. In this respect, they are in striking contrast to the grandfather's generation of workers. But *Number Two* conveys the hope that something new, something better grounded, might come out of this isolation. Because it forces the family to focus on itself—because it obliges its six members to interrogate their sexual and other interactions with each other, and what they signify—the possibility for a new politics is created.

KS: The enabling role that such auto-reflections can perform with respect to the political becomes apparent in a scene shot from the balcony of the apartment. This scene dramatizes an exchange between Sandrine and a neighbor in the courtyard below. The neighbor invites Sandrine to a meeting about the mistreatment of women political prisoners in Chile. Sandrine declines to come, saying she's too busy, and anyway not interested. The neighbor persists, without avail, and finally gives Sandrine a handbill on the subject. After the neighbor leaves, Sandrine reads the handbill aloud: "Everyday [the women political prisoners] pass in the hall from their cells to the toilet, single file, a hand on the shoulder, blindfolded. They have no right to see, but try to walk straight, proud, despite obscene jeers from the guards, who make them stumble. They have to relieve themselves in record time while the guards joke. They return silently, handled by the soldiers, who beat and torture them." Until this scene, Sandrine has stubbornly individualized her problems, functioning as if she were the only woman in the world. Now, for the first time, she realizes that she is not alone. "Other women exist . . . " she says out loud, after reading the handbill.

HF: This scene is depicted on the left monitor. At first, the right shows only a disturbance, but later a shot in which Sandrine fellates Pierre. This second image interacts complexly with the first. It can be read as a critical commentary upon Sandrine's initial indifference to the condition of the Chilean women—"she does not fight for other women, she only sucks cocks." But it also functions as an externalization of the

Fig. 31

thought which presumably permits Sandrine to make a connection
between herself and the political prisoners, and so to say: "Other
women exist." Through the image of fellatio, the film suggests that
while reading the handbill she recollects the sexual services she performs for Pierre, and the narrowness of her world, and says to herself
something like: "I, too, live in a prison, confined and sexually abused!"
Later in the film, we will be in a better position to understand why it
should be an image of fellatio rather than the anal rape which is made
to bear this meaning. We will learn then that Pierre does not gladly
provide his wife with a comparable pleasure.

KS: Several scenes later, a conversation occurs which further extends
the network of meaning radiating outward from the anal rape. Sandrine is shown sitting at the kitchen table in her by-now familiar
white bathrobe, gloomily drinking an unidentifiable liquid (figure
31). Pierre, who is only partially visible in the right of the frame,
holds out to her some laxatives in the form of suppositories, which
he offers to insert. She responds: "It's my kitchen, my kids, my ass.
Too much there." He protests: "But you've got to shit." She answers:
"It's more complicated than that . . . It reminds me of filth." Earlier,

Fig. 32

Sandrine leaves without trying to understand Pierre's work. Now, he leaves without trying to grasp what her constipation means.

HF: After Pierre is gone, Sandrine explains to her son that she has been constipated for two weeks. This scene indicates that the two everyday meanings of number two—shit and woman—have become inextricably linked for Sandrine, presumably through the anal rape and her husband's general interest in her buttocks. Her constipation represents an attempt to disentangle those two signifiers. It also signifies her difficulty with respect to production, a topic which will become more important toward the end of the film. Industry and metabolism are related; in both cases, things flow in and out.

KS: Sandrine could be said to be blocked at the level of production—not to produce, in the conventional sense of the word.[15] Alternately, we could read her constipation as the unconscious renunciation of production, because she feels that what she produces is shit. As Freud tells us, and Godard repeatedly shows us, the psyche can attach multiple and even contradictory signifieds to the same signifier.[16] In the next scene, the image of Sandrine sitting at the kitchen table moves

to the right monitor. The left is given over to a scene of Sandrine masturbating (figure 32). These two images comment upon and complicate
each other. Masturbation is represented in part as a displaced expression of the need to excrete. As Sandrine comes into the bedroom where
she will masturbate, her voice-over narrates: "I came home. I was beside
myself. Really beside myself. Still loaded down . . ." A moment later, as
she pulls down her panties, she says: "I show my flower and unload."
But if what Sandrine produces is shit, and shitting can be compared to
masturbation, then masturbation can also be analogically linked back
to her production.

HF: Sandrine's production is onanistic because she's a solitary machine.
Godard establishes himself at the outset as a machine which plugs into
other machines. Sandrine does not. "Machinically" speaking, *Number
Two* suggests, she is onanistic.

KS: This is perhaps the film's way of saying that Sandrine has a troubled relation to production because she is outside symbolic
exchange. Her products do not circulate. *Number Two* will make this
crucial point again, in other ways, and it will later clarify the conditions under which a woman like Sandrine might be brought within
symbolic exchange, or—to use your metaphor—plugged into other
machines. But it's important to note that masturbation is no more
unequivocal a signifier in this film than is anal sexuality. It connotes
not only a noncirculable form of production, but also Sandrine's
retreat from the difficulties of sex with her husband, and an insistence upon her own pleasure.

HF: Yet another reading is possible. In this scene, as in the kitchen
scene, Pierre offers "help"; he comes into the room while Sandrine is
masturbating, and asks if she would like him to caress her. But for Sandrine, Pierre's suggestion that he caress her genitals is contaminated
by his earlier offer to insert the anal suppository.

KS: For her, to accept that caress would be to allow Pierre to put her
sexuality once again under the sign of anality, so she asks him to
leave the room, and satisfies her own sexual desires.

HF: As if to insist once again upon the multifaceted nature of sexuality,
Number Two cuts from the masturbation scene to one offering an

almost utopian account of the erotic. In this scene, Pierre and Sandrine introduce Nicolas and Vanessa to sexuality through the display of their naked bodies before sending the children off to school. The implication is that they have more to learn in the school of life than through formal education. Sandrine lies diagonally across the single image displayed on the screen, her head in the left upper corner. Pierre kneels to her right, with an obvious erection. His head is cropped. When Vanessa enters, she sits to the left of Sandrine. Nicolas assumes a position in the lower center frame. His head—like that of a spectator before the cinematic screen—partially obscures Sandrine's body, and so renders it more mysterious and interesting.

KS: In this scene, we are given an entirely new conceptual access to the body's most erotically coded parts. "See that?" Sandrine asks, pointing to her vulva, "They're lips. My sex lips." Touching his penis, Pierre explains: "See here, it's a kind of mouth. So this mouth and this one . . . you kiss your lover's lips. Understand?" Sandrine adds: "When we make love, he puts his sex's mouth in the lips of my sex as if we were kissing, like talking. . . . It's called love. Love gets us to talk." Pierre, finally, concludes: "When it's over, death touches the lips, and says: 'Be quiet.'" This account of the body privileges the metaphor of the mouth. To have sex is to kiss, or—better yet—to talk together.

HF: This scene reprises the first prologue, where the connection between language and love is already established. Everything in this film is magically repeated at least once; it is a film with a memory.

KS: For Sandrine and Pierre to compare their lovemaking to talking is to suggest that both are forms of communication, and that at least in the case of the caresses they exchange at the end of this scene, they are finally "listening" and "speaking" to each other. This scene thus dramatizes something which eludes Pierre and Sandrine at so many other moments in *Number Two*: relationality.

HF: In the very next scene specifically involving those two characters, we look again at a very different kind of image—the split image in which Pierre seemingly walks away from Sandrine to the nuclear demonstration, while she apparently sleeps with her back to him. Their conversation is clearly over.

KS: Relationality is not the only feature of the family sex scene which sets it apart from most of the rest of the film. Pierre and San-drine's behavior suggests that the more sex is talked about and seen, the less repression there will be, but at other times it seems as if the contrary is the case. The image of Vanessa's face bleeding into the image of the anal rape is a particularly potent reminder that sexual showing and telling can have traumatic effects. As in Jean Laplanche's account of the primal scene, adult sexuality here invades an unprepared psyche, and the only possible defence is repression.[17]

HF: The family sex scene is followed by one stressing the incommensura-bility of male and female desire, and the conflicting meaning for Pierre and Sandrine of the concept "home." What is normal for the wife, we learn, is totally inconceivable for her husband. Pierre is shaving in the bathroom, with the door open. From off-screen, Vanessa asks: "When you and mom fought, you said 'impossible.' What's 'impossible'?" Pierre answers: "When we fought over the washer, she said I don't help. True, it's hard for me to see her dirty panties, because it means her ass is dirty. For her, it's automatic—it's the factory for her. For me, it's home. That's why some things are possible and some impossible." Pierre's "impossi-ble" attests to a profound psychic intractability.

KS: This is an astonishing speech, given the fact that Pierre anally rapes Sandrine. On the one hand, he maintains her "shitlike" status; on the other hand, he insists that she facilitate his desire by present-ing herself to him only in the most ideal form. Here we see one of the classic double binds of femininity: the necessity for the norma-tive female subject to assume responsbility for representing simulta-neously everything that is most abject, so that the male subject can be "clean" and "proper," and everything that is most femininely desirable.[18] We also see how an identification with the "clean" and "proper" can quickly become a masculine alibi for having nothing to do with work connected to bodily functions and everyday life—for the so-called "separate spheres" of man's and woman's labor.

HF: At the end of this scene, Pierre turns on his electric razor. As we all know, when turned on, an electrical razor disturbs television transmis-sion. The next shot seems to show us just that: two video monitors with an identical flickering image. This flickering is then made a metaphor for the sexual excitement produced in Pierre when he reads the pornographic magazines his son brings home, and thinks about his wife's genitals. It's a kind of measurement device for tabulating desire.

KS: This train of thought, given to us by Pierre's voice-over, leads first to the recollection of Sandrine's infidelity, and his still-current jealousy, and then to a meditation on their sexual practices: "Fuck and be fucked. She's the man sometimes and I'm the woman. But since I'm a guy, then, sometimes it's like fucking another guy. That's why I like her finger up my ass. I ask her to." Pierre here makes absolutely explicit the homosexual underpinnings of his relationship to Sandrine. But since the thematization of Sandrine's production as masturbation, we are in a better position to understand what it means for Pierre to imagine that he is a man having sex with another man when making love to his wife. The wish that Sandrine be a man at such a moment can be read at least in part as Pierre's desire to bring their sexuality within symbolic exchange: the desire to be in bed with another fully social subject.

HF: Pierre comes close here to elaborating the conditions under which his sexual relations with Sandrine could achieve that transparent communication fantasized in the sex education scene. Unfortunately, he fails to do so. He can imagine being a man to Sandrine's woman, or a man to Sandrine's man. However, he can only for a second imagine being a woman to Sandrine's man, and fails altogether to articulate the other possible transmutation implicit in this paradigm—that he be a woman to Sandrine's woman.

KS: Not surprisingly, then, the very next scene dramatizes Pierre's inability to perform cunnilingis on Sandrine—to engage in that one form of sexual activity which is specific to her, rather than his own, pleasure. Equally significantly, he explains that his disaffection in this situation comes from the disgust he feels in having to say "I love you" all the time, once again conflating sexuality with speech. On this occasion, as on so many others, speech is blocked or strangulated.

HF: Near the end of Number Two comes another scene full of utopian potential, this time set in the kitchen, rather than the bedroom. For the first time, Sandrine is fully dressed, and we see Pierre helping her with the housework. Even more remarkably, Sandrine talks about herself, and Pierre listens. As she washes the dishes, and he dries them, Sandrine explains why she gave up her briefly held job at the pharmacy ("It's too fast and I don't understand, my eyes can't follow my hands"). She then goes on to describe her life in the apartment. After relating the activities she is good at—cooking, helping Nicolas with his home-work, cock-sucking—she concludes: "there's too much . . . too much and yet not enough." Too much family, and too little sociality. There is still one moment of conspicuous friction during this conversation, but it nevertheless points to the possibility of a new beginning.

KS: The camera cuts to two monitors. The one on the left shows the grandmother cleaning the floor, and the one on the right Sandrine performing fellatio—women's work. Sandrine continues speaking, now in voice-over: "I thought I was producing, but the goods had already been sold. I was producing at a loss." She thereby generates yet another metaphor for understanding that peculiar form of pro-duction which is housework, a form of production whose products are used rather than exchanged, and which are either so immaterial or so quickly consumed that they are scarcely visible as such. San-drine asks: "Who was profiting? Who? " She quickly answers: "Not him." In so doing, she once again prevents us from slotting Pierre into the category of "exploiter," and puts in that position instead "someone behind" and then, more abstractly, "something between us," which she characterizes as "work."

HF: There is a certain vagueness about these categories. Sandrine doesn't say "capital," or "the system," as we would have said in 1968. By 1975, it wasn't so easy to identify the forces of oppression as it had been a few years earlier. At one point, Sandrine even imagines solving her sexual difficulties through money; she tells Pierre that if she were rich, she would pay him to sleep with her.

KS: In the final shot of the story proper, we return once again to the scene where Sandrine sits in her white bathrobe at the kitchen table and speaks about her constipation. Now, it becomes even more evi-dent that constipation is a signifier both for her troubled relation to production ("Nothing happens in my ass. I make the food, it goes in and down, but not out"), and for her forced identification with excrement or waste ("I feel like a bitch and a shit"). But the next words she utters suggest that she is beginning to understand these difficulties in their gender specificity. She asks: "I wonder if many

Fig. 33

women are like me?" For the first time, she grasps not only that there
are other women in the world, but also that they, too, might feel as if
they are excrement, or produce excrement. In progressing from an
identification with a strictly private "me" to one with the category
"women," Sandrine assumes an overtly social identity. Simply by
virtue of grasping herself as a member of a group, she makes possible
a vast range of social, economic, and psychic transactions with the
world outside the family. Suddenly the door leading to symbolic
exchange is thrown wide open. In the epilogue, *Number Two* will
show Sandrine going through that door, and putting her discourse
into circulation. However, she will do so in her capacity not as the
protagonist, but rather as the lead actress of the film.

HF: At the end of the story about the proletarian family, the camera cuts
to Godard in his workroom. He sits with his head on the table, listening
to Sandrine's voice emanating from a tape recorder in front of him.
Behind him are two video monitors. At a certain point the one on the
left lights up with an image of Sandrine in the kitchen, and the one on
the right with an image of Vanessa taking a bath (figure 33). Sandrine is

no longer talking as her fictional character, but first as an actress in Godard's film ("my role is over . . . "); then seemingly as an actual wife ("always like him, who says 'wash up, go on strike, come home, let's fuck, go on vacation.' What's worse, I say it for him"); and, finally, as a cinematic spectator ("you go to a movie; you buy a ticket: you sell out to the producer. Turn on the TV, and you're an accomplice").

KS: But since the image of Sandrine in her white bathrobe is on the screen for much of this monologue, the actress also clearly speaks here for the character she plays. This scene offers us something like a "Sandrine complex."

HF: Increasingly, the theme of her lengthy monologue is the crime of letting others make the films you watch. *Number Two* seems to be suggesting that everyone should have access to the means of production, and be making films themselves, rather than depending upon others to do it for them.

KS: Many people gave voice to this belief in the late 1960s and early 1970s. But *Number Two* elaborates the familiar argument in new and gender-specific terms. Sandrine says that a man is in the place where she should be. As she puts it: "He's where he shouldn't be. . . . I ought to be there and I'm not." This someone else would finally seem to be Godard himself, or—in some more global sense—the masculine filmmaker. Again, Sandrine speaks not only for herself, but also for her fictional character, and—by implication—every other woman in an analogous situation.

HF: Elsewhere in her monologue, she explains what it means to allow someone else to be in your place: it means to permit that person to speak for you, rather than speaking for yourself.

KS: And to speak for yourself, and so to occupy that place, would seem to mean something like "to put your discourse into social circulation," or "to contribute to the production of public meaning." We can now understand better why Godard goes to such lengths in *Number Two* to divest himself of his authorial powers and prerogatives, and why—both in the second prologue and in the epilogue—he gives Sandrine's voice the metacritical function, rather than assuming it himself. Godard is trying to make a film without at the same time assuming the enunciatory position because he wants to give that position to a woman. *Number Two* stages not only an authorial divestiture, but also the accession of the female subject to the place where she belongs. As Sandrine continues talking about the necessity for women to speak for and about themselves, and—in the process—to participate in symbolic exchange, she realizes that she is doing just that. Significantly, she does not thereby "become" a "man," or occupy the "number one" position. Instead, because Sandrine comes to public discourse only after effecting an identification with the category "women," she steps into an altogether new position, one outside sexual difference as we know it. "Finally in my place," she says, "number three."

HF: For a moment, with Godard, we listen once more to some chords of a song from Ferré. Then the camera cuts to a close-up of Vanessa bathing. Pierre, partially visible in the frame, reads aloud the text to his rental agreement: "The renter will accept the locale as it is upon occupancy. It will be used only for his personal residence, and that of his family. He will answer to police and city requirements . . . [and be] a respectable citizen . . . " It's very much an idea of the 1970s that Pierre should be held to the obligation to be a good father by the social housing administration. It's analogous to another notion expressed by Godard during the same period—the notion that filmmakers should only make films they can show to their families.[19]

KS: For me, this is the most important scene in the film for understanding Pierre. When Pierre reads the rental contract, he makes something explicit which has until now been only implicit, signaled through his impotence. Like Sandrine, he is subject to a higher authority, which we might call the Law. This Law, which can assume an infinite variety of local forms, from his boss to his landlord, lays out his social, economic, and familial responsibilities for him in advance. Even the position of father transcends him; it will succeed him, just as it preceded him. It is a function which grasps him.[20] Once again, Godard refuses to conceptualize "number one" and "number two" in simple opposition to each other.

HF: But although this scene maps out the symbolic position into which Pierre has been socially slotted, it does not reduce him to a behaviorist exemplification of that function. Pierre's "fatherhood" is simultane-

ously articulated on a number of other registers. When finished reading, Vanessa asks: "When you die, will you still be my papa?" Pierre
answers: "Of course, don't worry," and he pats her reassuringly. We
see that for Vanessa he signifies not only "head of the family," or "sexual aggressor," but a protector whom she hopes will always be there.
It's complicated in the family.

KS: In the final moments of *Number Two*, Godard manipulates the
audio controls. Over the sound of Ferré singing, Sandrine carries on
a disembodied conversation, first with Vanessa, and then with Nicolas, now once again as their mother. Now that Sandrine-as-character
has understood herself to be a member of a collectivity, and now
that Sandrine-as-actress has succeeded in speaking for herself in a
form capable of circulating within the larger society, housework can
have a new meaning and value. It can be thought in relation to
other kinds of work. Perhaps it can even become something other
than production at a loss.

HF: To Vanessa, Pierre poses the question, "So is papa a landscape or a
factory?" a question also posed at the beginning of the film, but never
answered. In the final spoken line in the film, Vanessa obliquely
answers the question by deconstructing this last antithesis—by insisting once again upon "this" and "that": "There was . . . a factory.
Around it they put a landscape." As Vanessa speaks these words, we
hear the by now familiar sound of birdsong, through which Godard so
often puts the landscape around that most important of all factories:
the family.[21]

KS: After Sandrine, Vanessa, and Nicolas have stopped speaking,
Ferré half sings, half declaims a kind of musical coda to the film:
"Those eyes watching you night and day, said to be fixed on numbers and hate, those forbidden things you drag yourself to . . . will be
yours when you close the eyes of oppression." Still sitting at the controls, Godard closes the lid to the sound equipment, and puts his
film—like Nicolas and Vanessa—to bed.

HF: In the epilogue, he has seemingly become a simple conductor of
prerecorded music. No longer the heroic creator, he is content to control the volume, and turn the video and audio equipment on and off.
But even here, he does not altogether succeed in throwing off the man-

tle of authorship. Music in the film is associated both with wonder, and with the fourth dimension—with a larger life, and with the ability to see what can't be seen. And he is still the one who provides access to it.

KS: Perhaps the crucial question to ask in closing is not whether Godard succeeds in *Number Two* in altogether negating himself as the source of meaning or affect, but rather whether he manages to avoid being where he shouldn't be: whether he makes room for Sandrine, as character and actress, to be "finally in [her] place." It seems to me that he does.

seven

Moving Pictures

Passion (1981)

HF: *Passion* (1981) takes place in an ordinary town in Switzerland, during an unremarkable winter. But in a studio in that town, an extraordinary film is being made: masterpieces of art are "reproduced," staged with stand-ins assuming Rembrandt and Delacroix poses. The resulting images are spectacular, but the producer is unhappy with the production because it lacks a story. Jerzy (Jerzy Radziwilowicz) is dissatisfied for another reason: for him, the studio light is always wrong.

KS: The images which Jerzy reconstructs in his studio signify "high art," in every sense of that term. They depict tableaux in which human beings rise above their everyday condition, and they have a similar effect upon the spectator. Looking at them, we too feel exalted, expansive, jubilant. The world outside the film studio seems, by contrast, almost hyperbolically quotidian. But *Passion* does not allow us to conceptualize these two domains in opposition to each other. It links the set on which Jerzy is shooting his extraordinary film to the ordinary town in which it is located through a complex series of relationships. The stand-ins for Jerzy's film come mostly from a factory in the town. Isabelle (Isabelle Huppert), one of Jerzy's girlfriends, also works in the factory until she loses her job.

170

The film crew stays in a hotel owned by Hana (Hanna Schygulla), Jerzy's other girlfriend. And Hana is married to Michel (Michel Piccoli), who owns the factory where Isabelle and the stand-ins work. *Passion* explores all of these relationships in detail by crosscutting between studio, hotel, and factory.

HF: *Passion* is not just the narrative of Jerzy, Hana, Isabelle, and Michel, and their respective work sites, but also the narrative of Godard himself. The film's diegetic director is a surrogate in certain respects for its extra-diegetic director. For Godard, as for Jerzy, storytelling is the least interesting part of filmmaking. And for Godard, as for Jerzy, cinema is above all light. Finally, for Godard, as for Jerzy, art means creating texts which are in a dialogue with earlier texts. Godard underscores these metaphoric connections between himself and his protagonist by giving the same title to Jerzy's film as to his own. But the analogy is not absolute; whereas Godard completes his film, Jerzy does not.

KS: *Passion* is concerned with even more than human or authorial liaisons. It also obliges us to rethink the relationship between concepts which have been traditionally opposed. Often the human interactions seem subordinate to this conceptual reconfiguration, which is effected in part through the transformations to which the film subjects the paintings it reconstructs, and in part through the complex montage through which it moves from studio, to hotel, to town.[1]

HF: *Passion* opens with a shot filmed by Godard personally, with a camera built to his specifications by Jean-Pierre Beauviala. In this shot, which is given to us in four segments, an invisible plane inscribes a white line across a chiaroscuro sky. It was produced on the spur of the moment, without plan or preparation. Godard saw the exhaust trail of the plane, grabbed a camera, and filmed it. Here, the camera is subordinated to the pro-filmic event, which it can only follow blindly. The spontaneity of this shot is underscored by the unsteadiness of the camera's exploratory pans. They register the movements of Godard's eyes, scanning the sky to see what it can tell us, and never sure in advance what they will find.

KS: But as is so often the case in Godard's films, this documentary shot moves inexorably in the direction of fiction. The second segment of the shot, in which the exhaust trail does not appear, is so artificial in appearance that it could be mistaken for a studio shot from Jerzy's film. And, since Godard situates a series of shots introducing us to the main characters in the frame story of *Passion* between the four parts of the sky shot, the chiaroscuro expanse soon becomes the heaven above their heads.

HF: Still, at least for the duration of this sequence, the sky is more important than the earth, and light more significant than narrative. Regarded from the vantage point of the sun and clouds, the five characters to whom we are introduced are as insignificant as ants. And it is precisely from this vantage point that the astral music, Ravel's *Concerto for the Left Hand*, encourages us to look. This is especially pronounced in the last of the introductory shots, in which Jerzy and Laszlo (Laszlo Szabo), Jerzy's production manager, fight with the Italian producer. They are small shapes in the back of the image, which is dominated by a large flower bed.

KS: The opening sequence introduces us to two of the antitheses which *Passion* will most insistently dismantle: heaven and earth, and truth and fiction. It also deploys the two tropes through which it will most frequently put opposed terms in communication with each other. We have a time-honored word for the first of these tropes—oxymoron, the rhetorical figure through which two mutually exclusive things are simultaneously affirmed. It is dramatically at work in the sky pan, which signifies at the same time "real sky" and "imaginary world of Jerzy and Hana." We lack a category with which to characterize the second trope through which *Passion* undoes opposition, but it could be designated through any one of a number of words with the prefix "trans": "transferral," "transition," "transposition," "transformation," even "translation," in the biblical sense of that word. Through this trope, Godard asserts the derivation of a term from its ostensible opposite. In *Passion*, crosscutting is a privileged vehicle for establishing such derivations. In the opening sequence, Godard uses it to show that heaven comes from earth, and earth from heaven.

HF: The next scene takes place in the film studio. Jerzy is filming the first of the recreated masterpieces: Rembrandt's *Nightwatch* (1642). It is not surprising that Godard would begin with this painting, since it offers one of the most celebrated studies of light in the history of painting. It is also an image which would especially appeal to Godard because it is so "underlit." The *Nightwatch* shows how much light there is even in darkness. Indeed, it reveals that it is above all *within darkness* that light is to be found.

KS: But Godard seems ultimately less interested in duplicating this painting than in reconceiving it in filmic terms. The fixed vantage point of the painter gives way to the mobile camera, which can adopt multiple positions, pan across the surface of the image, and even invade the spectacle itself.[2] Rembrandt's figures are released from their frozen poses, and begin to move and breathe, and the banner draped in the background blows in the studio wind. *Passion* also cuts back and forth between the Rembrandt scene, and shots of Isabelle performing factory work, reminding us that montage is another feature of cinema which distinguishes it from painting.

HF: The central issue here seems to be "transformation," in the strictest sense of that word—the changes which occur when we shift from one form or textual system to another. And in the transformation from painting to cinema, movement is all-important—camera movement, movement within frame, and movement from one shot to another. *Passion* suggests as much by having one figure step out of the composition, and later return to it.

KS: Significantly, it is a female figure who leaves the position assigned to her in Rembrandt's painting: the little girl in the elaborate gold dress who joins the adult citizens in their nocturnal watch.[3] This is a recurrent motif; as Jean-Louis Leutrat observes, the studio scenes consistently show *"women in movement."*[4]

HF: As we look at the reconstituted *Nightwatch*, we listen to an off-screen conversation about it. Most of the participants in this conversation are members of Jerzy's crew, but one is a member of Godard's crew. This scene thus blurs the usual distinction between the "diegetic" and the "extra-diegetic." Jerzy's production manager, Laszlo initiates this unorthodox exchange with the query: *"Qu'est-ce que c'est cette histoire?"*[5] He means to ask: "What's the story here?" But Laszlo's listeners are no more concerned with narrative than Jerzy is. Instead, they treat Laszlo's question as if it signified something like: "What's the main issue in this painting?"

KS: Patrick (Patrick Bonnel), Jerzy's assistant, provides one answer to this question. He says: "Don't scrutinize the structure or the distance severely. Do what Rembrandt did: examine the human beings attentively . . ." For him, the *Nightwatch* signifies above all "fidelity to life," or "truthfulness." For Sophie, Jerzy's production assistant, the *Nightwatch* is rather "something imaginary." But she goes on a moment later to define the imaginary as not exactly the truth, but also not its opposite, thereby deconstructing the opposition to which she seems to contribute. She proposes that we think of Rembrandt's painting as something like a "true fiction."[6]

HF: Raoul Coutard, the cameraman who shot all of *Passion* except the opening sky shots, offers yet another response to Laszlo's query. What interests him about the recreated *Nightwatch* is what interests Jerzy: the light. However, whereas Jerzy is passionately unhappy with the way in which the tableau vivant has been illuminated, Coutard is entirely satisfied. The reconstituted *Nightwatch* is sufficient because it allows us to answer the question which preoccupied painters from Rembrandt to the Impressionists, the question: "Where does the light come from?" "The lighting's right," he insists, "from left to right, a bit from the top, a bit from behind."

KS: Since Coutard is not, strictly speaking, a character in the diegesis, but rather one of the enunciators of the larger film, his words carry considerable weight. There is a second enunciatory intrusion later in *Passion*, and one which again overtly overrules Jerzy on the topic of light. In the middle of the Goya scene, Jerzy yells "stop," and complains once more about the way it has been lit. *Passion* nevertheless not only continues its rapturous exploration of three recreated Goya paintings after this directorial intervention, but shows the diegetic camera doing so as well. It thereby affirms what Jerzy rejects.

HF: I have the sense that Jerzy and Coutard are not talking about the same thing when they refer to the light in the Rembrandt scene. When Jerzy complains about the light, he clearly means that provided by the studio lamps. But when Coutard praises the light, he seems to attribute it to the sun. He says that the reconstructed Rembrandt is not a *Nightwatch*, but rather a *Daywatch*.

KS: Jerzy and Coutard seem to be talking at cross-purposes because Jerzy is referring to the light in *his* film, but Coutard to the light in

Godard's film. And, although there are points of commonality between the two, there are also striking differences. Whereas Jerzy's film consists only of recreated masterpieces, Godard always cross-cuts between the tableaux vivants and the frame narrative. He also intersperses the studio scenes with scenes from the village. There is as a result a constant derivation of natural light from artificial light, and artificial light from natural light. The light in one scene could thus be said to come from the one before. It is in this sense that the reconstructed *Nightwatch* is really a *Daywatch*; it is illuminated with the sun of the sky sequence.

HF: It seems that for *Passion* the light is "right" when it is transferred in this way from elsewhere. We could indeed go further. The light is "right" when it derives from what it is habitually opposed to—in this case, the studio light from the sun, the artificial from the natural. The light in Jerzy's film is "wrong," on the other hand, because it is hermetic, closed in upon itself.

KS: The subtitle of Jerzy's film could be *A la recherche de la lumière perdue*; not the mother, but rather light, is his impossible lost object. He seeks to recover in the studio the illumination which was available to Rembrandt and El Greco, and will accept no substitutes. Godard, on the other hand, embraces the imperative to displace. He recognizes that the light which has been lost can never be found again in the same location, nor in the same form. Indeed, he understands that it is not situated punctually in any location or form, but only in transferal and transformation.

HF: Still, it is clear that the distinction between the two films is never absolute. The cinematic reconstitution of masterpieces is as much the project of Godard's *Passion* as it is of Jerzy's. Indeed, the reconstructed paintings often seem to belong more to Godard's than to Jerzy's film. As if to lay claim to them symbolically, Godard always shows us these paintings through his own camera, not Jerzy's. Godard and Jerzy are also in search of the same thing: what might be called the "sublime."

KS: Yes, but here again we find difference as well as similarity. Whereas Jerzy looks for the sublime in the light of Rembrandt, Goya, and El Greco, which he attempts to recreate, Godard knows that it isn't "in" things, even when they are as immaterial as light. Rather, it is "in" relationships. We access the sublime at those moments when the ordering principle of the binary is defeated: when contraries meet, either in time or space.

HF: At the end of the Rembrandt scene, Jerzy announces that he's quitting. A rapid traveling shot to the left across a stand of trees dramatizes this "running away." At first, the only illumination in this shot is provided by the few rays of light which can penetrate the branches of the trees. Then the camera breaks into the open, revealing a lake and the sun. Isabelle begins to speak to Jerzy in voice-over; she also has work difficulties, and has just lost her job at the factory. She tells Jerzy that a meeting has been planned for that evening to discuss problems at the factory, and asks him to come. Jerzy talks about his problems as well, but less to Isabelle than to himself. Although he's a Pole in the time of Solidarity, he doesn't seem to believe in collective action.

KS: This exchange, which continues over a shot of Isabelle walking beside Jerzy's car, and one of him driving, marks the beginning of *Passion's* experiments with asynchronicity. During these two shots, there is again no "marriage" of voice and image. But Jerzy and Isabelle's voices defy the categories of voice-over and voice-off. Godard creates a new vocal category with these voices, what might be called the "voice between." In the process, he suggests that voices do not speak "from" or "above" bodies, but in the interval which separates them. Although we are accustomed to thinking of speech as something highly individual and locatable, it is in fact intersubjective, traveling between a speaker and a listener.

HF: In silent films, there is always a disjuncture between the movements of a character's lips, and the accompanying intertitles. This prevents us from imagining that meaning either preexists its articulation, or is identical with it. Godard does much the same thing here; he separates the enunciation from what is enounced, and so allows us to see that meaning must be produced—that it entails *work*. As the conversation between Jerzy and Isabelle should help us to understand, "work" is a privileged category in *Passion*, and one which will also be subjected to a reconceptualization.

KS: The experimentation with sound continues in the scene in which Isabelle and her colleagues discuss difficulties at the factory, and devise a collective strategy for responding. Sometimes Isabelle's voice is aligned with her lips, but for the most part there is no attempt to assign words to their speaker. Rather, they float once again "between" all of those present. But in this scene "between-ness" assumes a new value. The difficulties which one character has at the factory are not specific to him or her; rather, they are almost always generalizable to everyone present, or even to "workers," in some more global sense. Godard consequently films the conversation in a way which discourages us from thinking of problems as "private property." Here, there is no ownership, but rather a socialism of speech.

HF: Socialism is also thematized in this scene through quotation. Early in the meeting, everyone starts quoting lines or titles which double as revolutionary slogans. The grandfather inadvertently initiates this group project with his "phrase": "the poor are usually right." Others provide "The Commune and the Military," "The Words Which Shook the World," "Poverty, the Nation's Wealth." In an unheroic moment like the present, where the worker has nothing to gain or to lose but a job, suddenly the entire history of the socialist movement is once again conjured forth.

KS: In an earlier historical period, such a conversation would have been accompanied by the *International*, but it is now only in a Bertolucci film that this song can be played without irony. Godard accompanies this conversation with a very different piece of music, one less militant than devotional: Mozart's *Requiem*. In other ways as well, this scene suggests that the truly revolutionary aesthetic is not social realist, but sublime, one which produces the sacral out of the everyday. Like the Rembrandt scene, this scene is once again nocturnal—not a "Nightwatch," but a "Night of the Proletariat," as the first of the slogans suggests.

HF: Isabelle lifts a hanging lamp when talking to her grandfather, and we register the subsequent swaying of the lamp in the play of light and shadows on her face. Later, she sits in front of a pole lamp, which silhouettes her form. Near the end of the scene, she draws the lamp closer to herself, and lowers the bulb, first illuminating her face and then extinguishing it. On each of these occasions, Isabelle's profile or features are sharply delineated. For some time now, Godard has been developing an art of cinematic portraiture, akin to that developed for painting by a painter like Vermeer. In addition to being a little essay addressing the art school question, "Where does the light come from?" this scene is part of that project.[7]

KS: It's interesting that *Passion* should deploy the art of portraiture in a scene devoted to the dramatization of a political meeting. Vermeer portraits usually offer glimpses of private life. But then this scene belies the opposition between "public" and "private." The meeting it dramatizes takes place in the intimacy of Isabelle's home, and must be delayed until her grandfather has finished his dinner.

HF: And this private room opens onto the world. The theme of worker revolt is inscribed into the film not merely through this and assorted other scenes which dramatize conflict between Michel and his workers, but also by various references to Poland and the Solidarity movement. Jerzy is always assumed to be automatically on the side of the workers, simply because he is a Pole. And although he generally disappoints such expectations, he does in fact inadvertently introduce the notion of an international proletariat into the film, and so provides a displaced inscription of that revolutionary song which, as you suggested, it is no longer possible to play. Manuelle asks Jerzy if Poland is beautiful, and he responds: "It's beautiful everywhere."

KS: The workers' scene would thus finally seem to signify something like "private publicness," or "intimate sociality."

HF: *Passion* cuts from the shot of Isabelle adjusting the standard lamp in her living room to a high-voltage lamp in Jerzy's studio, and Mozart's *Requiem* continues uninterruptedly from the one scene into the next. Again, terms which are generally assumed to be discrepant are shown to be in a generative relationship to each other: factory production and artistic creation. Three reconstituted Goya paintings are being simultaneously filmed: *The Nude Maja* (circa 1800), *The Parasol* (1777), and *Madrid, 3rd May, 1808: Executions at the Mountain of Prince Pius* (1814). In this scene, *Passion* proposes something like "The World of Goya."

KS: Like the Rembrandt scene, the Goya scene poses the question: "What is cinema?" And once again, the answer is something like "moving pictures." Goya's *Parasol*, one of the paintings which this scene animates, signifies "immobility." A woman sits tranquilly on the ground, with a dog on her lap. A servant holds a parasol, with which he protects her from the sun. Jerzy's film converts this passivity into activity; it depicts the woman strolling alone with her dog and parasol. In this scene, we are also reminded once again of other kinds of cinematic movement. The camera tilts down from the close-up of the studio lamp to figures from Goya's *Madrid, 3rd May, 1808*. Behind them, Jerzy's camera tracks to the right.

HF: And as with the *Nightwatch*, the camera shows us the reconstituted Goya images from perspectives unavailable to the spectators of the originals, making their two-dimensional inhabitants three-dimensional. We *enter* the world of Goya, rather than remaining at a fixed distance from it. For Godard, as for Béla Balázs, cinema differs from other art forms in offering "the changing distance, the detail taken out of the whole, the close-up, the changing angle."[8]

KS: Although we are at times virtually "inside" the images themselves, they remain mysterious and elusive. Every new shot reveals new aspects of the reconstituted paintings, but closes off previous aspects. We never have the sense that we are grasping them in their "totality." Consequently, although we come "closer" to them than we are able to come to the originals, they retain their "distance" or "aura."[9] The only image which provides a coherent tableau, the group portrait at the end of this scene reconstructing Goya's *The Family of Charles IV* (1800), is by contrast altogether quotidian, despite the fact that the camera shows it to us first in long shot, and then in extreme long shot.

HF: There is another way in which the recreated Goya paintings resist visual mastery: they cannot be circumscribed. With the exception of *The Family of Charles IV*, there is no implied frame around the images Jerzy films. Rather, the paintings interpenetrate. The woman with the parasol walks by the nude Maja and the soldiers aim their guns as if she were a nineteenth-century *flâneuse*, and they were some of the sights on which her eyes came to rest during an afternoon stroll (figure 34).

KS: As if to underscore this point, *Passion* exploits another of cinema's representational possibilities: it shows us most of this scene almost entirely from the mobile point of view of the woman with the parasol. In so doing, it codes looking as feminine, even in the case of an

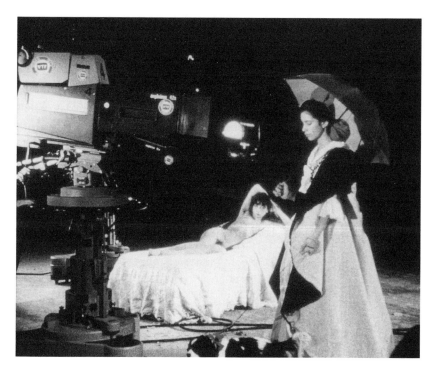

Fig. 34

image like *The Nude Maja*, which implies a male spectator. Here, for the first time, sexual difference overtly figures as one of the antitheses to whose reconfiguration *Passion* is devoted. By proposing something like the oxymoronic rubric "A Woman Looks," this scene undoes the conventional opposition of male look to female spectacle.[10]

HF: At the end of the Goya sequence, Jerzy tells Sophie to order the crew to stop filming. She objects that he's the boss. He responds: "I'm nothing, Sophie, nothing at all. I do absolutely nothing. . . . I observe, transform, transfer, I smooth the rough edges—that's all." Jerzy thereby distances himself emphatically from that kind of artistic production which is assumed to entail an *ex nihilo* creation. He suggests that he does not so much generate new images as give preexisting images a new form.[11]

KS: Sophie is not content with this formulation, but not because she clings to a more romantic notion of artistic creation. For her, the filmmaker is subject to certain rules, which he or she is not at liberty to break. Jerzy retorts that there are no rules in cinema.

HF: Does Jerzy really believe this, or does he just not want to hear about rules from an officious assistant? Godard himself doesn't seem to be beyond rules: the framing of his images accords with classical rules about harmony and tension. He knows that without them, there can be no "just" sounds or images.

KS: I don't think that Godard is any more interested in rules than Jerzy is. The only kind of art which interests the director of *Passion* is one which puts into motion what was hitherto stationary, whether that is conceptual (our binary categories), the human form, or point of view. This is by very definition filmic production. In the cinema, characters move, the camera moves, and the film strip moves through the gate of the projector. Every image but the first could also be said to "come from," and every image but the last to "go toward," another. *Passion* not only provides an extended interrogation of what it means to represent something filmically, rather than with canvas and paint, but it also uses cinema as a metaphor for what might be called "passage," or simply "transferral." It's less interested in arrival than embarkage; in destination than in travel. Sophie, on the other hand, with her rules, might be said to stand for destination and stasis: for the "end."

HF: So far, we have discussed shots and scenes which are sublime in one way or another. However, most of the scenes in the village are devoid of mystery. They show us epiphenomenal buildings from the late industrial period, buildings intended to last only a few years: a parking lot, a modern hotel, a gas station. These buildings do not display themselves to the public eye, or form an architectural ensemble; they are not striving for the mythology of a city. There are of course ways of photographing a gas station or a parking lot so that it becomes symbolic in some other sense, but Godard doesn't try to do this. Rather, he films the scenes in the village in a banal way, presumably so as to stress the "everydayness" out of which the sublime emerges. Perhaps he also means to suggest once again that art in the late twentieth century is only possible when it can reproduce a preexisting text in a new form, whether that be Mozart's *Requiem* or an Ingres painting. But these buildings not only have no interest in the future, they have also forgotten that there was a past.

KS: Although the scenes immediately following the Rembrandt scene are examples of precisely this diminished affect, they serve an important thematic function. These scenes dramatize a libidinal configuration which is at the heart of the film, and which they give us in a reversible form. In one, Sophie finds Patrick, her boyfriend, kissing Magali, one of the stand-ins, in his car. In another, Hana eats breakfast in her hotel with her husband, Michel, who complains about her interest in Jerzy. In the first, a man is "between" two women, and in the second a woman is "between" two men.

HF: Another scene in the hotel articulates the second of these tropes compositionally as well as verbally: Hana stands behind the bar, talking with Jerzy, who sits on the other side to the right. Michel enters from the left, behind the bar. Hana is now literally as well as metaphorically in the middle.

KS: But it is of course the relationship between Jerzy, Isabelle, and Hana which most dramatically represents *Passion's* primary libidinal paradigm. And Jerzy is not only "between" those two women, but also "between" the studio and the factory, and the studio and the hotel.[12]

HF: The pinball conversation between Magali, Sophie, and Patrick introduces another crucial antithesis. Sophie complains that her job at the factory isn't pleasant. Patrick responds "Love is one thing, work is another," as if to suggest that only the former is supposed to be enjoyable. As usual, this opposition is no sooner introduced than erased. Shortly after their conversation at the bar, Jerzy and Hana meet again, outside the hotel. Jerzy wants to continue with their "work." Hana responds: "The work you demand of me is too close to love." And a few moments later, Jerzy asserts the impossibility of distinguishing in any way between the terms Hana has brought together. Called away from his work with Hana to the telephone, he says to his producer: "To love, to work, to work, to love . . . show me the difference."

KS: The work which Jerzy and Hana perform in his hotel room is unlike that dramatized in the studio scenes. It involves video rather than film—a small television monitor rather than the "most expensive studio in Europe." It is private rather than public. And it involves looking at images rather than producing them. Jerzy and

Fig. 35

Hana view a videotape of Hana listening to and pretending to sing to a recording of Mozart's *Mass in UT Minor* (figure 35).

HF: Interestingly, when Jerzy first proposes to Hana that they work, she says that she doesn't want to, because it's boring getting undressed. We assume then that the work he wants her to perform is comparable to that of the actresses in some of the studio scenes—being nude before a camera. However, when we see Hana and Jerzy actually at work, she is fully dressed. We realize then that "to undress" is a metaphor for another kind of exposure—self-scrutiny, or even self-criticism. Perhaps Jerzy and Hana expend more effort looking at the video than they did making it. That activity has always seemed to me the biggest part of filmmaking.

KS: This scene also needs to be read in relation to *Passion*'s larger experimentation with asynchronicity. In it, Godard effects a "false" synchronization; he puts together Hana's body with another woman's voice. But this "putting together" is not at the service of coherence; rather, *Passion* attempts thereby to make it possible for us to "see" the Mozart—-to "see" the auditory or invisible.[13] The transfer between the senses of sight and hearing represents a crucial component of the Godardian sublime, and is once again a potentiality specific to cinema. However, it can only be effected once the norm of synchronization has been abolished—once the heterogeneity of seeing and hearing has been established. Until then, we are under the illusion that the relation between seeing and hearing is purely supplemental.

HF: Hana's performance, like Jerzy's film, involves quotation or reproduction. As is always the case, Schygulla imitates poses from German cinema of the 1940s and 1950s. She conjures forth suffering faces from earlier films as the visual correlative of the Mozart mass. Once again, we see that artistic production is only possible when it is based upon a prior textual model—here not only a sacral piece of music, but the exalted renditions of suffering women produced by actresses like Magda Schneider and Paula Wessely.

KS: At the same time, paradoxically, access to the sublime dimensions of these prior texts is dependent upon a certain loss of understanding. When, near the end of the video scene, Hana complains that she doesn't know how Jerzy wants her to dramatize the music, he responds: "Profit from that. If the sentence isn't formed, you can begin to speak, begin to live. . . . Perhaps it isn't very helpful to understand [comprendre]; it's enough to take [prendre]." To reproduce something with "understanding" is to be guided by its system of intelligibility—to play by its conventions or rules. It is to respect the boundaries put in place by that text's structuring antitheses, and its system of representation. "Taking," on the other hand, implies doing a certain violence to the text: allowing its contraries to interpenetrate, or to emerge out of each other.

HF: There is yet another feature of this scene which sets it apart from the studio scenes. The way Hana is shot in Jerzy's hotel room, both on video and within the larger film frame, is in sharp contrast to the way in which the female stand-ins are depicted in the studio scenes. Rather than shooting her from behind, as Godard usually shoots those other women, he gives her to us in an individuating close-up.

KS: In addition, Hana functions not simply as spectacle, but also as spectator. And Jerzy, too, appears on the television monitor; for the first time the film's most important male spectator is also a diegetic spectacle. As with the terms "work" and "love," "male" and "female" are thus shown to be "the same." For the second time, Godard uses analogy rather than oxymoron or transferral as the mechanism for dismantling opposition. But there is nothing sublime about similarity; it is not the point where contraries meet, but the site of their disappearance. *Passion* will later decisively renounce this trope.

HF: The hotel scene forms a unit with two others—the one beginning when Isabelle and two of her co-workers attempt to prevent Michel from driving into the factory driveway, and the one in which *Passion* provides its voluptuous recreation of Ingres' *Small Bather* (1826). Godard cuts back and forth between factory, hotel, and studio, once again stressing the necessity of conceptualizing these locations in relation to each other. He also puts figures whom we associate with one of them in another—Jerzy in Hana's hotel, and Sophie in Michel's factory. The factory scene provides a little allegory about class warfare. Isabelle, the representative of "Labor," struggles with Michel and the police, who stand for "Capital."

KS: At the end of the factory scene, Isabelle asks Sophie, who is there looking for more stand-ins, why film and television never show people at work. When Sophie responds that it's forbidden to shoot in factories, Isabelle says: "So I was right . . . work is like pleasure. It has the same gestures as love. Not necessarily the same speed, but the same gestures." As she speaks, *Passion* cuts to the studio scene. This scene once again undoes the opposition between work and love—between what is generally assumed to be utilitarian, and on the side of the forward march of civilization, and that which is usually regarded as nonutilitarian, and on the side of an asocial pleasure.[14]

HF: Godard does so by dramatically intensifying the erotic charge of the Ingres' painting, and thereby of the term "work." In the original painting, a woman sits on a stool by an outdoor pool, her naked back to the spectator. Her body is turned to the left, and her head to the right. She wears a red and white turban, and a white sheet or towel is wrapped around her left arm. Five other women bathers, some dressed and some undressed, can be seen in the distance. Godard reduces the cast of supporting characters to four women, all gathered around a pool of water. Two of these women are dressed in Oriental fashion, and two are nude. One of the nude women brushes the other's hair. The scene is evocative of a harem, or a Turkish bath.[15]

KS: Yes, within *Passion*, the basis for the analogy between love and work would seem to be libido, as much as gesture. In Freud, this similarity would immediately give way once again to antithesis, since work represents a "cool" or sublimated form of Eros, and love a "hot" or unsublimated form.[16] But *Passion* resists this distinction. There is nothing sublimated about work on the set of Jerzy's film.

HF: I am disappointed that Godard shows the similarity between work and the gestures of love by focusing on the reconstructed Ingres, rather than on the factory. It's a pity that he can't prove his point by showing machine work rather than naked women. All the old prejudices against filming inside industrial spaces are confirmed, even as they are deplored.

KS: It may be that Godard does not do much in this scene to alter our prejudices against industrial spaces. However, as will become clear when we have accounted for all the changes to which he subjects *Small Bather*, he really does show us more than "naked women." In addition to the modifications you have already mentioned, Godard makes the bather's turban white, and her towel red. He also alters her sitting position. Finally, he shows us not only the imaginary scene from which the painting might be said to derive, but also the bather's journey from scene to painting. She walks toward the prepared stool, is divested of a robe, ceremonially seats herself, and holds out her arm for the draped towel (figure 36). Once again, a woman *moves*.

HF: The next time we see Jerzy in the film studio, he still seems engrossed in thinking about sound/image relationships. He arranges for a nude stand-in to "do a star" in the pool of water earlier used for the Ingres scene, and before looking at her he orders a sound technician to play another excerpt from Mozart's *Requiem*. As soon as he has contemplated the girl floating in the pool, he commands the sound technician to turn off the music, making clear that the *Requiem* is that through which he attempts to "hear" what he would otherwise only see. Retroactively, we understand that just as the video scene makes it possible for us to "see" music, so the scenes inside Jerzy's studio help us to "hear" Rembrandt, Goya, and Ingres.

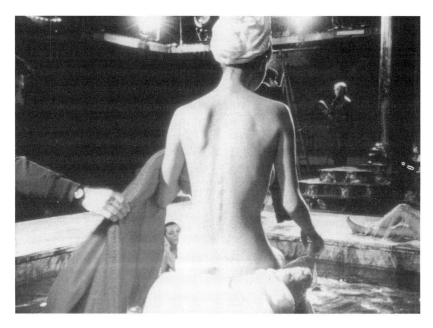

Fig. 36

KS: When Laszlo asks Jerzy what he's looking at, Jerzy responds not "a nude girl," but rather "the Universal Wound." It is very risky to bring together the terms "wound" and "female body" in this way in a film dedicated to the reconceptualization of sexual difference, even when it is specified as "Universal." But Godard is very careful here. As if knowing that seeing generally means believing in cinema, he does not allow us to visualize "woundedness" in the usual way,[17] but maintains it in its metaphoricity. Although Jerzy looks at the stand-in from the vantage point of her spread legs, the camera itself discreetly maintains its position on the other side of the pool.

HF: After Jerzy "sees" the Universal Wound, Laszlo sits down beside him. They both face away from the pool, toward a scale set of Constantinople. The two halves of the sky backdrop are open, for the first time admitting natural light into the studio. That light mixes imperceptibly with the artificial light of the film studio, so that it is no longer possible to distinguish between them. Language does not seem adequate to the task of designating the resulting oxymoron.

KS: Jerzy orders a technician to turn off all the studio lights, and to reduce the space between the two parts of the backdrop to a small opening. The contrast between the studio and the outside world is powerfully reasserted; it becomes literally a matter of black and white. Through the exchange between Laszlo and Jerzy which then takes place, *Passion* provides a new conceptual access to the second trope through which it effects the sublime conjuncture of contraries:

> *Laszlo:* . . . I see day and night.
> *Jerzy:* Like the two women, Hana and Isabelle. One open and
>   one closed . . . I'm between the two, searching.
> *Laszlo:* Everyone is searching. Everyone is in between.
> *Jerzy:* That's right. I'm like everyone else.

The notion of "betweenness" now explicitly emerges not only as one of the primary metaphors of *Passion*, but as one of the most central vehicles in the film for reconceptualizing the relationship between terms which are generally assumed to be antithetical. We have already seen that "betweenness" is something that characterizes both female and male characters in the film, and so overrides the gender distinction between Hana, on the one hand, and Jerzy and Patrick on the other. *Passion* also conceptualizes speech as something which is "between" a speaker and a listener. But in this scene, "betweenness" is generalized beyond the triangular situation within which Jerzy and Hana find themselves. It also becomes more than a metaphor for conceptualizing linguistic exchange. "Betweenness" now means something like "the interval" between antagonistic terms.[18] Everyone occupies this position; to be human is to reside within the interval. That does not mean to mediate between contraries until they can no longer be distinguished from one another. Rather, it means to have the possibility of "coming from" the black, and "going toward" the white. Unlike oxymoron, which insists upon the copresence or even interpenetration of opposites, and even less like similitude, which abolishes difference altogether, "coming from" and going toward" maintain those terms in their separateness. However, by simple virtue of his or her "betweenness," every human subject dramatizes the *continuity* between those distinct categories, and so definitively undoes the binary between them. Each one of us has the capacity to journey back and forth every day between the celestial and the terrestrial, the sublime and the quotidian, or fiction and documentary, which are placed in a relation of mutual derivation and consequence. Because we are "between," transferral is possible.

HF: At the end of the first part of the scene devoted to the reconstruction of Delacroix's *Entry of the Crusaders into Constantinople* (1840), in which we see crusaders walking with their half-dressed female captives, and others riding on horses through the miniature streets of Constantinople, there is another inscription of "betweenness." Standing to one side of the action, but still within the Constantinople set, Patrick reads to his daughter from a book: "[Delacroix] began by painting warriors, then saints; from there, he passed to lovers, and then to tigers. At the end of his life he painted flowers." The evolution described by Patrick is from the sublime of war toward the everyday of flowers. *Passion* itself here effects precisely the same transition. When Patrick completes his reading, the camera cuts from a scene of war to a greenhouse. But Patrick and his daughter belong neither to the sublime nor to the quotidian — or rather, they belong to both at the same time.

KS: Delacroix's *Entry of the Crusaders into Constantinople* is the painting with which *Passion* takes the greatest liberties. In the original, a group of crusaders on horseback have pulled up short before five abject townspeople: an older man, who reaches out imploringly for mercy; a woman — presumably his wife — who kneels beside him, clutching his garments, along with her child; and a half-clothed woman, who bends protectively over the lifeless or unconscious body of another woman, lying on her lap. The horses are champing at the bit, and it seems unlikely that their riders will halt for very long before this pitiful scene. In the background, at a considerable distance from the hill where this tableau is located, lie the buildings of Constantinople. As with Ingres' *Small Bather*, *Passion* shows something like the "coming to be" of *Entry of the Crusaders into Constantinople*.

HF: Here, Godard draws on countless other paintings from the history of Western art. Crusaders on horseback trot through the city streets, abducting naked virgins. The scene is a hyperbolization of traditional sexual relations. In the original painting, the buildings of Constantinople lie far in the background, and are scaled accordingly. That is also the case with the concluding tableau in *Passion*'s reconstitution of that painting. However, in the scene leading up to it, where the crusaders ride through the city, seizing fleeing women, those buildings are situated in the foreground of the image, but are as small as they would be if they lay far in the distance. The effect is almost comic, a denaturalization of the gender relations this part of the scene dramatizes.

KS: The camera tracks from one of the buildings, and a prostrate female figure on the ground, to the older man with wife and child. He reaches out to the crusaders, as in Delacroix's painting, but the gesture now has a new meaning. It is no longer an appeal for pity, but a warning to the horsemen not to come closer. The crusaders halt as a platform slowly descends from above in front of them. It holds *Passion*'s version of the group in the lower right of Delacroix's painting: one woman bent over the other, who lies on her lap. However, what was generative of pity is now conducive of awe. The two female figures have been transformed from helpless victims of male violence and sexual desire into a spectacle of inviolable beauty, one which belongs more to heaven than to earth. And on the faces of the crusaders can be read that emotion which Luce Irigaray suggests should always predominate in relations between men and women: wonder.[19]

HF: It is as if Godard has shown us not only what lies to the right of the family grouping—what the frame might be said to cut off—but also what lies above: the celestial. In so doing, he introduces an axis which does not at all figure in Delacroix's painting: the vertical. He also dramatizes intercourse between two categories which are initially opposed to each other in *Passion*—the celestial and the terrestrial.

KS: Commerce between the two domains happens via the figure of woman. The (unseen) transition from earth to heaven occurs by means of the cinematic translation of Delacroix's two very mortal women into the sublime figures who then descend from above. Thus, although Jerzy maintains that everybody is "in between," that seems more dramatically the case with the female than with the male subject.

HF: "Betweenness" is also coded feminine in a subsequent scene, in which Jerzy and Laszlo talk in Jerzy's hotel room. A tape of Hana talking is shown on the video monitor. After completing a telephone conversation, Laszlo reports: "They want a story." Jerzy's response is to gesture toward the image of Hana with the words: "Look, she'd be good for the Rubens; there are stories *and* light there." Hana thus provides the point of convergence for terms which have seemed until now irremediably binary.

KS: Laszlo does not understand the significance of Jerzy's remark. Instead, he tells Jerzy to forget Hana. Jerzy turns to the video monitor for help in this task. "I'm forgetting you, I'm forgetting you," he murmurs; "don't forget me." As he speaks, he repeatedly freezes the image of Hana.

HF: In arresting the flow of video images, Jerzy performs an action which is the reverse of what he does on the film set: rather than animating and bringing within time what is inanimate and outside time, he immobilizes and detemporalizes what is mobile and temporal. In the process, he mortifies Hana, shows the skull beneath her flesh.

KS: Jerzy's experiment doesn't have the desired result. We know from the end of the film that he doesn't succeed in forgetting Hana. And Jerzy's death drive will later be turned back upon himself. In the gas station scene early in *Passion*, where all of the major characters converge, he says that he is searching for a knife cut. This remark remains inexplicable until he "looks" at the Universal Wound. Retroactively, we understand Jerzy to be searching for the common denominator linking him to what is ostensibly antithetical: woman. He unexpectedly finds what he is looking for in the scene in the kitchen, where he talks with Manuelle, the maid. Through a slapstick comedy of errors, he is injured with the knife which she directs jokingly first against herself, and then against him. "Woundedness" now becomes as fully definitional of masculinity as it is of femininity, and so in fact universal. Once again, sexual difference is erased through analogy.

HF: The next scene begins in Isabelle's kitchen. Jerzy is ostensibly there to say goodbye to Isabelle; he has decided to abandon his film, and return to Poland. At the climactic moment in this scene, he asks her if she loves to work. When she responds in the affirmative, he queries: "When you say that you love to work, does 'to love [to work]' come from 'love'?" "It doesn't 'come from,'" Isabelle responds, "it 'goes toward.'" "Well, then, Isabelle," Jerzy urges, "let's go." The film itself then cuts back and forth from images of their lovemaking to images from the film studio, in a cinematic realization of the trope at the heart of their conversation.

KS: Isabelle might be said to "go toward" love twice. After she and Jerzy have left the kitchen downstairs for the bedroom upstairs, she must go downstairs again to deal first with Michel, and then with Hana. She then returns to the bedroom. But *Passion* does not show either ascent.

HF: Instead, as Isabelle begins to go to the bedroom for the second time, *Passion* cuts to Jerzy's studio, where a nude woman is helped up to a platform, before descending and climbing again to a higher one. Between these last two acts, the woman pauses for a moment, as if waiting for the music—Fauré's *Requiem*—to accompany her movement and mitigate her exposure. After she has reached the second platform, the camera cuts back to the kitchen, where Jerzy will soon say: "Well, Isabelle, let's go [upstairs]." She thus climbs the steps in anticipation of Isabelle's ascent to the bedroom; in fact, she climbs *for* Isabelle. Yet this woman will subsequently take her place in a reconstructed version of El Greco's *Assumption of the Virgin* (1608–1613). The principle of "nudity," which properly belongs to profane love, thus manifests itself in the reconstituted *Assumption*, not in the carnal exchange between Isabelle and Jerzy.

KS: This sequence repeatedly situates elements belonging to the *Assumption* in the scene in Isabelle's bedroom, and elements belonging to the sex scene in the biblical scene. For instance, *Passion* is at pains to establish Isabelle's virginity, rather than Mary's, and the Immaculate Conception transpires in her bedroom rather than on the set of Jerzy's film. In addition, before sexual intercourse, Isabelle and Jerzy both recite the Agnus Dei, underscoring the sacral dimensions of what is about to happen (figure 37). Carnal and divine love interpenetrate, like natural and studio light in the pool scene. The result is something like "sacred carnality."

HF: This represents perhaps the most scandalous of *Passion*'s oxymorons. It is made more so by Jerzy's suggestion that he sodomize Isabel rather than vaginally penetrating her, so that there be "no trace"—by his proposal, that is, to effect the Immaculate Conception in the "dirtiest" possible way.

KS: This suggestion would also seem a further step in the erasure of the terms "male" and "female." The anus is what man and woman

Fig. 37

have in common, the corporeal site at which antithesis gives way to similitude. It could even be called the "Universal Wound."[20] However, a moment after Jerzy makes his proposal, something extraordinary happens. Godard decisively repudiates analogy as a trope for undoing the opposition "male/female," and insists upon the specificity of the female body. The camera cuts back to *The Assumption of the Virgin* as Jerzy says, off-screen, "No, it doesn't work. It's not the right passage. I have to keep searching for the opening."

HF: Perhaps the search must be continued because sexual difference is in excess of any one opposition. Identifying a particular aspect as that which links man to woman threatens to blind us to the antinomies which continue to structure our thinking at other points.

KS: Or perhaps Godard does not finally want to dismantle gender entirely. It would seem that once again his project is the debinarization, but not the abolition, of difference. It may even be that, in order to undo all of the other antitheses in *Passion*, Godard must maintain the distinction between "male" and "female." We have seen that "woman" is the most privileged site for the convergence of antinomies in *Passion*, whether they be story and light, the celestial and the terrestrial, or—in the case of this scene—sacred and profane love.

HF: Apart from the addition of the nude woman, Godard doesn't effect as many visual changes in El Greco's *Assumption of the Virgin* as he does in Ingres's *Small Bather*, or Delacroix's *Entry of the Crusaders into Constantinople*. Already, the original has two features which are very germane to his project. First, the painting is characterized by an extreme elongation. Here is the vertical access which Godard was obliged to add to the Delacroix, and which dramatizes the straining of the terrestrial toward the celestial. The body of the Virgin Mary is so extended that her head almost touches the sun. The topic of the painting is also immediately germane to Godard's purposes, and already implies feminine movement: Mary's ascent to heaven. Godard is content to stress precisely these two features of the original in his cinematic adaptation.

KS: Interestingly, El Greco's *Assumption of the Virgin* is described by one art historian as a "perpetual Assumption";[21] the Virgin goes ever higher, never reaching her goal, much like the characters in Godard's film. It is also important to know that some scholars believe the El Greco painting to be an Annunciation, rather than an Assumption.[22] There is thus a certain undecidability in the original about whether the celestial is approaching the terrestrial, or the terrestrial the celestial. *Passion* exploits this ambiguity through its simultaneous references to heavenly ascent, and the Immaculate Conception.

HF: Finally, the painting depicts two angels with musical instruments. Perhaps this suggested to Godard the idea that *Passion* should make it possible for us to hear paintings, and see sounds.

KS: At the end of the film, Hana searches for Jerzy in a snowy meadow. Underneath the snow can be seen grass; winter coexists with summer. This is not the only visual oxymoron: an old-fashioned ship with sails and actors in eighteenth-century costume mix anachronistically with a tractor, bringing together the pre-industrial with the industrial, and making the earth simultaneously a sea.

HF: In the meadow, one last masterpiece of art is reconstituted: Watteau's *Pilgrimage to Cythera* (1719).[23] But now the studio and the world are fully imbricated, and costumes and props which were destined to be filmed with artificial light are irradiated by the sun.

KS: In the original painting, a group of lovers prepare to depart for Cythera, the Greek island of love. A statue of Aphrodite, Cythera's presiding deity, stands at the extreme right, and a ship with pink sails at the extreme left. But the idyllic landscape in which the human figures are situated, and their obsessive heterosexual coupling, suggest that they have already arrived at their destination.[24]

HF: In his reconstitution of *Pilgrimage to Cythera*, Godard retains only the ship, whose sails he shades red, and some of the human figures. He rearranges many of these figures into less conventional groupings, and he gives pride of place to the solitary figure of Hana, whom he adds to the picture.

KS: Hana runs through the meadow looking for Jerzy, making the larger scene unambiguously one of quest and unsatisfied desire. Like the *flâneuse* in the Goya sequence, whose umbrella she seems to have borrowed, Hana takes in the view along the way. Again, mobility and the look are coded feminine.

HF: Soon, there will be a literal embarkage: three of the lovers in the film will depart for their island of love: Poland. Once, the inhabitants of that country dreamt of going to America. Now only Laszlo wants to go to the land of Sternberg light. For the other central characters, Poland has become the new America. Manuella and Jerzy will travel there on a magic carpet, or perhaps in the ship with sails, like the original Pilgrims. Hana and Isabelle adopt a more conventional means of transportation—Isabelle's car. But they travel together, in acknowledgement of what is "between" them.

KS: Movement is the dominant metaphor of the final scenes of the film. In addition to the ship, and the running figure of Hana, we see two cars, and a plane, all in motion. And in an important reminder of what makes cinema the textual form most suited to this late twentieth-century sublime, the camera is also hyperbolically mobile. In the *Assumption* scene, it repeatedly cranes up and down the grouping of Virgin and angels, providing a formal inscription of the double meaning implicit in the original. And in the meadow scene, the camera constantly tracks vertically, first to the left, and then to the right. Once again Godard underscores the "trans" implicit in his textual transformation.

HF: Although many miracles are enacted in the final moments of *Passion*, they occur in the midst of the ordinary. Apart from the magic meadow, all we see in the last scenes of the film are an inconspicuous airport, an ordinary country road, and a car with chains. But now we understand that this quotidian landscape itself leads to heaven. Perhaps Poland will be the site of the next Annunciation.

eight

The Same, Yet Other

New Wave/Nouvelle vague (1990)

KS: Most of *New Wave* (l990) takes place on a large country estate facing Lake Geneva. It is owned by Elena Torlato Favrini (Domiziana Giordana), a wealthy Italian industrialist. Her lover (Alain Delon), who goes under the name Roger Lennox in the first half of the film, and Richard Lennox in the second, lives on the estate with her. Elena and Lennox are not so much "characters," in the usual sense of the word, as archetypes; they represent the heterosexual couple at the end of the twentieth century. This couple is still defined through dominance and submission. However, the roles of "man" and "woman" no longer seem fixed. The one who dominates in the first half of the film later submits, and *New Wave* ends on a note of undecidability with respect to the question of power.

HF: *New Wave* refers several times to Raymond Chandler's *The Long Goodbye*, a novel about a man who is assumed to have been killed during the war, but who later reappears with a different face. It also includes a character named "Della Street," in homage to the stories of E. S. Gardner. These stories are full of people who are believed to be dead, but who live on in a different guise. Pulp novels in which people switch their identities are always ontological projects; the detective asking "Is A really A, or B?" is a mask for the philosophical question: "Is a human being really him or herself?" As Godard's allusions to Chandler and Gardner help us to see, this question is also at the heart of *New Wave*.

KS: The film is divided into two parts, each culminating in a boating scene on Lake Geneva. In the first of these, Elena catapults Lennox into the water, and ignores his subsequent appeals for help. In the second, Lennox knocks Elena into the water, and eventually rescues her. Making this a recurring series is an earlier episode, in which Elena saves Roger after an automobile accident. But this is only one of the forms repetition assumes in *New Wave*. Virtually every line is a quotation, from sources as diverse as Dante, Proust, Chandler, Schiller, de Rougemont, Marx, Hemingway, Lacan, and Rimbaud.[1] Many of these lines are spoken more than once, sometimes by the same and sometimes by different characters. Certain images are also reprised. Finally, the same two pieces of music—Dino Saluzzi's *Andina-Winter* and David Darling's *Journal October/Far Away Lights*—are played at the beginning and at the end, and many other scenes are placed in a metaphoric relation to each other through musical echoes.

HF: Godard once said that we should take cinema where it isn't.[2] With *New Wave*, he does just that. It is a "new wave," or fresh beginning. Although the film deploys modernist strategies like quotation, temporal discontinuity, and repetition, which are familiar to us from many earlier Godard films, it has strict rules. Indeed, it is almost mathematical. At the same time, *New Wave* has the grace and harmony which we associate with an earlier period of representation. Its depiction of nature recalls the great landscape painters. It is thus not so easy to say what the film "is." Perhaps it will be fifty years before we have the language to do so.

KS: *New Wave* begins with words which consign what follows to memory. A disembodied male voice, which we will later recognize as that of Lennox, says to the accompaniment of Dino Saluzzi's meditative *Adina-Winter*: "But I wanted this to be a narrative. I still do. Nothing from outside to distract memory. I barely hear, from time to time, the earth's soft moan, one ripple breaking the surface. I am content with the shade of a single poplar, tall behind me in its mourning."[3] At first, we see nothing but white credits against a black screen. But after Lennox has decisively banished the "outside," in favor of recollection, Godard paradoxically shows us an image of a park in summer, with a luxuriant and most unpoplar-like tree filling most of the frame, and two blue horses in the background.

HF: The next two images are also suggestive more of an outer than and inner scene. In the first, an outstretched hand is framed, palm upward, against the green of a meadow. Another hand enters the frame, and seemingly places something in it. This shot is followed by a stationary shot of a pool of water in a green field, surrounded by rushes waving in the wind. A dog barks off-screen, and thunder menaces.

KS: These images have an unusually intense sensory appeal, both visual and acoustic. But because they are at the same time placed so emphatically under the sign of memory, they trouble the usual oppositions between "interior" and "exterior." The film suggests that the outer world manifests itself to us most profoundly from within, via recollection. As we subsequently learn, the issue of memory is at the heart of *New Wave*.

HF: Whatever the status of the landscape, it seems more central to *New Wave* than do the human figures. It is as if, in making the film, Godard was attempting to answer the question: "How does this place look at different times of the day, and different seasons of the year?" Or: "What possibilities does it provide for a narration?

KS: It's not finally so easy to differentiate the landscape from the human characters in *New Wave*. At first, the film seems to tell two stories—that of Elena and Lennox, and that of the house, park, and lake. Sometimes one is more prominent, sometimes the other. But through the operations of memory, Elena and Lennox come to occupy the landscape, in the most profound sense of the word.[4] And then the two stories become one.

HF: Yes, but the film keeps a strange distance from its characters. Usually films are "human-centered systems." Here, the center is elsewhere. It is as if Elena, Lennox, and the others are incidentally included in the film because they happen to inhabit the estate, like dwarfs, animals, and ghosts in a fairy tale forest. The film attends to them much as servants attend to their masters; sometimes maids or butlers listen quite closely to what their employers say or do, but always with a certain detachment, knowing that it does not pertain directly to them. Perhaps this metaphor occurs to me because Jules, the gardener (Roland Amstutz), often seems to represent *New Wave*'s point of view.

KS: Significantly, for your reading, Jules is the first character to appear in the film. He pulls up in his green tractor in front of Elena's house. He is joined almost immediately by his daughter, Cécile (Laurence Cote), who rides into the frame on a bicycle; his wife, Yvonne (Violaine Barret), who drives up with newspapers in a vintage Citroën; and the chauffeur, Laurent, who washes the window of a black Mercedes sedan. Elena herself emerges from the house only after the servants have been assembled. She announces her intention to drive alone. This first glimpse of La Contessa makes clear that she belongs to the new, working rich.

HF: Jules is not only the first character to appear in *New Wave*, but also the first character to speak within the narrative proper. As is typical, he addresses no one else, and seems uninterested in the human events unfolding around him. Jules's preoccupation throughout the film is with the garden in which he labors, and for which he attempts to find an adequate language.

KS: Sometimes that language is poetic, and sometimes philosophical. Here, he is a poet: "We've had no time to discover, like a lamp just lighted, the chestnut tree in blossom, or a few splashes of bright ochre, strewn among the jade-green shoots of wheat . . . "

HF: Jules is only the most extreme example of a principle which obtains throughout *New Wave*: the characters do not really attempt to communicate with each other. Even when one character does address another, he or she is likely to be answered by a third. Sometimes this displacement is so extreme that it is more words that speak to other words than characters to other characters. There is even a figure—Dorothy Parker (Laure Killing), the writer and wife of a doctor who is also one of Elena's business associates—whose primary function is to recognize, and applaud others for recognizing, the texts from which they quote, thereby further underscoring the autonomy of language in *New Wave*.

KS: This scene adds five iron horses to the two flesh-and-blood ones we see in the first shot—in addition to those already mentioned, a white Mercedes sedan, and a black Mercedes cabriolet. And, as Elena drives off in the last of these vehicles, the camera—which tracks right along a parallel meadow—discloses another iron horse, and one which is a more fitting mate to the romantic horses in the first shot: a white Cadillac.

HF: Cars are almost as important in this scene as they are in *Weekend*. But here, rather than being piled up in modernist wreckages on the highway, they are signifiers of luxury and wealth. In addition to telling the story of the landscape, and dramatizing today's battle of the sexes, *New Wave* shows us the beauty that only money can buy.

KS: As the sound of Elena's car dies away at the end of this scene, it is replaced by Darling's *Journal October/Far away Lights*, which continues until it is drowned out by more traffic sounds. We see first a green field between two strips of a country road, and then the distant figure of Lennox walking on the shoulder of one of the strips. The shot gives primacy to the field over either the pedestrian or the cars traveling in both directions. Then the camera tracks right, until our access to Lennox is entirely blocked by a tree trunk. In the ensuing sequence, he is forced against the tree, and eventually knocked to the ground by speeding cars. But even now the camera focuses insistently on the tree, through whose branches we at one point glimpse the sun and sky. Is as if Lennox can't be seen properly because he hasn't yet found a way of being "in" this landscape.

HS: As Elena drives by, she sees Lennox lying on the ground. She brakes dramatically and backs her car up to where he is lying, but she does not immediately get out of her car. Instead, she looks up twice at the branches of the tree beside which he lies, and the camera eagerly follows. It stays there even after Elena leaves her car, and asks Lennox if he is injured. Only when he obliquely responds does the camera begin to tilt down to the human grouping below. The tree which is the focus of all this attention is a kind of heathen god. Or better: *New Wave* treats nature as if it were animated by the spirits of the dead.

KS: When Lennox fails to respond to Elena's inquiries, she begins to turn away, presumably to find help. What then transpires explains

Fig. 38

why the opening of the film gives such emblematic importance to an open hand. Lennox reaches upward toward Elena, and as he does so she says: "How wonderful, to give what you don't have."[5] In a reverse shot we see his outstretched hand against the blue, brown, and green of mountains and a field, and Elena clasping it with her own (figure 38). As their fingers touch, Lennox responds: "Miracle of empty hands." This luminous moment stands altogether outside the psychodynamics of power. Since what is given is not owned, it cannot indebt or obligate. It is even unclear who has given, and who has received, this purest of all gifts. Lennox suggests that the act has been reciprocal; the gift comes not from one hand, but from both.

HF: The image of Elena and Lennox's hands reaching out to each other is shot as if it were a painting. Usually when hands are shown in close-up, the background is closed down rather than opened up. They are held against a body, or rest on a musical instrument or table. But Lennox's and Elena's hands are shot as if they were human or mythological figures in a three-dimensional space.

KS: The title of this metaphoric painting could be "Hands in a Land-scape." For a moment, the story of the lovers and the story of the estate are one. Elena's attention to the tree seems to have made possible this miraculous convergence.

HF: *New Wave* here quotes not only Renaissance portraiture, but also Michelangelo's fresco of the creation in the Sistine Chapel, in which God reaches out to Adam. It thereby suggests that what is given in this scene is somehow life itself. But here the force of creation is human rather than divine love. With their delicate movements, Elena's and Lennox's hands perform a kind of ballet, in which the prince meets the princess.

KS: The next scene takes place some months later, and is very different in spirit. Not only is it located far from nature, in the Torlato Favrini factory, but it also shows the relationship between the prince and princess to be well-established, and showing signs of strain. This scene also introduces some new characters—the CEO, Della, the Secretary of State, a nameless functionary. Again, we are shown representatives of what, in an earlier epoch, would have been an oxymoron: the working rich.

HF: The camera tracks back and forth laterally, which has the surprising effect of strongly differentiating the foreground from the background. But the scene itself is very much at odds with the expectations created by this visual delineation. What happens in the background is not subordinated to what happens in the foreground, nor the secondary to the primary characters. Rather, we are given equal access to what the CEO (Jacques Dacqmine) says to Lennox, the CEO to the Secretary of State (Raphael Delpard), Della, the CEO's assistant (Laurence Guerre), to the functionary, and the Secretary of State to Elena. There is also no real narrative progression. The characters are assimilated to their functions: the factory director directs, the Secretary of State ministers, the Contessa rules. They inhabit less a diachronic than a synchronic order.

KS: All of the conversations revert to two topics, which we are clearly being asked to conceptualize in relation to each other: love and money. It is perhaps more surprising that the CEO should philosophize about love than that the economic should provide a vocabulary for conceptualizing the erotic. Ever since the publication of Freud's *Three Essays on a Theory of Sexuality*, we have become accustomed to thinking of affective relations in the language of capital: we invest libido in objects, thereby increasing their value but reducing our own psychic reserves, sometimes to the point of absolute bankruptcy.[6] However, whereas terms like "investment," "value," and "bankruptcy" are for Freud only metaphors for the erotic, *New Wave* again refuses to subordinate one term to another. The economic is not merely metaphoric, but literal as well, and it not only signifies, but is signified by, the erotic. The cross-references which this scene sets up between the two domains also put in place a very different psychic "ledger" than that described by Freud, as well as one in sharp contrast to the pure gift of the preceding scene. As we will see later, libidinal investment in *New Wave* generally implies a greater loss for the recipient than for the donor. Bankruptcy is therefore more likely to be experienced by the one who receives than by the one who gives.

HF: Near the end of the factory scene, an exchange takes place between Elena and Lennox which consolidates the equation between love and life. He says: "So it's not me you place your trust in, but in love." She responds: "[Love] doesn't die, it's people who die. It goes away, when you're not good enough." Whereas the accident scene represents the arrival of love as a creation, this scene associates the departure of love with death.

KS: In the short scene that follows, the death drive once again surfaces dramatically. This scene introduces the theme of dominance and submission which will be so central to the rest of *New Wave*. Cécile walks back and forth in the garden behind Elena's house with a tray of glasses, under her mother's harsh supervision, her hands trembling convulsively. Yvonne shouts: "Better than that! Discipline, Cécile! We're poor—don't forget it!" Here, sadomasochism provides a vehicle for theatricalizing the difference between masters and servants.

HF: But elsewhere it provides the vehicle for denying this difference. In an almost immediately adjacent scene, Raoul speaks to Lennox about Elena's "destructive" nature, and her desire "to be conquered" for once "in her own eyes." It seems that although sadomasochism can be deployed for the purpose of representing class relations, it is itself no respecter of socioeconomic boundaries.

KS: Indeed, the category of "slave" will ultimately be instantiated more fully by Elena and Lennox than by Jules, Yvonne, or Cécile. *New Wave* undoes the opposition between masters and servants in a number of other ways as well. It is not only the wealthy characters who worry about currency exchange rates, but Cécile as well; and not only Dorothy Parker who speaks in quotations, but also Jules. *New Wave* deals with class relations within a late-capitalist framework. All of the traditional alibis separating rich from poor have disappeared. Now, the only support for that difference is wealth. The film says as much at the end of the scene with Cécile and Yvonne. Cécile asks: "But are the rich then so different from us?" and Yvonne responds with a famous line from Hemingway, "Yes, they have more money."[7]

HF: At the same time, words spoken several times in voice-over by the CEO indicate that in the world of *New Wave* class still makes a *psychic* difference: "One can take as defunct the society that we inhabit. If it is evoked in future ages, it will appear as a charming instant in the history of men. One will say: 'It was a time when there were still rich and poor, fortresses to take . . . things . . . well enough protected to conserve their value. Luck was in the running.'"

KS: Yes, class still has a psychic purchase in *New Wave*, and that is perhaps what is being theatricalized in the scene with the glasses. These lines from the CEO explain why. In withholding wealth and material goods from the poor, the rich produce in them a longing to possess those things, and so the servant class as such. Because it is the CEO who then adds that "luck was in the running," *New Wave* seems at first to be suggesting that it is the rich who profit from this arrangement. But the lyricism of the images which accompany these lines, as well as their anticipatory nostalgia, suggest that they contain a profounder truth. It seems that, from the vantage point of *New Wave*, it is ultimately the poor for whom luck is in the running, since they are the richest in the only lasting good: desire. Although this view of things is inimical not merely to Marxism, but to all conventional forms of morality, it is fully in keeping with the teachings of psychoanalysis.[8]

HF: Immediately after the exchange between Cécile and Yvonne, the gardener utters words which he will repeat once more at the end of the film: "The summer was early this year, and a little unruly. Everything bloomed at once . . . " He thereby characterizes the season in which the characters find themselves in terms of a difference within repetition. But it is only when he speaks these lines a second time that we will register the importance of such a transformative repetition, because only then will the figures of Elena and Lennox participate in the unruliness of the summer.

KS: After these two little episodes involving servants, *New Wave* focuses once again on the masters. Elena, Lennox, Raoul, and Raoul's girlfriend are shown returning to the Torlato Favrini estate, where the camera will henceforth remain. As he makes his way toward Elena's house, Raoul says, in seeming reference to Lennox: "In love, we generally find out too late if a heart has only been loaned to us, given to us, or sacrificed to us." *New Wave* thereby indicates that love can assume radically different forms. It can be a gift, freely given, in which case it implies no debt on either side. But it can also be provisional, subject to repossession; so lacking in reciprocity that it undoes the one who gives; or a mechanism for imposing indebtedness on the one who receives.

HF: In this scene, Raoul's girlfriend asks, in a refrain which will often be repeated: "What shall I do?" This line, which echoes one spoken by Anna Karina in *Pierrot le fou*, reminds us that not all of the rich have an active function in *New Wave*. Some have no other "job" than to admire nature, the architecture, the light. *New Wave* cultivates the same indolent wonder in us. Time flows by, and suddenly something starts happening which has nothing to do with narrative. Raoul moves through the garden, Lennox stands in front of the door making droll faces, we see the photograph of Elena's parents, and then a shot of the interior staircase. The effect is comparable to a day on which you sit outside and watch the clouds: after a while their pattern imperceptibly changes, producing a completely different atmosphere.

KS: The immediately following scene takes place inside the house. In the living room, Elena dances with Raoul without music while smoking a cigarette. She blows smoke aggressively in his face, prompting him to slap her and walk away. Unruffled, she commands Lennox—who is standing in a corner of the room—to play music. He complies, and they begin to dance to Werner Pirchner's deeply romantic *EU, Sonata of a Rough Life*. The ensuing exchange is filmed with a camera which tracks back and forth from Lennox and Elena to the adjacent hallway, where Raoul and his girlfriend—and later, Cécile as well—stand listening.

HF: Sometimes the camera cuts from this tracking shot to a pan over water. It is as if Lake Geneva were in the next room. At other times, we hear the water without seeing it, or the camera cuts from the waves to Cécile listening. Enchantment is in the air: not only can humans and a lake inhabit adjacent rooms, but the camera can also pass effortlessly through a thick wall. Raoul and his friend miraculously listen through the same wall, their faces transected by melodramatic shadows. A bell rings and a dog barks, after which the camera cuts to an image of the lake at night, with rolling waves. And when it returns to Elena and Lennox, they are frozen first in one dramatic tableau, and then in another. They seem under a spell, as do those listening in the other room.

KS: As the camera tracks for the first time away from Elena and Lennox to Raoul and his friend, Elena seats herself in front of Lennox, in a position of gratitude, and kisses his hand. She says, in voice-over: "It matters not that I am born. You become visible in the place where I am no more." She thereby articulates—and in very psychoanalytic language—the master/slave logic which for the most part triumphs in her relationship with Lennox.[9] The success of one of those characters generally implies the subordination or even the negation of the other. For once, Elena submits to her own extinction rather than decreeing Lennox's. But then, as the camera first holds on Raoul and his friend, and subsequently tracks back to the living room, she once again asserts her preeminence. She does so by offering to *work* for Lennox. "I'll work for you the livelong day," she promises. "At night you'll reproach me for my faults one by one." As we will see over and over again in the first half of *New Wave*, it is above all through her prowess as a businesswoman that Elena negates Lennox.

HF: This is at first glance a surprising but seemingly straightforward inversion of Hegel's account of the master/slave relationship in *Phenomonology of Spirit*, which can be explained by the very different value which our century attributes to work. In the *Phenomenology*, it is the slave who works. In *New Wave*, on the other hand, it is the master who works.

Fig. 39

KS: Yes, but there are some curious inversions within the inversion. In Hegel, the work of the slave at least initially accrues to the credit of the master. It also signifies the slave's subordination to the master.[10] But in *New Wave*, the master's work accrues to his own credit. The more the master does for the slave, the more the slave owes him. And the greater the slave's debt, the more profound is his subordination. This particular economic metaphor holds sway in virtually all domains of life within *New Wave*. The CEO articulates the reigning ideology of Lennox's and Elena's world when he says, in the factory scene, "We must impose the idea of debt."

HF: With the words "one by one," the camera cuts to the nocturnal image of the lake. The lake is the site where the struggle for the positions of master and slave will be most decisively played out. When the camera returns to Lennox and Elena, they are frozen in a tableau suggestive of her triumph: Lennox is bent over so that his back can serve as the support for Elena's outstretched leg (figure 39). The camera again tracks away from this image to Raoul and his friend. But when it returns to the living room, Elena and Lennox have formed a new tableau: Lennox is standing in front of Elena, who from a kneeling position reaches up beseechingly to him. We hear the sound of the lake even before the film cuts back to it. This second tableau anticipates later events, when it will be Lennox rather than Elena who works, and thereby dominates and indebts.

KS: On one of the occasions when the camera focuses on Raoul and his friend, Elena says: "By holding in our hands this beginning of happiness, we may be the first to destroy it." The emphasis here seems to be on the word "holding." The moments at which love is productive of life are those in which it is given and received. Such transcendent moments cannot be sustained, *New Wave* will repeatedly assert; once possessed, love soon lapses into a more everyday form, in which the economic principle triumphs. But if it is possible to descend from the extraordinary to the ordinary, it is also possible to rise again from the ordinary to the extraordinary. Elena does just that a moment later, when she says to Lennox: "Thank you for accepting." In so doing, she acknowledges that it is often more blessed to receive than to give in *New Wave*.

HF: Part of the magic of this scene has to do with the lighting. When one returns to a beach house or a country house after a long walk, perhaps to eat a meal or take a nap, the beauty of the day is always still present through the light that pours in through the windows. *New Wave* captures this quality here, partly because it was shot with natural light, and partly because—in order to make that possible—Godard must have spent many days in the house doing nothing more than learning where the sun falls at different hours of the day. Godard and his team make use of its rays as one would make use of a sundial.

KS: If the scene inside Elena's house somehow brings the outside inside, the subsequent scene in the park initially creates an inside out of the outside. Elena and Lennox walk and talk under a stand of trees, still moist from rain, through whose thick boughs the sun can barely penetrate. The sound of birds singing acts as a synesthetic prompt to remember what is usually beyond cinema's evocative powers: the fragrant smell of wet earth and trees. Elena hands Lennox postcards from Dorothy Parker and the doctor, who are as

Fig. 40

usual traveling apart. Eventually we see a close-up of the postcards, which provide a striking case of non-identical repetition. They both show a reproduction of a Gauguin nude, but in differing hues.

HF: For almost forty years, now, Godard has alternated between long shots and close-ups, without any mediating medium shots. One of the results is that, when a close-up is provided, it can have a very surprising, or even disorienting effect. Another is that the production values of narration are kept, but not the narration itself—much like Picasso paintings of a particular period, which give us the lines of three women at a beach, without the women themselves. The way the postcards are shot is a good example of this. Lennox and Elena stand next to a tree, naively wondering why such a simple painting should be so valuable. We see Lennox and Elena in medium shot, but the postcards in long shot, and have only a vague impression of what they show. The identifying close-up comes only much later in this scene, as Della, shown sitting in a car, meditates upon love. Including such a close-up at this point, rather than earlier, is a bit like making a headline out of the words in a phrase. It permits them to assert their independence from the narrative, to escape semantic subordination.

KS: Later in this scene, Elena and Lennox sit on a bench outside the stable, next to a tethered horse (figure 40). Their conversation focuses upon memory, which now begins to emerge as the principle both of tragedy and salvation. Lennox says: "Memory is the sole paradise we can't be expelled from." Elena responds, wryly: "That's not always true." Lennox nods his head slightly in acknowledgment of her point, and does a complete *volte-face*: "Memory is the only hell to which we're condemned in all innocence." A moment later, it becomes clear that Lennox and Elena are somehow saying farewell to each other. Lennox asks Elena if she has any regrets. She responds with the cruelest of the film's economic thematizations of love: "Regret is seldom anything other than the consciousness of having paid too high a price for indifferent value." The irony of this formulation is that it is only when we have withdrawn our libidinal investment in someone that we are able to perceive him or her in this way. Indeed, by reclaiming our psychic "chips," we ourselves have brought about that person's "depreciation."

HF: Although Elena and Lennox have just said good-bye to each other, for all intents and purposes, the conversation continues under another of the film's animistic trees. Here, we have one of *New Wave*'s most striking examples of words speaking to words. In voice-over, the gardener declaims: "All of them, silhouetted against the summer's luxuriant green, and the royal blaze of autumn, and the ruin of winter, before spring flowers anew, are dirty now." There is a short pause, during which Elena asks Lennox for a "phrase," and he begins: "It occurred to him, that she . . ." In the long interval before he finishes his sentence, the chauffeur and the gardener then complete the text begun by the gardener, in a kind of "canon": "Dirty now, blackened by time and weather and use, yet calm, inscrutable . . . not protecting with their monolithic mass the living from the dead, but rather the dead from the living . . . from anguish and pain, and the inhumanity of the human race." As they speak, Lennox looks up at the upper branches of the tree, and the camera follows his look. When it returns again to the humans at the base, it is to focus on the rapt expression of Elena's upturned face. Lennox, too, looks at Elena before ending his sentence: "She had the impression that her happiness, if ever she hesitated, might well in its turn vanish as swiftly as the leaves burned by the unsettled summer." As he utters these words, he and Elena gaze once again out of frame. The next shot, which begins after the word "vanish," shows us what they ostensibly see: a cluster of trees, still green with summer leaves.

KS: In this scene, we have one of those important convergences of the two stories of *New Wave*—the story of Elena and Lennox, and the story of the Torlato Favrini estate. It is not only that Lennox metaphorizes the fragility of Elena's happiness through the mortality of the leaves, but also that the two of them are engrossed in the landscape in a way which is reminiscent of the accident scene. In finding themselves there, they momentarily achieve something very much at odds with the words "indifferent value." As Elena and Lennox look upward at those trees, whose solemnity is thematized by the chauffeur and gardener, they align themselves with "the dead" over and against "the living"; they solicit protection, as it were, from their own cruelty and inhumanity.

HF: When the camera cuts to the cluster of trees, it first pans across them, and then cranes slowly upward before beginning its descent. But when it cranes down, it is on the other side of the trees. We see a road, along which Cécile bicycles. Jules runs across the road, and it is suddenly apparent that—without a cut—a new scene has begun.

KS: And this new scene is radically different in tone. In the next shot, we see Elena and Lennox standing next to a car, wearing the same clothes. Cécile rides up in her bicycle, and Jules runs by. Elena talks on the phone, absorbed in a conversation about currency exchange, and Lennox assures himself in voice-over that he is help-ing her, although actually reduced to inactivity. We are once again deeply within the quotidian.

HF: And returning to it, we have occasion to notice once again that, although Delon is approaching sixty, and time has ineradicably marked his features and body, there is still something very boyish about his appearance. He has found an interesting way to be a forever youngish man who knows how to deal with the humiliations of time. Delon therefore fits into the role of a dressed-up "nobody" singularly well.

KS: Since the central characters of *New Wave* say their farewells to each other in the park scene, there is a certain narrative necessity to the scene in which Elena knocks Lennox into the water, and ignores his appeals for help. When love goes away, people die, as we have learned in the factory scene. At the beginning of this scene, Elena begins for the first time to quote from Dante's *Divine Comedy*, always in Italian. She speaks the first lines from that text on her way to the lake: "Now—in the hour that melts with homesick yearning/The hearts of seafarers who've had to say/Farewell to those they love, that very morning-/Hour when the new-made pilgrim on his way/Feels a sweet pang go through him, if he hears/Far chimes that seem to knell the dying day . . ." These lines appear at the beginning of Canto VIII of the *Purgatory*,[11] and are part of an epic simile. As is the case with many of the quotations from *The Divine Comedy*, this simile contains a marine reference: "seafarers." In the original text, this word is metaphoric. Here, it is literalized, not only by the boat ride that follows, but by the two images of the lake which accompany the quotation.

HF: This scene also literalizes the metaphor of death in the epic simile, and the line "Farewell to those they love" refers back to the forest scene.

KS: But what is perhaps most important about this quotation is the yearning desire which it introduces into the film. It is as if, in anticipating Lennox's death, Elena is looking forward to the moment when she will once again be able to love him.

HF: Lennox himself also recites lines of poetry as he waits at the dock for Elena. "Alas, I waste away in impotent striving,/To return to the confusion from which I strayed./How often will I die, yet go on living?/Do you know the crime, by which you are betrayed?" he declaims, first to himself, and then to Cécile. These words, too, are full of anticipation. They speak not only of a crime, but also of a victim who eagerly awaits the fate which will befall him.

KS: Lennox seems "half in love with easeful death," as Keats would say.[12] But the line "How often will I die, yet go on living?" suggests that the death which Lennox will undergo in the lake will not really kill him, but provide the opportunity for another kind of life.

HF: After Elena gets into the boat that will carry Lennox to his death, he removes his shoes, and throws them over the wall. He then descends the few steps from the dock to the water. The camera pans from an overhead angle across the green depths of the water to Jules, who sits in another boat, staring into those depths. He asks, "What are these images?" As usual, he is "elsewhere." The camera continues its overhead pan slowly over the water, until a boat of burnished wood comes partially into frame. From an unseen and unexplained vantage, Lennox steps from the right frame into it. We can only imagine that he has been carried there in another boat—perhaps in Jules's. Again, we have the principles of narration without the actual narration. This ellipsis works with Jules's question and the strains of Darling's *Journal October/Solo Cello* to freight the embarkage with mystery.

KS: As Lennox steps into the boat, the chauffeur asks from off-frame, "Have you ever been stung by a dead bee?" Lennox's bafflement will later be shown to signify a failure to remember. The chauffeur suggests that Elena could also once have answered the question. "She knew," he shouts after the disappearing boat.[13]

HF: The moments leading up to Lennox's drowning are fully represented. We see Elena dive into the lake, and call out to Lennox to join her. We hear Lennox repeatedly remind Elena that he can't swim, and Elena escalate her demands. We also observe Lennox's wary response when Elena asks him to help her climb back into the boat. But *New Wave*'s depiction of the ostensible climax of this scene is typically anti-actionist. We do not see the actual moment of Lennox's fall into the water, or the moment at which he is finally submerged.

KS: At a crucial juncture, Godard even cuts away to Cécile and Jules, who are sitting on the ground staring into space. "Cécile, what are these images, sometimes free, sometimes confined, this vast space, where shapes pass, while colors shine?," Jules asks. *New Wave* cuts back to this pair a moment later so that we can hear Cécile's answer, as if it is at least as important as what is happening on the lake: "It's space."

HF: But it is not necessary that we see Lennox's death. What is important here are the images of his hand extended in vain for assistance (figure 41).

KS: The camera does not return to Lennox and Elena after the second time it cuts away to Cécile and Jules. Instead, it remains with

Fig. 41

them as Cécile says, meditatively: "Let the wail of the wind, the sigh of the wave, the gentle perfume of your sweet-scented air, all we see, hear and breathe, all, everywhere, let it say: they have loved." Towards the end of this speech, we see a now tranquil lake, through the trees, and—with the words "they have loved"—the wooden boat, empty of human inhabitants. Earlier, we were asked to understand Lennox's death as the precondition for his and Elena's future love. Now we are asked to understand it as an affirmation of their previous love. It is becoming more and more evident that death in this film signifies something other than simple physical extinction.

HF: The drowning scene is followed by a sequence suggestive of violence and conspiracy—Yvonne chops the head off a dead fish, and Raoul tries to dispose of the shoes Lennox left behind when he got into the boat. This sequence gives way to a nature montage. Over the first image in this sequence, a green meadow in late summer or early autumn, Elena quotes the famous lines from the beginning of Dante's *Inferno*: "Midway through this way of life we're bound upon/I woke to find myself in a dark wood,/Where the right road was wholly lost and gone./Ay me! how hard to speak of it—that rude/And rough and stubborn forest! The mere breath/Of memory stirs the old fear in the blood;/It is so bitter, it goes nigh to death . . . "[14] Six images of the land and water follow, suggestive of the coming of fall, and then winter. Like the Dante passage, the landscape tells simultaneously its own and Elena's story—her dark night of the soul. Then Jules's voice indicates that winter is almost gone, and—over an image of the veranda of her house in the midst of April showers—Elena speaks the immediately following lines from Dante's *Inferno*: "Yet there I gained such good, that, to convey /The tale, I'll write what else I found therewith" (p. 71). This passage signals a dramatic change of mood.

KS: As Elena's monologue progresses, we see first the title "*Veni Creator*" ("Come, Creator") over black, and then images of Raoul arriving at Elena's estate on a late spring or early summer day. The Dante text and the images of a regenerated nature tell us that another creation is about to occur.

HF: Although the creator has been summoned, he has not yet announced himself. But as we look at the words "*Veni Creator*," we hear the CEO saying the following words: "We plot within set E of an algebraic structure by connecting two random points: x and y of E. This corresponds to a third: Function (x,y)." We know then that it is from the miraculous convergence of x and y, or Elena and Lennox, that life will issue.

KS: The nature montage concludes with an extraordinary stationary shot of a pool in which trees and rushes are reflected. Pollen floats in the air above the water. Delon enters, via his reflection, and stands above the pool, with his legs authoritatively spread (figure 42). He will subsequently claim to be not Roger Lennox, Elena's former lover, but Richard Lennox, Roger's brother.

HF: Through the way in which this character walks and stands throughout the second half of the film, he repeatedly takes imaginary possession of Elena's house and estate.

KS: The next shot is an intertitle, against black, which reads: "*Je est un autre*" ("I is an other").[15] This famous line from Rimbaud is usually used to theorize the otherness of the self—the external derivation

Fig. 42

both of desire and identity.[16] That Lennox is given to us here as a reflected image suggests that the Rimbaud quotation still carries these connotations. But the quotation also serves as the provocation to pose a number of by now urgent questions: Why does the man who stands above the pool of water seem the same, although ostensibly other? Is he really the brother of Roger Lennox? Or is he in fact Roger, returned to life?

HF: We learn shortly after why Raoul has come to Elena's estate. The entire cast of business partners has been assembled to deal with the crisis created by Lennox's appearance/return. In a series of little scenes inside Elena's house, *New Wave* stitches together something much more approximating a conventional narrative than anything it has given us until now. Lennox has clearly arrived to claim Elena, but also to demand a cut of the business in exchange for remaining silent about his brother's death. The other characters stop philosophizing about love. Instead, they plot, scheme, and eavesdrop on each other. They interrogate Lennox, under the guise of ascertaining whether he is a fit partner. He must repeat everything he was in a position to learn in the first half of the film. This is more than a simple repetition. It might be character-ized as a "memory test." Earlier, on the boat, he failed such a test. Now he demonstrates his ability to provide on demand the birth name and employment record of Della Street, and an account of the subatomic particle the Torlato Favrini factory thinks it has discovered.

KS: This is an everyday kind of memory. But immediately after Lennox's display of recollective powers, a conversation takes place in which he gestures toward a more redemptive form of memory. Walk-ing back and forth on the steps outside her house, Elena repeats words spoken earlier in the park by Lennox: "Memory is the only paradise we can't be expelled from." He responds, from off-frame: "It's not enough to have memories, one must forget them when they are numerous, and wait for them when they return. Because memo-ries are not just that. It is only when they become, in us, blood, look, gesture, when they have no longer a name, and can no longer be dis-tinguished from us . . . it is then that it can happen, in a very rare hour, in the middle of them . . ." Lennox does not finish his sen-tence, but *New Wave* does so for him. It suggests that it is only when memories become blood, look, and gesture—only when Elena and Lennox are prepared to assume them as their very substance—that their story and the story of the estate can become one. But their way of behaving with each other shows that they are not yet figures in the landscape.

HF: During the interrogation of Lennox, he provides one of those speeches which would seem as significant within the psychic as within the economic domain. He says: "It's getting harder to cope with imbalances running out of control. Central banks are puppets; raising lending rates is just like pulling strings. Except people die. In the past, such rampant manipulation of credit and debt always led to major dis-aster." As we will see, Lennox is speaking here as much about his new relationship with Elena as about corporate capital. It is not merely that this relationship once again imposes debt on the recipient, but also that it is governed by the principle of quid pro quo. Richard Lennox seems determined to extract a profit from his liaison with Elena equal to the losses earlier suffered by his ostensible brother.

KS: As Elena walks up and down on the veranda, Dorothy Parker pro-vides an implicit commentary upon this state of affairs. "There's a price to be paid for being good," she says, "the same as for being bad. . . . And it's the good who can't refuse the bill when it arrives. The bad, they can refuse. No one expects them to pay, now or later. But the good can't do that." With these words, she reminds us that we have traditionally moralized economic relations: those who pay—whether with their lives, their money, their libido, or their work—are "good," and those who don't are "bad." But no one is really prepared to pay forever. We expect present losses to be offset by future profits. For centuries, those who paid in this life believed that they would reap extravagant rewards in heaven. They also took comfort in the thought that those who did not pay on earth would be obliged to do so in hell.

HF: But the world which Dorothy Parker describes—which is also, of course, our world—is one where these promises no longer hold. The good pay without the assurance of future recompense, and the bad need fear no retribution for not paying.

KS: Yes, the inhabitants of this world no longer believe in an eternity in which divine justice will rectify the imbalances of human existence. However, they still cling to the belief that those who pay are good, and those who don't are bad, as well as to the corresponding belief that the good must ultimately be rewarded. Since there is no afterlife, the field of human relations must now itself provide the domain within which all losses are recouped, and all payments fully recompensed. But this is a fundamentally impossible state of affairs, since one person's recompense always means another person's loss. And, as *New Wave* repeatedly shows, a fatal ambiguity surrounds the terms "donor" and "recipient." Who in fact pays in an economy in which receiving implies loss, and giving a gain? Who has the truest claim upon "goodness"?

HF: The relationship between Elena and Lennox provides a vivid dramatization of the dangers of conducting libidinal affairs as an "economy." But Lennox's speech about memory seems to hold out the possibility for something else—for another kind of life.

KS: It also seems to hold out the possibility for another kind of erotic relationship. We are given a glimpse of what that relationship might entail in the nocturnal sequence shot of Elena's house.

HF: In that shot, the camera tracks the full length of the house first to the right, and then to the left, in a reprise of the earlier tableau scene. Lights illuminate every room the camera passes as it makes its outward journey. On its return journey, Cécile comes along, moving at approximately the same speed. She extinguishes light after light, and yet—thanks to the miracle of the new Kodak film with which Godard filmed *New Wave*—we can still see an astonishing amount. At one moment, Cécile's face is rendered a pool of brightness as she bends over a lamp, a moon swimming in black. We are forced to relinquish our belief that darkness is the opposite of light—to understand that there are only degrees of illumination.

KS: The opening of Schönberg's *Transfigured Night* accompanies this shot, suggesting that it represents another of those moments when the central characters succeed in transcending their everyday limits. Godard quotes only the most harmonious parts of this modernist symphony—the parts which could come from the nineteenth century.

HF: Again he insists simultaneously on modernism and classicism. As in the tableau scene, the sound of crashing waves can also be heard. They contain a threat, but also a promise—the threat and the promise of the destiny the characters carry within themselves, but which is dramatized by the lake.

KS: The tableau scene occurs before the drowning of Lennox. Therefore, it can function anticipatorily, but not retrospectively. Now things are different. We hear the drowning in the waves, what was in what is. We are not alone. What Lennox and Elena say during this shot suggests that the memory of what happened on the lake is growing within them. After passing three rooms on its outward journey, the camera arrives at the doorway where they are standing. Because Elena is behind a glass door, her image has the instability of a watery reflection, as if she inhabits the lake.

HF: Lennox says: "The positive is given to us. It's up to us to make the negative." I take the "positive" as denoting life, and the "negative" as referring to those definitionally human things with which we produce the fatality of meaning: words, images, ideas, or even—as in Hegel—work.[17]

KS: As the camera tracks to the left, it eventually comes once again to the figures of Lennox and Elena. One last light is still burning, and in its illumination Elena can be seen to face Lennox, her head leaning against his chest. She says: "There's no judge anywhere. What's not resolved by love remains forever in suspense." This means: "We inhabit a post-metaphysical world. There is no higher arbiter to determine what is wrong or right, who must pay and who can profit. Love is the only court of appeal, and in this court competing claims are not weighed against each other, but rather 'resolved.'" The metaphor here is musical, suggestive of the reestablishment of harmony. In the court of love, debts are not paid, but canceled. Violence is not punished, but neutralized.

HF: It seems that this shot makes a religion of love, and thereby reintroduces the metaphysical.

KS: In holding out the possibility of transcending the binaries of donor and recipient, and master and slave, through a libidinal resolution, *New Wave* does propose something like an ethics of love. But this principle of transcendence is immanent; it resides within the characters themselves, not in some higher sphere. And in overcoming their everydayness, Elena and Lennox do not leave the terrestrial behind; rather they become adequate to it, assume their "in the worldness." Finally, transcendence inexorably gives way to more "fallen" forms of being, from which it must be once again won. I take the word "fallen" from Heidegger, who uses it to designate not a postlapsarian condition from which we can be permanently redeemed, but rather the everyday human condition to which we will always revert.[18]

HF: I wonder: is there a resolution? This particular scene ends on a very irresolute note. After Elena says the words "forever remains in suspense," the camera cuts to the title "Since the Beginning," suggesting that since the origin of the world lovers have been metaphorically drowning each other in lakes. And rather than allowing a musical resolution with the end of the scene, Godard postpones that resolution until two shots later.

KS: As you noted, near the beginning of the Schönberg shot, Lennox says: "We have been given the positive, it's up to us to make the negative." This is a classic example of thesis/antithesis. The film in its entirety provides another. Thesis: Elena knocks Lennox into the water, and he appeals for help. Antithesis: Lennox knocks Elena into the water, and she appeals for help. It is to that last scene that we must ultimately look to determine whether or not there is a resolution of this opposition, and—if there is—what form it takes. But first we must discuss the scene which most fully foregrounds the negative: the one where a prospective buyer visits Elena's house.

HF: In this scene, Elena is at home alone, standing beside an almost completely shuttered window. Her posture and her position suggest that she is waiting for someone to arrive. She thereby fulfills the "woman" function, as traditionally conceived; singers sing, dancers dance, and women wait for the return of their men. We hear footsteps, and their owner says, from off-frame: "I have a meeting with Mr. Lennox." In the subsequent exchange, the unseen man treats Elena as if she were a servant in the house, someone with whom he is entitled to be impatient and a bit brusque. Elena is strangely resigned to this treatment. Lennox arrives, and orders Cécile to fetch the newspapers. Della appears with a document for him to sign. Lennox's activity contrasts sharply with Elena's inactivity. Elena goes slowly, almost somnolently, to meet him. Lennox embraces her, while proudly proclaiming: "Four million dollars." It is as if he is quantifying his love.

KS: As is further demonstrated by the conversation which takes place inside the house a moment later, the debit and credit system is firmly in place:

> *Elena:* Your face . . .
> *Lennox:* What, my face? . . .
> *Elena:* I don't see you.
> *Lennox:* But look at me, please!
> *Elena:* No, I don't see you; not yet . . .
> *Lennox:* Let's go outside, one can't see anything here . . .
> *Elena:* If he didn't have your face . . . I wouldn't be obliged to
>   love you. Even if you were . . . not another, you would *be* . . .
>   You have stolen my existence!
> *Lennox:* Because I take care of everything?
> *Elena:* In delivering me from my existence, you have stolen it . . .
>   You arrived from outside, and, through love, you installed
>   yourself in me, and I welcomed you through love . . .

Once again, we see that the liberation love promises can turn into a new form of oppression, and its gifts into a mountain of debt. And once again we see that it is paradoxically through his labor that the master dominates the slave. In the second half of the film, it is Lennox who goes on business trips, writes checks, amasses millions, while Elena has less and less to do. Finally, whereas she earlier addressed him with the familiar form of the second-person singular pronoun, and he addressed her with the unfamiliar, here that is reversed.

HF: All of this shows in Lennox's physical appearance. In the first half of *New Wave*, he is primarily defined by the boyish charm with which he wears clothes, assumes the pensiveness or innocence the moment demands, and produces "phrases." His only job is to please. Now he is the master, and there is no further need for any of these blandishments. Elena, on the other hand, becomes paler and paler, and more and more lethargic in the second half of the film. It is as if she is losing her life substance.

KS: Significantly, Elena is under a compulsion to love the man who purports to be Richard Lennox not because of anything he does, but because he has the face of Roger Lennox—because he is the reincarnation of the what-has-been. Like the past about which Heidegger writes, this face comes to Elena from the future, in the form of her destiny.[19]

HF: It is for this reason that, after Elena utters the words "in delivering me from my existence, you have stolen it," Lennox says, in voice-over: "The presence you have chosen admits of no adieu." In one form or another—either as himself, or in the guise of the men who will replace him—Lennox is shackled to Elena forever. One of them will be forever knocking the other into the lake, and refusing to reach out to the hand that seeks assistance.

KS: But *New Wave* suggests that this scenario will compulsively repeat itself only so long as Lennox manifests himself as the other who is at the same time the same—as the stranger named Richard Lennox, who is entitled to be Elena's lover because he has his brother's face. There is another option here, which the film elaborates through the Rimbaud quote, and that is for Lennox to be once again Roger, yet simultaneously other.

HF: We are not surprised to find Lennox and Elena climbing once again into their boat immediately after their exchange inside the house; their relationship clearly cannot continue in its present form. At first history seems to be replaying itself in reverse: Elena's shoes are left behind, just as Lennox's were; Elena falls into the water off-screen, just as Lennox earlier did; and Lennox at first ignores Elena's outstretched hand, as she previously did his. But then we notice the many differences in the way this scene is staged. The weather is less fine, and the lake choppy. Lennox throws Elena almost violently into the boat, while giving voice to some of the paradoxes of their love: "I'm a trap for you," "The more faithful I am, the more I'll deceive you," "My candor will ruin you." In the water, he demands a kiss from Elena, who refuses with the contradictory expression of someone who loves him, yet fears that he will take her life. But the most important and saving of the many differences comes at the end of the scene: Lennox reaches out and grabs the hand that appeals for help. As in the accident scene, once again a pure gift is given.

KS: So we see that there is in fact a resolution. Elena and Lennox escape the logic of quid pro quo by grasping that the only thing that can in fact be given belongs to no one. They are able to do so because they have finally assumed their past, let memory become blood, look, and gesture. Knowledge of what they have been makes it possible for Elena and Lennox to take certain transformative liberties with the narrative which is their destiny—to repeat it less obsessively, and less exactly. It even makes it possible for them to transcend the roles of master and slave, donor and recipient. As Lennox says in third-person voice-over as he and Elena make their way from the lake back to the house, "It was as if they had already lived all this. Their words seemed frozen in the traces of other words from other times. They paid no heed to what they did but to the difference which set today's acts in the present [apart from] parallel acts in the past. They felt tall, motionless . . . above them past and present: identical waves in the same ocean."

HF: As Elena and Lennox walk in extreme long shot across the park, she recites another text from Canto I of *The Inferno*, again one dominated by an aquatic metaphor which the narrative of *New Wave* literalizes: "as a swimmer, panting, from the main/Heaves safe to shore, then turns to face the drive/Of perilous seas, and looks, and looks again,/So, while my soul yet fled, did I contrive/To turn and gaze on that dread pass once more/Whence no man yet came ever out alive." These lines function to thematize what happens on the lake as a miraculous escape. Elena and Lennox have survived an experience which has always previously led to death.

KS: And now, at last, we understand what death signifies in *New Wave*. Death is the enervation which we experience when we fail to make use of the creative potentiality love gives us. It is the fading away of our life-force which occurs when we prove inadequate to the capacity which Eros gives us for enacting an old story in a new way. When Elena and Lennox are unable to sustain their relation in the mode of a pure gift, which neither indebts nor obligates, love leaves, taking its generative force with it. But in the miraculous landscape which they inhabit, love always comes again, and gives them another chance. That is why death signifies not only an ending, but also the possibility of a new beginning.

HF: Near the end of this scene, the camera cranes up and away from Elena and Lennox, until a large tree blocks our access to them. But this time the tree does not seem to cancel out the human figures, but rather to speak for them. If Elena and Lennox feel tall and motionless, it is in an implied analogy with the trees in the park. And the crane shot which finally gives such a prominent place to one of those trees provides nothing so much as a formal inscription of precisely this "tallness."

KS: Jules's primary function in the film is to articulate ever anew for us the question: What is the relationship between the two stories of the film—the story of man, and the story of nature? Sometimes, he proposes that grass and trees are nothing more than a human projection, the product of naming. At other moments, he suggests that naming is a violence which words do to things, and that the world should be left without human markers. However, the film does not finally endorse either of these positions. The world is neither "inside" us, nor "outside" us. It is, rather, what we inhabit when we assume our "thereness." Lennox acknowledges as much when he says, at a crucial moment of the lake scene, "It happens here, on water and land."

HF: In the final scene, Elena says good-bye to her servants. She has sold the estate, which can now become the site where some other set of

Fig. 43

lovers drown and save each other. Lennox mimics a professional tennis player as the servants drive off, and as Elena bends down to tie his shoes he compares himself to Art Larson, who once jumped the net to let his opponent tie his shoes (figure 43). His competitive juices are clearly flowing once again. But the camera returns to the magical landscape as Elena quotes one last time from *The Divine Comedy*: " . . . I still clung closely to my faithful guide;/How had I sped without his comradeship? . . . My mind, till then in one strait groove compressed/ Expanded, letting eager thought range free,/And I looked up to that great mountain, soaring/Highest to Heaven from the encircling sea."[20] Again, the characters transcend their everydayness.

KS: As Elena speaks these lines, Lennox repeats words he spoke once before in the film, and which are by now rich in meaning: "My mother once said: 'Giving a hand was all I asked of joy.'" Elena responds: "So, it was you." She uses the familiar form of the second-person pronoun, which earlier in the film would have obliged Lennox to use the unfamiliar, to effect this temporal condensation. However, Lennox says instead: ""*C'est toi, c'est moi*"—"it's you, it's me."

HF: But this rare moment of equality cannot be sustained. Elena immediately responds: "I'll lead."

KS: Although Lennox assumes his old role, it is under different conditions. He now understands that he is playing one: "The exchange is exchanged," he says wryly. And when the chauffeur asks an old question, which Lennox was never able to answer—"Were you ever stung by a dead bee"—Lennox shows that he now knows his lines. To the chauffeur's "If you walk barefoot," Lennox quickly adds, "it stings as if it were alive—[provided that] it died in a rage."

HF: And, after announcing that she will lead, Elena surprisingly gets into the passenger seat, leaving the driver's seat for Lennox.[21]

KS: The final line in *New Wave* is spoken by the chauffeur. It consists of words which we are only now in a position fully to understand: "He's not the same, he's an other."

Notes

Notes to Chapter 1

1. James Blue, "Excerpt from an Interview with Richard Grenier and Jean-Luc Godard," in *Jean-Luc Godard: A Critical Anthology*, ed. Toby Mussman (New York: E. P. Dutton, 1968), p. 249.

2. Jean-Luc Godard, "Propos Rompus," in *Jean-Luc Godard par Jean-Luc Godard*, ed. Alain Bergala (Paris: Cahiers du Cinéma-Editions de l'Etoile, 1985), p. 470. Translation by Kaja Silverman.

3. The notion of "empty speech" derives from Jacques Lacan. In "The Function and Field of Speech and Language in Psychoanalysis," in *Ecrits: A Selection*, trans. Alan Sheridan (New York: Norton, 1977), pp. 42–45, he characterizes empty speech as a use of language in which the imaginary predominates over the symbolic—in which the *moi* or ego takes priority over the *je* or subject of desire.

4. When quoting dialogue from *Vivre Sa Vie*, we have consulted the script of the film published in *L'Avant-Scène Cinéma*, no. 19 (October 15, 1962).

5. Godard, "The Scenario of *Vivre Sa Vie*," in Mussman, ed., *Jean-Luc Godard: A Critical Anthology*, p. 77.

6. André Bazin, "The Evolution of the Language of Cinema," in *What Is Cinema?* vol. 1, ed. Hugh Gray (Berkeley: University of California Press, 1967), pp. 23–40.

7. These words come from Bazin, "The Ontology of the Photographic Image," in *What Is Cinema?*, vol. 1, p. 15.

8. A diegetic element is one that is internal to the fictional world, or diegesis, of a film. An element that is external to the diegesis (e.g., a disembodied voice-over) is extra-diegetic.

9. Arthur Rimbaud, "Lettre à Paul Demeny, 15 Mai 1871," in *Œuvre complètes*, présentées et établies par Louis Forestier (Paris: Robert Laffont, 1992), p. 230.

10. Quoted by Marilyn Campbell in "Life Itself: *Vivre sa vie* and the Language of Film," *Wide Angle*, vol. 1, no. 3 (1976): 32.

11. In *Four Fundamental Concepts of Psychoanalysis*, trans. Alan Sheridan (New York: Norton, 1978), p. 115, Jacques Lacan remarks that "*man's desire is the desire of the Other.*" It is through conforming to this axiom that we enter the symbolic order.

12. By "personal desire" I do not mean desires which are totally unique to a particular subject, but desires which have been claimed as his or her own.

13. Lacan also opposes empty speech to a more authentic form of speech, which he calls "full speech" (see "The Function and Field of Speech and Language in Psychoanalysis," pp. 46–48). However, "full speech" is not equivalent to what *My Life to Live* calls "true speech." It means speech within which the symbolic function reigns supreme.

14. Susan Sontag objects to this fracturing of the fiction in "On Godard's *Vivre sa vie*," in Mussman, ed., *Jean-Luc Godard: A Critical Anthology*, p. 99. As we have attempted to show, it is fractured from the beginning.

Notes to Chapter 2

1. Albert Moravia, *A Ghost at Noon*, trans. Angus Davidson (New York: Farrar, Straus and Young, 1955), p. 81.

2. Passages which undergo this kind of reattribution in *Contempt* can be found on pp. 142, 180, 181, 183–84, and 205–206 of the Moravia novel.

3. Jean-Luc Godard, "*Le Mépris*," in *Jean-Luc Godard par Jean-Luc Godard*, ed. Alain Bergala (Paris: Cahiers du Cinéma-Editions de l'Etoile, 1985), p. 249.

4. In quoting from the film, we have relied upon the French script, published in *L'Avant-Scène Cinéma*, nos. 412/413 (1992).

5. Jose Luis Guarner maintains that it was Levine in particular who insisted on nude shots of Bardot. See "*Le Mépris*," in *The Films of Jean-Luc Godard*, ed. Ian Cameron (New York: Frederick A. Praeger, 1969), p. 59.

6. Toby Mussman also suggests that *Contempt* tells the story of the fall in "Notes on *Contempt*," in Mussman, ed., *Jean-Luc Godard: A Critical Anthology* (New York: E. P. Dutton, 1968), p. 156.

7. A yellow blanket appears in the middle part of this shot, when there is a full range of colors.

8. "An Interview with Jean-Luc Godard," by *Cahiers du Cinéma*, trans. Rose Kaplin, in Mussman, ed., *Jean-Luc Godard: A Critical Anthology*, p. 113.

9. James Monaco suggests that Godard cast Francesca in *Contempt* as a safeguard against dubbing. See *The New Wave: Truffaut, Godard, Chabrol, Rohmer, Rivette* (New York: Oxford University Press, 1976), p. 138.

10. Godard, "Scénario du *Mépris*," in *Jean-Luc Godard par Jean-Luc Godard*, p. 246.

11. Freud attributes to the drives a "'daemonic power,'" and character-izes them as a "malignant fate" in *Beyond the Pleasure Principle*. See *The Standard Edition of the Complete Psychological Works*, trans. James Strachey (London: Hogarth Press, 1955), vol. 18, p. 23.

12. This exchange is based on Maurice Blanchot's analysis of "Vocation of the Poet" in "L'itinéraire de Hölderlin," in *L'espace littéraire* (Paris: Editions Gallimard, 1955), pp. 283–92.

13. We have been able to locate only the second and third of these vari-ants. The second in fact reads: "*so lange der Gott uns nah bleibt.*" The third reads: "*so lange, bis Gottes Fehl hilft.*" See Friedrich Hölderlin, *Sämtliche Werke und Briefe*, ed. Michael Knaupp (Munich: Hanser, 1992), pp. 271 and 331.

14. See Moravia, *A Ghost at Noon*, p. 66.

15. The French word "*revoir*" means literally "to see again."

16. Jacques Aumont also compares *Contempt* to *Voyage in Italy* in "The Fall of the Gods: Jean-Luc Godard's *Le Mépris*," in *French Films: Texts and Contexts*, ed. Susan Hayward and Ginette Vincendeau (New York: Rout-ledge, 1990), pp. 219–20.

Notes to Chapter 3

1. Susan Sontag, *Styles of Radical Will* (New York: Farrar, Straus & Giroux, 1969), p. 182.

2. In quoting from the film, we have relied upon *Alphaville: A Film by Jean-Luc Godard*, trans. Peter Whitehead (New York: Simon & Schuster, 1966).

3. Quoted by Jean-Luc Douin in *Jean-Luc Godard* (Paris: Editions Rivage, 1989), p. 161. Translation by Kaja Silverman.

4. Richard Roud, in "Introduction," in *Alphaville: A Film by Jean-Luc Godard*, p. 12.

5. Other critics have also stressed that *Alphaville* is more about the past than the future. For James Monaco, Lemmy Caution is "less . . . a traveler in the future than . . . a man from the past visiting in the terrible present" (*The New Wave: Truffaut, Godard, Chabrol, Rohmer, Rivette* [New York:

Oxford University Press, 1976], p. 156). For Robin Wood, Lemmy Caution is "a man from twenty to thirty years ago transported suddenly into the world of today" ("Society and Tradition: An Approach to Jean-Luc Godard," in *Jean-Luc Godard: A Critical Anthology*, ed. Toby Mussman (New York: E. P. Dutton, 1968), p. 186. And Marie-Claire Ropars-Wuilleumier writes that *Alphaville* is really about a time long ago, when there was absolute poetry ("La Forme et le fond, ou les avatars du récit," in *Etudes Cinématographiques*, ed. Michel Estève (Paris: Lettres Modernes, 1967), pp. 26–27.

6. For Ferdinand de Saussure, who makes the distinction between *langue* and *parole*, *langue* denotes the abstract language system, and *parole* the concrete discursive instance. See *Course in General Linguistics*, trans. Wade Baskin (New York: McGraw-Hill, 1966), pp. 7–20.

7. Roland Barthes writes in "Rhetoric of the Image" that the photograph attests to a *"having-been-there."* See *Image-Music-Text*, trans. Stephen Heath (New York: Hill and Wang, 1977), p. 44.

8. For this linguistic account of repression, see Sigmund Freud, "The Unconscious," in *The Standard Edition of the Complete Psychological Works*, trans. James Strachey (London: Hogarth Press, 1957), vol. 14, pp.166–204.

9. Henri's last words to the seductress—"I love you"—also link him to surrealism. As Michael Benedikt has observed, "Love was . . . the central Surrealist doctrine" (*"Alphaville* and its Subtext," in Mussman, ed., *Jean-Luc Godard: A Critical Anthology*, p. 214).

10. For Saussure, these relationships are unmotivated or "arbitrary" (*Course in General Linguistics*, p. 67).

11. For a discussion of the operations of the primary process, which Freud associates with the unconscious, see *The Interpretation of Dreams*, in *The Standard Edition*, vol. 5, pp. 588–609.

12. The "Lands Without" is how residents of Alphaville refer to other parts of the world.

13. Freud repeatedly emphasizes the mutability of memory, the vulnerability of the past to a subsequent rewriting. See, for instance, his *Project for a Scientific Psychology*, in *The Standard Edition*, vol. 1, pp. 352–57; and "Screen Memories," *The Standard Edition*, vol. 3, pp. 303–22.

14. *Alphaville* seems to attribute not only these lines, but Natasha's subsequent monologue to *Capital of Pain*. At the end of the scene, Natasha is shot through a window of Lemmy's hotel room, holding a copy of that volume. However, only two of the passages seemingly imputed to *Capital of Pain* are direct citations from it, and they are both poem titles: "death in conversation," and "to be trapped by trying to trap." As Rob Miotke suggested to us, the other passages are more readings *of* than readings *from* the poems. For the French edition of *Capital of Pain*, see *La Capitale de la douleur* (Paris: Librairie Gallimard, 1926). The English version is *Captital of Pain*, trans. Richard M. Weisman (New York: Grossman, 1973).

15. In *How to Do Things with Words* (Cambridge: Harvard University Press, 1962), J. L. Austin defines performative speech as speech that, rather than describing a reality, creates it.

16. In *Beyond the Pleasure Principle*, in *The Standard Edition*, vol. 18, pp. 7–36, Freud associates the psychoanalytic cure with the linguistic "binding" of affect.

17. In "Jensen's 'Gradiva'," in *The Standard Edition*, vol. 9, pp. 88–90, Freud discusses the "cure by love."

18. In the transference, the patient "remembers" in the mode of a displaced repetition. See Freud, "The Dynamics of Transference," in *The Standard Edition*, vol. 12, pp. 99–108, and "Observations on Transference-Love," in *The Standard Edition*, vol. 12, pp. 159–71.

19. As Monaco says in *The New Wave*, "Alpha–60 is made in the image of its creators" (158).

Notes to Chapter 4

1. Because *Weekend* has no credits, we have been unable to determine the names of all actors. When we do not provide this information, that is because it is unavailable.

2. In "*Weekend*," Robin Wood writes: "*Weekend* is not about the end of the world—it is simply about the end of *our* world" (*The Films of Jean-Luc Godard*, ed. Ian Cameron [New York: Frederick A. Praeger, 1969], p. 169).

3. In quoting from *Weekend*, we have relied upon the text as transcribed in *Weekend: A Film by Jean-Luc Godard*, trans. Marianne Sinclair (New York: Lorrimer Publishing, 1972).

4. Georg Simmel, *The Philosophy of Money*, 2nd ed., trans. Tom Bottomore and Davis Frisby (London: Routledge, 1990), p. 66.

5. Guy Hocquenghem, *Homosexual Desire*, trans. Daniella Dangoor (London: Allison and Busby, 1978), p. 87.

6. Claude Lévi-Strauss was the first to theorize women as objects of exchange—as commodities circulating between families, and making out of them a society (see *The Elementary Structures of Kinship*, trans. James Harle Bell, John Richard von Sturmer, and Rodney Needham [Boston: Beacon Press, 1969], pp. 36, and 496). See also his "Language and the Analysis of Social Laws," in *Structural Anthropology*, trans. Claire Jacobsen and Brooke Grundfest Schoepf (New York: Basic Books, 1967), p. 60. Gayle Rubin and Luce Irigaray have written important feminist critiques of the notion of woman as commodity (see Rubin, "The Traffic in Women: Notes on the 'Political Economy' of Sex," in *Toward an Anthropology of Women*, ed. Rayna R. Raiter [New York: Monthly Review Press, 1975], pp. 157–210; and Irigaray, "Women on the Market," in *This Sex Which Is Not One*, trans. Catherine Porter with Carolyn Burke [Ithaca: Cornell University Press,

l985], pp. 170–191). Irigaray's reading of woman as an object of exchange, which is conducted within a Marxian frame of reference, is especially germane to our discussion of *Weekend*.

7. I of course use the word "gold" here metaphorically rather than literally. It signifies not "precious metal," but "money."

8. I draw here on Jean-Joseph Goux's important book, *Symbolic Economies: After Marx and Freud*, trans. Jennifer Curtiss Gage (Ithaca: Cornell University Press, 1990). Goux argues that gold is the general equivalent within the domain of commodities, the phallus the general equivalent within the domain of objects, the father the general equivalent within the domain of subjects, and language the general equivalent within the domain of signs. In all four of these domains, "an identical syntax allows one of [its] members . . . to accede to power and govern the evaluations of the set from which it is excluded" (p. 24).

9. Marx refers to gold as the Lord of commodities in *A Contribution to the Critique of Political Economy*, trans. N. I. Stone (New York: International Library, l904), p. 166.

10. I take the notion of the "disenchantment" of the world from Max Weber, who attributes it to the ever-increasing "intellectualization and rationalization" brought about by "scientific progress." See his *Essays in Sociology*, trans. H. H. Gerth and C. Wright Mills (New York: Oxford University Press, l946), pp. 138–39. Max Horkheimer and Theodor W. Adorno also speak of the disenchantment of the world, and attribute it to the program of the Enlightenment (*Dialectic of Enlightenment*, trans. John Cumming (New York: Continuum, l991), p. 3.

11. As Simmel says in *The Philosophy of Money*, "if the object is to remain an economic value, its value must not be raised so greatly that it becomes an absolute" (p. 72).

12. I am theorizing here what we will later call "anal capitalism." Anal capitalism should be understood as a category for understanding the operations of the commodity general equivalent, not as a comprehensive account of anal sexuality. There can be no such account. All forms of sexuality can be put to infinite metaphoric uses, as Godard repeatedly shows. *Weekend, Number Two, Every Man for Himself*, and *Passion* all find different ways of symbolizing anal sexuality. The only thing which these systems of symbolization have in common is that they all represent anality as an inadequate solution to the complexities of heterosexuality. Once again we should be wary of transforming this into a general principle. Godard seems to be working through something personal here. What is interesting is that he consistently problematizes what seems to obsess him most sexually.

13. See Sigmund Freud, *Three Essays on the Theory of Sexuality*, in *The Standard Edition of the Complete Psychological Works*, trans. James Strachey (London: Hogarth Press, l953), vol. 7, pp. 179–206.

14. Sigmund Freud, "On Transformations of Instinct as Exemplified in Anal Erotism," *The Standard Edition*, vol. 17, p. 128.

15. In "Towards a Non-Bourgeois Camera Style," Brian Henderson argues that *Weekend* refuses depth of field (*Movies and Methods*, ed. Bill Nichols [Berkeley: University of California Press, 1976], pp. 422–38). For Henderson, this signifies a rejection of bourgeois interiority and values. We are here advancing a contrary argument—the argument that *Weekend* attributes "flatness" to the world constructed by late capitalism. At those moments when we are given compensatory access to a noncommodified, or only partially commodified, nature, *Weekend*'s images have a marked depth of field.

16. "When the Goods Get Together" is the title of a chapter of *This Sex Which Is Not One*. In it, Luce Irigaray describes what would happen if women were suddenly to refuse to be objects of exchange.

17. In *The Thief's Journal*, trans. Bernard Frechtman (New York: Grove, 1964), Jean Genet describes a tube of vaseline taken from him by the police, which was for him "the sign of a secret grace," and the contents of which brought to his mind "an oil lamp . . . of a night light beside a coffin" (p. 20).

18. Marx's son, Paul Lafargue, wrote a book defending laziness (see *The Right to Be Lazy* [1883], trans. Fred Thompson [Chicago: C.H. Kerr, 1975]).

19. The UNR stands for "Union Nationale Républicaine," the Gaullist Party.

20. For us, singularity has nothing to do with use value. Use value, like exchange value, with which it is intimately conjoined, must be socially produced. Our "needs," as Jean Baudrillard argues in *For a Critique of the Political Economy of the Sign*, trans. Charles Levin (St. Louis: Telos, 1981), pp. 63–87, and 130–42, are always ideologically generated. Singularity or absolute value is something altogether different. It, too, is an effect of the signifier. However, its production is private rather than social, and ontological sacrifice rather than economic or semiotic exchange is the means of that production.

21. Wood uses the word "enclosure" to describe the way in which this sequence is shot, and the relationship of the courtyard to the rest of the film (p. 169).

22. Marx, *Capital*, trans. Ben Fowles (New York: Random House, 1977), vol. 1, p. 165.

23. Sigmund Freud, *Totem and Taboo, The Standard Edition*, vol. 13, pp. 1–161.

Notes to Chapter 5

1. *Gay Knowledge* was coproduced by ORTF, and destined for television transmission. However, the film was never shown on French television. See Marc Cerisuelo, *Jean-Luc Godard* (Paris: Editions de Quatre-Vents, 1989), p. 142.

2. This argument is advanced by Christian Metz in *The Imaginary Signifier: Psychoanalysis and the Cinema*, trans. Celia Britton, Annwyl Williams, Ben Brewster and Alfred Guzzetti (Bloomington: Indiana University Press, 1977), pp. 7-16.

3. In 1969, Godard formed a filmaking group named after the Soviet filmmaker Dziga Vertov. The most important films produced by the group are *British Sounds* (1969), *Pravda* (1969), and *Wind from the East* (1969).

4. James Monaco, *The New Wave: Truffaut, Godard, Chabrol, Rohmer, Rivette* (New York: Oxford University Press, 1976), p. 206.

5. These are only a few of the books out of which Godard makes *Gay Knowledge*. As Susan Sontag argues in *Styles of Radical Will* (New York: Farrar, Straus & Giroux, 1969), Godard does not distinguish between books and other, more conventional profilmic objects; for him, "books and other vehicles of cultural consciousness are part of the world; therefore they belong in films" (p. 154).

6. The German title of the Nietzsche volume is *Die Fröhliche Wissenschaft*. It has been translated by Walter Kaufmann under the title *The Gay Science* (New York: Vintage Book, 1974). Although there are good reasons for this choice of title, the English word "science" does not precisely correspond to "*Wissenschaft*," since that latter word also designates the humanities. The French word "*savoir*" is closer to "*Wissenschaft*," since it implies knowledge of an objective sort. See the discussion of "*savoir*" and "*connaissance*" below.

7. Godard initially planned to base *Gay Knowledge* on Rousseau's great treatise on education, *Emile* (see Colin MacCabe, *Godard: Images, Sounds, Politics* [Bloomington: Indiana University Press, 1980], p. 20).

8. And, as Ian Cameron intimates in "*Gay Knowledge*," hearing may be even more crucial here than seeing, since the film's soundtrack "contains all manner of echoes from the events of May 1968" (*The Films of Jean-Luc Godard* [New York: Frederick A. Praeger, 1969], p. 174).

9. Jean-Luc Godard, "Premiers 'Sons Anglais,'" in *Jean-Luc Godard par Jean-Luc Godard*, ed. Alain Bergala (Paris: Cahiers du Cinéma-Editions de l'Etoile, 1985), p. 338.

10. "La Chance de repartir pour un tour," in *Godard par Godard*, p. 408.

11. James Roy MacBean maintains that *Gay Knowledge* not only reflects a certain disregard for aesthetic concerns, but launches a deliberate assault on the "cult of the 'masterpiece.'" For him, it is a "purposely flawed" text (*Film and Revolution* [Bloomington: Indiana University Press, 1975], p. 73).

12. As Ruth Perlmutter observes in "'Le Gai Savoir': Godard and Eisenstein: Notions of Intellectual Cinema," *Jump Cut* no. 7 (May–July 1975), neologism is in a sense Godard's motto, whether he is dealing with words, sounds, images, or film form (p. 17).

13. By underlining the zero, Godard emphasizes what a central concept it will be in *Gay Knowledge*. As Monaco observes, it is "the key to the constellation of concepts which is [that film]" (p. 205).

14. *Gay Knowledge* is especially indebted to Derrida's *Of Grammatology* here. The English edition of that text has been translated by Gayatri Chakravorty Spivak (Baltimore: Johns Hopkins University Press, 1976).

15. René Descartes, *Discourse on Method and Meditations on First Philosophy*, ed. David Weissman (New Haven: Yale University Press, 1996), pp. 21–22.

16. Karl Marx and Frederick Engels, *The German Ideology*, ed. C. J. Arthur (New York: International Publishers, 1970), p. 47.

17. *The German Ideology*, p. 55.

18. Michel Foucault, *The Order of Things: An Archaeology of the Human Sciences*; no trans. (London: Tavistock, 1970), p. 385.

19. Appropriately, this new chapter begins with an indirect reference to Jacques Lacan's assertion that "the unconscious is structured like a language" (*Four Fundamental Concepts of Psycho-Analysis*, trans. Alan Sheridan [New York: Norton, 1978], p. 149). Patricia announces that she and Emile are to be guided by chance in their selection of sounds and images, since "chance is structured like the unconscious." And the rest of the film makes clear its commitment to a linguistic notion of the unconscious.

20. In "Silences of the Voice," trans. Philip Rosen and Marcia Butzel (in *Narrative, Apparatus, Ideology*, ed. Rosen [New York: Columbia University Press, 1986], Pascal Bonitzer suggests that the voice-over lends itself to this kind of epistemological aggrandizement, "since it resounds from offscreen, in other words from the field of the Other" (p. 322).

21. See, for instance, *Quotations from Chairman Mao Tsetung* (Peking: Foreign Languages Press, 1972), p. 21, where Mao writes: "Revisionism, or Right opportunism, is a bourgeois trend of thought that is more dangerous than dogmatism. The revisionists . . . pay lip-service to Marxism. . . . But what they are really attacking is the quintessence of Marxism."

22. Louis Althusser is another representative for the leftist "scientism" which figures so centrally in *Gay Knowledge*. In *For Marx*, trans. Ben Brewster (London: New Left Books, 1969), Althusser at times associates dialectical materialism with "scientific truth" (see especially pp. 163–216).

23. Wilhelm Reich, *The Mass Psychology of Fascism*, ed. Mary Higgins and Chester M. Raphael, M.D. (New York: Farrar, Straus & Giroux, 1970).

24. Herbert Marcuse, *Eros and Civilization: A Philosophical Inquiry into Freud* (New York: Vintage, 1963), pp. 11 and 16.

25. This formulation echoes that articulated by Louis Althusser in "Ideology and Ideological State Apparatuses," in *Lenin and Philosophy*, trans. Ben Brewster (London: Monthly Review Press, 1971), pp. 127–86.

26. Jacques Lacan, "The Mirror Stage as Formative of the Function of the I as Revealed in Psychoanalytic Experience," in *Ecrits: A Selection*, trans. Alan Sheridan (New York: Norton, 1977), pp. 1–7.

27. This is an expression coined by Laura Mulvey in "Visual Pleasure and Narrative Cinema" (*Visual and Other Pleasures* [Bloomington: Indiana University Press, 1989], p. 19).

28. The film in fact says "are true," but the context in which these words are spoken indicates that "seems true" is meant.

29. For Jean Collet, *Gay Knowledge* consistently pits language against the imaginary, or the regime of the mirror (see Jean Collet and Jean-Paul Fargier, *Jean-Luc Godard* [Paris: Editions Seghers, 1974], p. 55.

30. The theorists who brought about this revaluation of the linguistic signifier include not only Derrida, Foucault, and Lacan, but also such figures as Julia Kristeva and Roland Barthes. The French journal *Tel Quel* also played a crucial role in shifting attention away from the signified to the signifier.

31. Of course, since *Gay Knowledge*, Godard has devised many strategies for affirming two images at the same time, most of them made possible by video technology. We discuss some of these strategies in chapter 6.

32. Hannah Arendt, *The Human Condition* (Chicago: University of Chicago Press, 1958), p. 9.

33. The Croix Lorraine is a symbol of Gaullism. The line drawing offers an implicit critique of police violence under de Gaulle.

34. Thomas M. Kavanagh makes the same point in *"Le Gai Savoir," Film Quarterly*, vol. 25, no. 1 (1971), p. 52.

35. Karl Marx, *The Eighteenth Brumaire of Louis Bonaparte* (New York: International Publishers, 1963), p. 15. The passage in question reads: "Men make their own history, but they do not make it just as they please; they do not make it under circumstances chosen by themselves, but under circumstances directly encountered, given, and transmitted from the past."

36. The molotov cocktail sequence was perhaps inspired by a passage from Lacan's second seminar, in which he defines the subject stripped of imaginary accoutrements as "acephalic" or "headless." The subject who grasps his or her linguistic bases could thus be said to be without a face. See *The Seminar of Jacques Lacan: Book II, the Ego in Freud's Technique of Psychoanalysis, 1954-1955*, trans. Sylvana Tomaselli (Cambridge: Cambridge University Press, 1988), p. 170.

37. In *Four Fundamental Concepts*, Lacan maintains that speech induces a "fading" or disappearance of the subject's being (pp. 209–29).

Notes to Chapter 6

1. Wolfried Reichart, "Interview mit Jean-Luc Godard," trans. Michael Klier, *Filmkritik* no. 242 (February 1977): 61.

2. Stephen Heath, *Questions of Cinema* (Bloomington: Indiana University Press, 1981), p. 62.

3. Reichart, "Interview mit Jean-Luc Godard," p. 67.

4. As James Monaco points out in *The New Wave: Truffaut, Godard, Chabrol, Rohmer, Rivette* (New York: Oxford University Press, 1976), p. 215,

this collective really included only Godard and Jean-Pierre Gorin, and every film produced by it is hyperbolically Godardian. *Number Two* represents in my view a more serious attempt at authorial divestiture than any of these films.

5. "Deux heures avec Jean-Luc Godard," in *Jean-Luc Godard par Jean-Luc Godard*, ed. Alain Bergala (Paris: Cahiers du Cinéma-Editions de l'Etoile, 1985), p. 335. Translation by Kaja Silverman.

6. Reichart, "Interview mit Jean-Luc Godard," p. 56.

7. Colin MacCabe, "Interview with Godard," in *Godard: Images, Sounds, Politics* (Bloomington: Indiana University Press, 1980), p. 103. Anne-Marie Miéville is Godard's partner and frequent collaborator.

8. Gerhard Theuring, "*Numéro deux,*" *Filmkritik* no. 242 (February 1977): 102.

9. Reichart, "Interview mit Jean-Luc Godard," p. 56,

10. For a further elaboration of the status of the traditional author, and of what it means for this author to be relocated within the text, see Kaja Silverman, *The Acoustic Mirror: The Female Voice in Psychoanalysis and Cinema* (Bloomington: Indiana University Press, 1988), pp. 187–234.

11. Laura Mulvey and Colin MacCabe also comment on the film's "relentless insistence on *showing* . . . the place of sex in the home" in MacCabe, *Godard: Images, Sounds, Politics*, p. 98.

12. In *Studies on Hysteria*, in *The Standard Edition of the Complete Psychological Works of Sigmund Freud*, trans. James Strachey (London: Hogarth Press, 1955), vol. 2, pp. 166–81, Freud maintains that in hysteria the body speaks in place of the psyche. In effect, it articulates what cannot be otherwise expressed.

13. Germaine Greer, *The Female Eunuch* (London: Paladin, 1971), pp. 318 and 55.

14. MacCabe and Mulvey also note the homosexual dimension of the anal rape in MacCabe, *Godard: Images, Sounds, Politics*, p. 98.

15. MacCabe and Mulvey also read Sandrine's constipation as a socioeconomic metaphor in MacCabe, *Godard: Images, Sounds, Politics*, p. 99.

16. See, for instance, Sigmund Freud, *The Interpretation of Dreams* in *The Standard Edition of the Complete Psychological Works*, vol. 4, pp. 119–20.

17. Jean Laplanche, *Life and Death in Psychoanalysis*, trans. Jeffrey Mehlman (Baltimore: Johns Hopkins University Press, 1976), pp. 25–41, and 102.

18. For a discussion of the operations of abjection, and the association of the category of the abject with the feminine, see Julia Kristeva, *Powers of Horror: An Essay on Abjection*, trans. Leon S. Roudiez (New York: Columbia University Press, 1982).

19. Jean Collet and Jean-Paul Fargier, *Jean-Luc Godard: Cinéma d'aujourd'hui* (Paris: Editions Seghers, 1974), p. 169.

20. This is a very Lacanian understanding of fatherhood. See Jacques Lacan, "Function and Field of Speech and Language in Psychoanalysis," in *Ecrits: A Selection*, trans. Alan Sheridan (New York: Norton, 1977), p. 67.

21. Jonathan Rosenbaum suggests that *Number Two* is itself "a factory-landscape where anything becomes possible" in *"Numéro deux," Sight and Sound*, vol. 45, no. 2 (1976), 125.

Notes to Chapter 7

1. Godard has suggested that the true subject of *Passion* is "liaison." See Jean-Louis Leutrat, *Des traces qui nous ressemblent* (Bodoni: Editions Comp'Act, 1990), p. 60. Marc Cerisuelo makes a similar claim in *Jean-Luc Godard* (Paris: Lherminier, Editions des Quatre-Vents, 1989), p. 207.

2. As Peter Wollen observes in *"Passion 1," Framework* no. 21 (1983), p. 4, "In *Passion*, the look . . .moves. Moreover, it moves not simply through space exterior to the tableau, but into it and within it."

3. In the original painting, there is a second girl behind the first, who is difficult to make out. She is similarly dressed.

4. See Leutrat, *Des traces qui nous ressemblent*, p. 28.

5. In quoting dialogue from *Passion*, we have relied upon the script published in *L'Avant-Scène Cinéma*, no. 380 (1989).

6. Leutrat makes a similar point in *Des traces qui nous ressemblent*, p. 16. Sophie's lines come from Eugene Fromentin, *Maîtres d'autrefois* (Paris: Le Livre de Poche, 1965), p. 317.

7. Leutrat also notes the Vermeer-like qualities of this scene (*Des traces qui nous ressemblent*, p. 27).

8. Béla Balázs, *Theory of the Film: Character and Growth of a New Art*, trans. Edith Bone (New York: Dover, 1970), p. 46.

9. Walter Benjamin associates the aura with precisely such a distance-in-closeness in "The Work of Art in the Age of Mechanical Reproduction," in *Illuminations*, ed. Hannah Arendt (New York: Schocken, 1969), pp. 222–23. For Benjamin, cinema is definitionally anti-auratic, but Kaja Silverman has argued otherwise in *The Threshold of the Visible World* (New York: Routledge, 1996), pp. 83–104.

10. As Laura Mulvey was the first to point out, in Hollywood cinema it is usually men who look, and women who are looked at (*Visual and Other Pleasures* [Bloomington: Indiana University Press, 1989], pp. 14–26).

11. This is one of the moments in *Passion* where Jerzy functions as a stand-in for Godard. As Leutrat suggests in *Des traces qui nous ressemblent*, what Godard wrote about Anthony Mann and his relationship to the Western also applies to himself and his relationship to prior texts: "He *reinvents it*. It would be better to say 're-invents': he displays at the same

time as to he dismantles, innovates at the same time as he copies, critiques at the same time as he creates" (pp. 22–23). Translation by Kaja Silverman.

12. Gilles Deleuze suggests that, in general, Godard's method is "the method of BETWEEN, 'between two images', which does away with all cinema of the One. It is the method of AND, 'this and then that', which does away with all the cinema of Being. . . . Between two actions, between two affections, between two perceptions, between two visual images, between two sound images, between the sound and the visual" (*Cinema 2: The Time-Image*, trans. Hugh Tomlinson and Robert Galeta [Minneapolis: Minnesota University Press, 1989], p. 180).

13. These kinds of sensory transfers are typically Godardian. In a conversation with Hanna Schygulla ("Passion Kino oder die Harte, alles zu registrieren," ed. Heinz Trenczak, *blimp* [March 1985], p. 8), Godard also imagines speaking with one's ears, and seeing with one's mouth.

14. The text which has most influenced contemporary thinking in this respect is Freud's *Civilization and Its Discontents*, in *The Standard Edition of the Complete Psychological Works*, trans. James Strachey (London: Hogarth Press, 1961), vol. 21, pp. 64–145.

15. This scene actually combines details from a series of Ingres' paintings. In addition to *Small Bather*, it draws upon *Half-Length Study of a Woman* (1807); *Valpincon Bather* (1808); and *Interior of a Harem* (1828). All of these paintings give the central position to the woman shown in *Small Bather*. In *Half-Length Study of a Woman*, this figure again turns to the left, and her face is visible. In *Valpincon Bather*, she sits alone on a bed in a curtained space, wearing only a red and white turban. Again, a white towel or sheet is wrapped around her left arm. In *Interior of a Harem*, the woman is nude except for a turban, and once again her body is turned to the left, and her head to the right. She sits with a group of other women around a pool. This last painting would seem to provide a particularly important prototype for the Ingres scene in *Passion*, suggesting—among other things—the "harem" idea.

16. Again, see *Civilization and Its Discontents*.

17. As Freud makes clear in "Some Psychical Consequences of the Anatomical Distinction between the Sexes," in *The Standard Edition*, vol. 19, pp. 248–58, our culture generally maps "woundedness" onto the female genitals.

18. As Paul Willemen puts it, the "between" is what "connects inside and outside, here and there . . . the psychic and the physical, phantasy and the real." It is thus "the ultimate refusal of binarism" (*"Passion 3," Framework* no. 21 [1983], p. 7).

19. Luce Irigaray, "Sexual Difference," in *The Irigaray Reader*, ed. Margaret Whitford (Cambridge, Mass.: Basil Blackwood, 1991), p. 171.

20. Willemen makes a similar point in *"Passion 3,"* p. 7. For a further discussion of anality, and its gender ramifications, see chapter 4 of the present volume.

21. See Leo Bronstein, *El Greco* (New York: Harry N. Abrams, 1950), p. 126.

22. Again, see Bronstein, *El Greco*, p. 126, as well as José Gudiol, *El Greco, 1541-1614*, trans. Kenneth Lyons (London: Secker & Warburg, 1973), p. 252.

23. There are three versions of this painting. The one upon which Godard drew would seem to be the one in Schloß Charlottenburg in Berlin. The other two are in the Louvre, and in the Städtisches Kunstinstitut in Frankfurt.

24. In *The Complete Paintings of Watteau*, intro. John Sutherland (New York: Harry N. Abrams, 1971), Sutherland argues that it is unclear whether this painting shows an embarkage to or a departure from the island of love. Giovanni Macchia makes the same point in *Antoine Watteau (1684-1721): Le peintre, son temps et sa légende*, ed. H. A. Millon, P. Rosenberg, and F. Moureau (Paris: Editions Clairefontaine, 1987), p. 187.

Notes to Chapter 8

1. In a German press conference, Godard indicated that he is working with a complex notion of quotation in *New Wave*: "I tried to establish a balance between literary quotations, verbal quotations, and also quotations from nature. In this film, there is the quotation of water, the quotation of trees" ("Es Wiederfinden," German trans. Hans Zischler, *Taz*, November 22, 1990). English translation by Kaja Silverman.

2. Godard's precise words are: "The cinema must leave the quarters where it is and go to those where it isn't" ("Lutter sur deux fronts," in *Jean-Luc Godard par Jean-Luc Godard*, ed. Alain Bergala [Paris: Cahiers du Cinéma-Editions de l'Etoile, 1985], p. 320). Translation by Kaja Silverman.

3. In quoting from the film, we have relied upon the script published in *L'Avant-Scène Cinéma*, nos. 396/397 (November/December 1990).

4. Our reading of *New Wave* draws here and elsewhere upon Martin Heidegger's *Being and Time*, trans. John Macquarrie and Edward Robinson (New York: Harper and Row, 1962). Heidegger argues there that we are *Dasein*, beings who have a specific *"da"* or "there." We will be arguing that the landscape signifies Elena and Lennox's *"da."*

5. The idea of love as the gift of what one doesn't possess comes from Jacques Lacan, *Le séminaire, livre VIII: le transfer*, ed. Jacques-Alain Miller and Judith Miller (Paris: Seuil, 1991), p. 147.

6. See Sigmund Freud, *Three Essays on the Theory of Sexuality*, in *The Standard Edition of the Complete Psychological Works*, trans. James Strachey (New York: Hogarth Press, 1953), vol. 7, pp. 217–18.

7. In *The Crack-Up, with Other Uncollected Pieces, Note-Books and Unpublished Letters*, ed. Edmund Wilson (New York: New Directions, 1945), p. 125, F. Scott Fitzgerald records the following exchange between himself and Ernest Hemingway:

Fitzgerald: "The rich are different from us."
Hemingway: "Yes, they have more money."

8. The notion that the all-important human project is to sustain desire is central to Lacan's psychoanalytic ethics. See *The Seminar of Jacques Lacan, Book VII: The Ethics of Psychoanalysis, 1959-1960*, trans. Dennis Porter (New York: Norton, 1992), pp. 291–325.

9. Lacan suggests that the imaginary logic subtending the master/slave relationship takes the following form, which Elena's declaration echoes: "*If it's you, I'm not. If it's me, it's you who isn't*" (*The Seminar of Jacques Lacan, Book II: The Ego in Freud's Theory and in the Technique of Psychoanalysis, 1954-1955*, trans. Sylvana Tomaselli [Cambridge: Cambridge University Press, 1988], p. 169).

10. See Georg F. W. Hegel, *Phenomenology of Spirit*, trans. A.V. Miller (New York: Oxford University Press, 1977), pp. 111–19. In Hegel, the slave ultimately triumphs through work.

11. *The Comedy of Dante Alighieri, the Florentine: Purgatory*, trans. Dorothy L. Sayers (New York: Penguin, 1955), p. 126. We have used this translation for all quotations from *The Divine Comedy*.

12. This phrase comes from John Keats's "Ode to a Nightingale."

13. The story about the dead bee, which will be completed only later in the film, comes from Howard Hawkes's *To Have and Have Not* (1944).

14. *The Comedy of Dante Alighieri, the Florentine: Hell*, trans. Dorothy L. Sayers (London: Penguin, 1949), p. 71.

15. Arthur Rimbaud, "Lettre à Paul Demeny, 15 Mai 1871," in *Œuvres complètes*, présentées et établies par Louis Forestier (Paris: Robert Laffont, 1992), p. 230.

16. See, for instance, Jacques Lacan, "Aggressivity in Psychoanalysis," in *Ecrits: A Selection*, trans. Alan Sheridan (New York: Norton, 1977), p. 23.

17. For Hegel, the slave's work is that through which he "posits *himself* as a negative in the permanent order of things, and thereby becomes *for himself*, someone existing on his own account" (*Phenomenology of the Spirit*, p. 118).

18. Heidegger, *Being and Time*, p. 220.

19. Heidegger, *Being and Time*, p. 373.

20. Dante, *Purgatory*, p. 88.

21. "*Conduire*" means "to drive" as well as "to lead."

About the Authors

Kaja Silverman is Chancellor's Professor of Rhetoric and Film at the University of California at Berkeley. She is the author of several books, including *The Threshold of the Visible World*, *Male Subjectivity at the Margins*, and *The Subject of Semiotics*. Berlin-based director and film essayist Harun Farocki has made over seventy films, including *Still Life*, *Workers Leaving the Factory*, *Videograms of a Revolution* and *Images of the World and the Inscription of War*.